Prentice Hall
Reference Guide
to Grammar
and Usage

Second Edition

Muriel Harris

Purdue University

Prentice Hall
Englewood Cliffs, New Jersey 07632

Library of Congress Cataloging-in-Publication Data

Harris, Muriel
    Prentice Hall reference guide to grammar and usage / Muriel Harris.—2nd ed.
       p. cm.
    Includes index.
    ISBN 0-13-225624-X
    1. English language—Grammar. 2. English language—Usage.
I. Title.
[PE1112.H293   1994]   93-34200
428.2—dc20   CIP

Production supervision: Keith Faivre
Interior design: Design Lab
Acquisitions editor: Alison Reeves
Production coordinator: Tricia Kenny
Cover design: Pentagram Design Inc.

*To Sam, Becky, and David (and now Dan too)
as always — and ever*

Printed in the United States of America
10 9 8 7 6 5 4 3 2 1

ISBN 0-13-225624-X (with exercises)
ISBN 0-13-399817-7 (without exercises)

Prentice-Hall International (UK) Limited, *London*
Prentice-Hall of Australia Pty. Limited, *Sydney*
Prentice-Hall Canada Inc., *Toronto*
Prentice-Hall Hispanoamericana, S.A., *Mexico*
Prentice-Hall of India Private Limited, *New Delhi*
Prentice-Hall of Japan, Inc., *Tokyo*
Simon & Schuster Asia Pte. Ltd., *Singapore*
Editora Prentice-Hall do Brasil, Ltda., *Rio de Janeiro*

Contents

To the Instructor

While writing this reference guide to grammar and usage, and again while revising for this second edition, I've kept in mind the countless numbers of students whom I've worked with elbow to elbow as a writing lab tutor and also the stacks of papers I've read as a teacher. Included here are all the points of grammar and rules I have seen students struggling with and all the suggestions, proofreading techniques, and cautionary advice about pitfalls to avoid that I've passed along to them. Drawing on the experience derived from more years than I care to count, I've given special emphasis to topics that I know are major sources of confusion and included strategies I also know students find useful. This book is thus the result of many years of field-testing.

The book is also the result of my efforts to produce a reference guide that all writers can use even when they don't know much grammatical terminology. In our writing lab we answer hundreds of grammar hotline calls and sit with hundreds more students who know the word or phrase or punctuation usage they want to check, but who don't know how to find the page or section they need in a handbook. Where possible, students should be able to actively consult a guide to grammar while they are editing their writing, which—of course—is the best time, not wait passively for someone else to locate and name their errors.

To help students, I've created two guides, "Question and Correct" and "Compare and Correct." In the "Question and Correct" list they can find many of their questions with accompanying references to the sections in the book they need. But it is sometimes difficult to phrase a question, so I have also included another means to locate the appropriate pages in the book, "Compare and Correct." Here students will find examples of typical troublesome constructions that may be similar to theirs. Again, references will guide them to appropriate places in the book.

Students who have had an instructor or writing lab tutor help them identify the point of grammar or usage they want to check can use the index, the table of contents, and the list of correction symbols to find the appropriate page or section.

The organization of the book is also intended to help writers easily locate the information they need. **Parts of Sentences** explains parts of speech, grammatical terms having to do with single words, and concepts about phrases, clauses, and sentence types. **Revising Sentences for Accuracy, Clarity, and Variety** provides rules and suggestions for constructions beyond the word level. **Punctuation and Mechanics** covers guidelines for the most frequently used forms in these areas. **Spelling** covers proofreading, useful spelling rules, and a guide to using the dictionary. **Style and Word Choice** offers suggestions for avoiding sexist language, wordiness, and clichés, along with guidelines on tone and word choice. **Special Writing Concerns** serves as a reference of guidelines on documentation format and style and business writing. An appendix on **Paper Format** and **Glossaries of Usage and Grammatical Terms** round out the handbook.

Students will find this book to be user friendly, clear, and concise. In the HINTS boxes they'll find useful strategies and errors to avoid, and in the exercises paragraphs they will learn interesting bits of information about lighter topics—such as the origins of the phrase "it's a doozy" and the increasing popularity of pigs—and about relevant, current topics—such as the problems of waste disposal and the potential of phone systems to deliver consumer information. For ease of self-checking, the answers to the exercises are at the end of each chapter. The exercises are set up so that students can practice several different types of skills: proofreading, sentence combining, and in the "pattern practice," writing their own sentences using various rules.

This version of the book is what publishers call the "second edition," but those of us involved with writing call these later drafts "revisions." As with other revising I do, this was an opportunity to clean up minor infelicities, to clarify some explanations, and—most important—to add material where needed. Some of the additions are aimed at helping students who speak and write English as a second language (ESL). These students need reference guides that also include explanations of aspects of English grammar that can be stumbling blocks for speakers of other languages. Thus, they can now find help with prepositions, articles, count and noncount nouns as well as the adjectives that accompany these nouns, and verbs with gerunds and infinitives. The extensive new chart of verb tenses should be more helpful for them as well, and there is now an ESL index at the back of this handbook. For all student writers I've added more material on transitions, especially at the paragraph level and between paragraphs. In addition, there is now a more extensive discussion of plagiarism as well as more on differences between summary and paraphrase, documentation of sources, levels of formality, and abstract and concrete language. The need for these additions reflects the growing emphasis on the kinds of informative and persuasive discourse being emphasized in writing courses as well as in writing assignments in other fields. With these additions and the inclusion of more material for non-native speakers of English, I now feel confident that the book is more inclusive both in terms of the audience it is aimed at and the types of writing assignments for which it can offer help. I'm delighted that I had this opportunity to revise.

This book, then, is a guide to the editing or proofreading stage of writing, and as I explain to students in the "To the Student" introduction, editing is only one of the writing processes and is most commonly performed after writers have composed their thoughts into words on paper. My advice to students is to attend to editing at the last stages when they are close to a final draft of a paper. But research has made us aware of how non-linear writing processes are, and some degree of editing and polishing may occur throughout various drafts. Our job, as teachers, is to keep our students from thinking that editing for grammatical correctness is the heart of writing. We also need to remind our students that reference guides are useful and necessary tools, but ultimately no book can answer all questions or include every sticky or unusual case. Having an instructor or a writing lab tutor to talk to is also necessary.

Among the useful supplements to this handbook available from Prentice Hall are the following:

- *Practicing Grammar and Usage* (by Muriel Harris). This booklet of supplementary exercises accompanies the Second Edition of the *Prentice Hall Reference Guide to Grammar and Usage,* matching both topics and approach. You'll find all exercises in paragraph form with answer keys at the back. These booklets can be purchased by students, or you can copy individual exercises from your free booklet as needed when you adopt the *Reference Guide.* (The pages are formatted for ease of copying.)

- *Prentice Hall Workbook for ESL Writers* (by Stacey Hagen and Bernice Ege-Zavala). This workbook, available for purchase by students, offers exercises on grammar and writing problems particularly troublesome to non-native speakers of English.

- *The Research Organizer.* This booklet provides guidance on the research process and assists that process by providing students with space to assemble notes, citations, outlines, and drafts of a research paper. It is available for purchase by students, or professors using the *Reference Guide* may copy it for free for their students.

- *Model Research Papers* (by Janette Lewis). This collection of eleven student research papers in various fields offers models of documentation, stylistic conventions, and formal requirements for various disciplines. Again, this is available either for sale or can be copied for students using the *Reference Guide.*

- *Prentice Hall/Simon & Schuster Transparencies for Writers* (by Duncan Carter). This set of one hundred color transparencies contains exercises, examples, and suggestions for student writing that focus on various aspects of the writing process and includes coverage of grammar, punctuation, and mechanics.

- *On-line Handbook.* This computerized reference system is compatible with most word processing packages and permits students to access information in the *Reference Guide* as they compose on a word processor. (Also in both Macintosh and IBM versions.)

- *Blue Pencil* and *Blue Pencil Authoring System* (by Robert Bator and Mitsura Yamada). *Blue Pencil* is an interactive editing program that allows students to practice their writing skills by making revisions in paragraph-length passages on the computer screen. If students have trouble with a particular concept, they can request additional instruction from the program. *The Blue Pencil Authoring System,* a for-sale item for professors, allows you to create your own exercises for the *Blue Pencil* program.

- Student Economy Packages. When you adopt the *Prentice Hall Reference Guide to Grammar and Usage* and another Prentice Hall composition text, the publisher makes them available in a shrinkwrapped package at a 10% discount off the total price.

- *Webster's Compact Dictionary* offer. This dictionary is available at only $2.50 above the price of the *Reference Guide* when the two are shrinkwrapped together.

- *Webster's Dictionary 3rd College Edition* offer. Your students can purchase this dictionary at a substantially discounted price when ordered with the *Prentice Hall Reference Guide to Grammar and Usage.*

- *Bibliotech.* This computerized Bibliography Generator for MLA, APA, and CBE Documentation styles is available for both the IBM and Macintosh.

Acknowledgements

This book first took shape in the mind of Phil Miller, the Editor in Chief, Humanities, as he patiently listened to all my griping about grammar handbooks. His quiet wisdom and calm persistence brought this book into existence. Lynn Greenberg Rosenfeld, Senior Editor, English, saw the manuscript through many formative stages, and her level-headed good sense still pervades the book. Kate Morgan, the Development Editor, took on the heroic task of page-by-page editing as well as huge-scale matters of organization and content. Her refinements grace the pages, though I still claim domination over any faults she did not weed out. I've benefited also from the useful comments, corrections, and suggestions of reviewers who have added their voices and insights throughout this book: Robert Dial, University of Akron; James Helvey, Davidson County Community College; Michael Williamson, Indiana University of Pennsylvania; Connie Eggers, Western Washington University; Christopher Thaiss, George Mason

University; Lyle W. Morgan II, Pittsburg State University; Joe Lostracco, Austin Community College; Joyce Powell, North Lake University; Marion Perry, Erie Community College; Carol Franks, Portland State University; Donald Fucci, Ramapo College; Vivian Brown, Laredo Junior College; Walter Beale, University of North Carolina at Greensboro; Tracy Baker, University of Alabama at Birmingham. Others who were particularly helpful as I prepared the second edition are Rebecca Innocent, Southern Mississippi University; Jami Josifek, University of California at Irvine; and Barbara Moreland, University of Texas at Arlington. I am also glad to have this opportunity to acknowledge the help of Virginia Underwood Allen (Iowa State University) with methods of explaining grammar, and the input of tutors from the Babson College writing center, under the direction of Joel Nydahl, who offered useful additions to the questions in the "Question and Correct" guide. I also owe a large debt of gratitude to the Production Department staff who transformed my sheets of computer printout into visually attractive, visually informative pages. Finally, I must acknowledge the extensive amount of assistance I've gotten from student writers who over the years have patiently listened to my attempts to help them and who revised the endless questions, doodles, diagrams, handouts, and bits of advice I kept giving them into coherent explanations and suggestions. As for my husband, Samuel, and our children, David and Rebecca and her husband Daniel, I prefer to think that my appreciation for them and for what they mean to me is always evident in our lives, not on pages of books.

THE NEW YORK TIMES and **PRENTICE HALL** are sponsoring **A CONTEMPORARY VIEW,** a program designed to enhance student access to current information of relevance in the classroom.

Through this program, the core subject matter provided in the text is supplemented by a collection of time-sensitive articles from one of the world's most distinguished newspapers, **THE NEW YORK TIMES.** These articles demonstrate the vital, ongoing connection between what is learned in the classroom and what is happening in the world around us.

So that students can enjoy the wealth of information of **THE NEW YORK TIMES** daily, a reduced subscription rate is available. For information, call toll-free: 1-800-631-1222.

PRENTICE HALL and **THE NEW YORK TIMES** are proud to co-sponsor **A CONTEMPORARY VIEW.** We hope it will make the reading of both textbooks and newspapers a more dynamic, involving process.

To the Student

This grammar handbook may look like others you've used or seen, but there are some differences in this book that will make it easier for you to use:

This handbook is designed for easy use.

- It is arranged so that you can look up answers to your questions without knowing the necessary grammatical terms. (There is, of course, an index if you know the point of grammar you want to check.)
- Most of the grammatical terms you need are explained in the first chapter. Others are explained as you need them.
- The explanations in this book are stated as concisely as possible. You won't be spending extra time reading a lot of unnecessary prose.
- The information is presented with visual aids such as charts, different ink colors, etc. to help you locate what you need quickly.

This handbook concentrates only on the most essential points of grammar and the most frequently made errors.

- This book focuses on the questions and problems writers most frequently have.
- You won't find an exhaustive list of grammatical terms of seldom-used rules in this book. However, if you want definitions of grammatical terms such as *participle, gerund,* and so on, see the Glossary of Grammatical Terms at the back of this book.

This book offers explanations and strategies.

- Rules are explained, not just stated.
- This book is intended to answer most questions, though you may need to consult your teacher or writing lab tutor for further explanation or specific information.

This book includes HINTS to help you use grammatical rules.

- You will find frequent HINTs to help you use various rules. These strategies are intended to help you use the rules that are explained.
- Some of the HINTs are reminders to help you avoid errors that are frequently made.

This book offers exercises in a useful format.

- To practice your understanding of various topics, try the exercises at the end of each chapter and check your answers with the Answer Key at the end of each part.
- You'll notice that the exercises are not lists of separate sentences. Instead, you'll be checking your understanding by practicing proofreading and pattern practice skills with paragraphs. The subjects of these paragraphs are of general interest and may even add to your storehouse of minor facts with which to amaze your friends. (For example, you'll read about the magnificent old Duesenberg automobile, the Turkish origins of Santa Claus, the art of whistling, the popularity of pigs as pets, and nonimpact aerobics.)

As you can tell from this description, the goal of this handbook is to be a useful companion for writers. As you edit your papers before turning them over to your readers, you may have questions such as "Do I need a comma here?" or "Something doesn't seem right in that sentence—what's wrong?" If you don't know the grammatical terms to look up in the index, try the suggestions for using this book in the next section. If needed, browse through the "Question and Correct" or "Compare and Correct" sections.

Some Cautionary Advice

All textbook writers would like to think that what they have written supplies all the answers and solves all the reader's problems. Their book is all that students need. That must be a great feeling, but you and I know that in the case of any reference guide to grammar and usage, such as this book, knowledge of grammar is only one aspect of writing—and not the most important one either. The writer's real task is to use writing to give shape to thoughts, to focus on topics and present them clearly and coherently. For most writers, this means moving through a variety of processes to compose, develop, and organize ideas and writing several drafts—at least—with feedback, when possible, from readers as the drafts are revised and evolve into more finished products.

The most effective time to use this book, then, is when you are working on final or near-final drafts, polishing them for grammatical correctness, proofing for correct punctuation and spelling, and sharpening your word choices and sentence constructions. At the earlier stages of composing, you don't want to interrupt your thought processes or the flow of the ideas evolving on the page to worry about choosing the right pronoun. There is also no point in checking the punctuation of a sentence in an early draft that may disappear in the next draft. When you have a well-developed, well-organized topic and have done all the necessary revision, you are finally ready to concentrate your attention on matters such as sentence correctness, word choices, punctuation, and spelling, or the appearance of the page. Then, you can benefit from this book which is designed to help you edit your writing to conform to standard English. When your sentences are clearly phrased and correctly punctuated and when your words are appropriately chosen and correctly spelled, your readers can more easily understand—and appreciate—your ideas.

1

Parts of Sentences

If you have a racing bike, you probably know about *derailleurs* and *caliper brakes*, and if you know about computers, you know about *modems, bytes*, and *machine language*. The more we know about a subject, the more specialized terms we learn, and this is true of grammar as well. However, to be users we don't all need to be specialists. But as we learn to effectively use our bikes, our computers, and our language, we do need to understand some basic concepts about each of them. Having a working vocabulary of some terms speeds us through explanations of these concepts.

In this chapter, you will learn both the basic terms you'll need and useful concepts about sentence parts. With this background knowledge, you'll understand the explanations of grammatical rules here and in later chapters. The topics covered in Part 1 are the following:

1. Verbs
   a. Verb Phrases
   b. Verb Forms
   c. Verb Tense
   d. Verb Voice
   e. Verb Mood
   f. Modal Verbs
   g. Phrasal Verbs
   h. Verbs with *-ing* and *to* + Verb Forms
2. Nouns and Pronouns
   a. Nouns
   b. Pronouns

1 Verbs (v)

A **verb** is a word or group of words that expresses action, shows a state of existence, or links the subject (usually the doer of the action) to the rest of the sentence.

The first step in distinguishing complete sentences from incomplete ones is recognizing the verb. Many sentences have more than one verb, but they must have at least one. Verbs provide several kinds of essential information in a sentence:

- *Some verbs express action.*

  Tim **jogs** every day.
  I **see** my face in the mirror.

- *Some verbs (called linking verbs) indicate that a subject exists or link the subject (the who or what) and the rest of the sentence together.*

  She **feels** sad.

  The shark **is** hungry.

- *Verbs indicate time.*

  They **went** home. (past time)
  The semester **will end** in May. (future time)

- *Verbs indicate number.*

  Jerry always **orders** anchovy pizza.
     (singular—only one doer of the action, Jerry)
  Flora and Terry always **order** sausage pizza.
     (plural—two doers of the action, Flora and Terry)

- *Verbs indicate the person for the subject (the who or what, usually the doer of the action).*

  First person: I or we
     I **love** to cook.
  Second person: you
     You **love** to cook.
  Third person: he, she, it, they
     He **loves** to cook.

HINT: You can find the verb (or part of it when the verb has more than one word) by changing the time expressed in the sentence (that is, by changing the sentence from the present to the past, from the past to the future, and so on). In the following examples note the word that changes. That word is the verb, and you can tell whether the sentence expresses something about the past or present because of the form of the verb that expresses time.

Present	*Past*
Tim *jogs* every day.	Tim *jogged* every day.
I *see* my face in the mirror.	I *saw* my face in the mirror.
She *feels* sad.	She *felt* sad.
The shark *is* hungry.	The shark *was* hungry.

1a Verb Phrases

A **verb phrase** is several words working together as a verb.

He **has gone** home.
I **am enjoying** my vacation.
They **should have attended** the movie with me.

1b Verb Forms

Verb forms are words that are not complete verbs in themselves. Verb forms may either be part of a verb phrase or appear elsewhere in the sentence.

(1) *-ing* Verbs

Forms of the verb that end in *-ing*, called *gerunds*, are never complete verbs by themselves. To be part of the verb phrase, they need a helping verb. They may also be used alone elsewhere in the sentence.

The computer program **is working** smoothly.
    Working is a verb form because it is only a part of the verb phrase. *Is working* is the whole verb phrase because of the helping verb *is*.
Feeling guilty is one of his favorite pastimes.
    Feeling is part of the subject. It is a verb form but not a verb.
Everyone enjoys **laughing.**
    Laughing is the direct object of the verb. (The direct object completes the meaning or receives the action of the verb.) *Laughing* is a verb form but not a verb.

1b
v

HINT: Some incomplete sentences, called *fragments*, are caused by using only an *-ing* verb form with no helper.

Fragment: Harlan, with his fast track record yesterday, **showing** all the practice and effort of the last three months.

(This is not a complete sentence because it does not have a complete verb.)

Revised: Harlan, with his fast track record yesterday, **is showing** all the practice and effort of the last three months.

-or-

Harlan, with his fast track record yesterday, **shows** all the practice and effort of the last three months.

For more information on fragments, see Chapter 13.

(2) *-ed* Verbs

To show past tense, most verbs have an *-ed* or *-d* added to the base form. (The base form is the one found as the main entry in the dictionary.) But there is another *-ed* form of the verb that needs a helping verb such as *has* or *had*. It can be part of the verb phrase or used elsewhere in the sentence.

She **has jumped** farther than any other contestant so far.
   (*Jumped* is part of the verb phrase and *has jumped* is the complete verb phrase.)
I forgot to read the second chapter, the one **added** to last week's assignment.
   (*Added* is not part of the verb phrase.)

(3) *to* + Verb

Another verb form, called the *infinitive*, has *to* added to the base form.

I was supposed **to give** her the ticket.
   (*Was supposed to give* is the whole verb phrase.)
To forgive is easier than **to forget.**
   (*To forgive* and *to forget* are not part of the verb phrase.)

Exercise 1.1: Proofreading Practice

To practice your ability to identify verbs, verb phrases, and verb forms, underline the verbs and verb phrases in the following sentences. Circle the verb forms both in verb phrases and elsewhere in the sentence. As an example, the first sentence is already marked. Remember, many sentences have more than one verb or verb phrase.

Remember to ask yourself the following questions:

- *To find a verb or verb phrase:*

  Which word or group of words expresses action, shows a state of existence, or links the subject, the doer of the action, to the rest of the sentence?

- *To find a verb form:*

  Which words end in *-ing* or *-ed* or have *to* + verb?
  Which of these are not complete verbs in themselves?

(1) For a long time psychologists <u>have</u> (wondered) what memories <u>are</u> and where they <u>are</u> (stored) in the human brain. (2) Because it is the basis of human intellect, memory has been studied intensely. (3) According to one psychologist, memory is an umbrella term for a whole range of processes that occur in our brains. (4) In particular, psychologists have identified two types of memory. (5) One type is called declarative memory, and it includes memories of facts such as names, places, dates, even baseball scores. (6) It is called declarative because we use it to declare things. (7) For example, a person can declare that his or her favorite food is fried bean sprouts. (8) The other type is called procedural memory. (9) It is the type of memory acquired

1c
v

by repetitive practice or conditioning, and it includes skills such as riding a bike or typing. (10) We need both types of memory in our daily living because we need facts and use a variety of skills.

Exercise 1.2: Pattern Practice

The following paragraph is in the present tense. Change it to the past tense by underlining the verbs and writing the past tense verb above the word that is changed. As an example the first sentence is already marked.

    (1) To learn more about memory, a psychologist <u>studies</u> studied visual memory by watching monkeys. (2) To do this, he uses a game that requires the monkey to pick up a block in order to find the food in a pail underneath. (3) After a brief delay the monkey again sees the old block on top of a pail and also sees a new block with a pail underneath it. (4) Only the new block now covers a pail with bananas in it. (5) The monkey quickly learns each time to pick up the new block in order to find food. (6) This demonstrates that the monkey remembers what the old block looks like and also what distinguishes the new block. (7) The psychologist concludes that visual memory is at work.

1c Verb Tense

Verb tense is the form of the verb that expresses time. The time indicated is past, present, or future.

**1c
v**

The four kinds of tenses for the past, present, and future described here are as follows:

Simple

Progressive: *be* + *-ing* form of the verb

Perfect: *have*

had + the *-ed* form of the verb

shall

Perfect progressive: *have*

had + *been* + *-ing* form of the verb

VERB FORM CHART

	Present	*Past*	*Future*
Simple:	I walk	I walked	I will walk
Progressive:	I am walking	I was walking	I will be walking
Perfect:	I have walked	I had walked	I will have walked
Past progressive	I have been walking	I had been walking	I will have been walking

VERB TENSE CHART

(1) Present Tense

Simple Present

- Present action or condition: She **counts** the votes. They **are** happy.
- General truth: States **defend** their rights.
- Habitual action: He **drinks** orange juice for breakfast.
- Future time: The plane **arrives** at 10 P.M. tonight.
- Literary or timeless truth: Shakespeare **uses** humor effectively.

Form: This is the form found in the dictionary and is often called the base form. For third person singular subjects (he, she, it), add an -*s* or -*es*.

I, you, we, they **walk.**
He, she, it **walks.**

I, you, we, they **push.**
He, she, it **pushes.**

Present Progressive

- Activity in progress, not finished, or continued:
The committee **is studying** that proposal.

Form: This form has two parts: *is* (or) *are* + -*ing* form of the verb.

We **are going.**
He **is singing.**

Present Perfect

- Action that began in the past and leads up to and includes the present: The company **has sold** that product since January.

- Habitual or continued action started in the past and continuing into the present: She **has** not **smoked** a cigarette for three years.

Form: Use *have* (or) *has* + -*ed* form of regular verbs (called the past participle)

I **have eaten.**
He **has** not **called.**

Present Perfect Progressive

- Action that began in the past, continues to the present, and may continue into the future: They **have been considering** that purchase for three months.

1c
v

Form: Use *have* (or) *has* + *been* + *-ing* form of the verb.

He **has been running.**
They **have been meeting.**

(2) Past Tense

Simple Past

- Completed action: We **visited** the museum during the summer.

- Completed condition: It **was** cloudy yesterday.

Form: Add *-ed* for regular verbs. See the list of irregular verbs for other forms.

I **walked.**
They **awoke.**

Past Progressive

- Past action that took place over a period of time: They **were driving** through the desert when the sandstorm hit.

- Past action that was interrupted by another action: The engine **was running** when he left the car.

Form: Use *was* (or) *were* + *-ing* form of the verb.

She **was singing.**
We **were running.**

Past Perfect

- Action or event completed before another event in the past: When the meeting began, she **had** already **left** the building.

Form: Use *had* + *-ed* form of the verb (past participle).

He **had** already **reviewed** the list when Mary came in.

Past Perfect Progressive

- Ongoing condition in the past that has ended: The diplomat **had been planning** to visit when his government was overthrown.

Form: Use *had + -ing* form of the verb.

They **had been looking.**
She **had been speaking.**

(3) Future Tense

Simple Future

- Actions or events in the future: The recycling center **will open** next week.

Form: Use *shall* (or) *will* + base form of the verb. (In American English *will* is commonly used for all persons, but in British English *shall* is often used for the first person.)

I **will choose.**
They **will enter.**

Future Progressive

- Future action that will continue for some time: I **will be expecting** your call.

Form: Use *will* or *shall* + *be* + *-ing* form of the verb.

He **will be studying.**
They **will be driving.**

Future Perfect

- Actions that will be completed by or before a specified time in the future: By Thursday, we **will have cleaned** up the whole filing cabinet.

Form: Use *will* (or) *shall* + *have* + *-ed* form of the verb (past participle).

They **will have walked.**

Future Perfect Progressive

- Ongoing actions or conditions until a specific time in the future: In June we **will have been renting** this apartment for a year.

Form: Use *will* (or) *shall* + *have* + *been* + *-ing* form of the verb.

They **will have been paying.**

(4) Irregular Verbs

The most often used irregular verbs have the following forms:

	Present		Past	
	Singular	*Plural*	*Singular*	*Plural*
to be	I am	we are	I was	we were
	you are	you are	you were	you were
	he, she, it is	they are	he, she, it was	they were
to have	I have	we have	I had	we had
	you have	you have	you had	you had
	he, she, it has	they have	he, she, it had	they had
to do	I do	we do	I did	we did
	you do	you do	you did	you did
	he, she, it does	they do	he, she, it did	they did

Irregular Verbs

Base (or Present)	Past	Past Participle
arise	arose	arisen
awake	awoke	awaken
be	was, were	been
beat	beat	beaten
become	became	become
begin	began	begun
bend	bent	bent
bet	bet	bet
bind	bound	bound
bite	bit	bitten (or) bit
bleed	bled	bled
blow	blew	blown
break	broke	broken
bring	brought	brought
build	built	built
burst	burst	burst
buy	bought	bought
cast	cast	cast
catch	caught	caught
choose	chose	chosen
cling	clung	clung
come	came	come
cost	cost	cost
creep	crept	crept
cut	cut	cut
deal	dealt	dealt
dig	dug	dug
dive	dived (or) dove	dived
do	did	done
draw	drew	drawn
drink	drank	drunk
drive	drove	driven
eat	ate	eaten
fall	fell	fallen
feed	fed	fed
feel	felt	felt

Base (or Present)	Past	Past Participle
fight	fought	fought
find	found	found
fling	flung	flung
fly	flew	flown
forbid	forbade	forbidden
forget	forgot	forgotten
forgive	forgave	forgiven
freeze	froze	frozen
get	got	gotten
give	gave	given
go	went	gone
grind	ground	ground
grow	grew	grown
hang	hung	hung
have	had	had
hear	heard	heard
hide	hid	hidden
hit	hit	hit
hold	held	held
hurt	hurt	hurt
keep	kept	kept
know	knew	known
lay	laid	laid
lead	led	led
leave	left	left
lend	lent	lent
let	let	let
lie	lay	lain
lose	lost	lost
make	made	made
mean	meant	meant
meet	met	met
mistake	mistook	mistaken
pay	paid	paid
prove	proved	proved (or) proven
put	put	put
quit	quit	quit
read	read	read
ride	rode	ridden

Base (or Present)	Past	Past Participle
ring	rang	rung
rise	rose	risen
run	ran	run
say	said	said
see	saw	seen
seek	sought	sought
sell	sold	sold
send	sent	sent
set	set	set
shake	shook	shaken
shed	shed	shed
shine	shone	shone
shoot	shot	shot
shrink	shrank	shrunk
shut	shut	shut
sing	sang	sung
sink	sank (or) sunk	sunk
sit	sat	sat
sleep	slept	slept
slide	slid	slid
speak	spoke	spoken
spend	spent	spent
spin	spun	spun
split	split	split
spread	spread	spread
spring	sprang	sprung
stand	stood	stood
steal	stole	stolen
stick	stuck	stuck
sting	stung	stung
stink	stank	stunk
strike	struck	struck
swear	swore	sworn
sweep	swept	swept
swim	swam	swum
swing	swang	swung
take	took	taken
teach	taught	taught
tear	tore	torn

Base (or Present)	Past	Past Participle
tell	told	told
think	thought	thought
throw	threw	thrown
understand	understood	understood
wake	woke	waken
wear	wore	worn
weep	wept	wept
win	won	won
wind	wound	wound
wring	wrung	wrung
write	wrote	written

Exercise 1.3: Proofreading Practice

In the following paragraph, choose the correct verbs from the options given in parentheses. Remember that the time expressed in the verb has to agree with the meaning of the sentence.

The way children (1. learn, will learn) to draw seems simple. But studies show that when given some kind of marker, young children (2. have begun, will begin, begin) by scribbling on any available surface. At first, these children's drawings (3. are, should be, had been) simple, clumsy, and unrealistic, but gradually the drawings (4. have become, should become, become) more realistic. One researcher who (5. will study, could study, has studied) the drawings of one- and two-year-olds concludes that their early scrawls (6. are representing, may represent, had represented) gestures and motions. For example, the researcher notes that one two-year-old child who was observed (7. took, has taken, had taken) a marker and (8. is hopping, hopped, had hopped) it around on the paper, leaving a mark with each imprint and explaining as he drew that the rabbit (9. was going, had gone, could have gone) hop-hop. The researcher (10. had concluded, has concluded, concludes) that the child was symbolizing the rabbit's motion, not its size, shape or color. Someone who (11. had seen, sees, might see) only dots on a page (12. would not see, has not seen, had not seen) a rabbit and (13. should conclude, would conclude, had concluded) that the child's attempts to draw a rabbit (14. have failed, had failed, failed).

Exercise 1.4: Pattern Practice

The following paragraph is written in present tense. At the beginning of the paragraph add the words "Last year" and rewrite the rest of the paragraph so that it is in past tense. To do so, change all the italicized verbs to past tense.

   One of the most popular new attractions in Japanese recreation parks *is* a maze for people to walk through. For some people this *can be* twenty minutes of pleasant exercise, but others *take* an hour or two because they *run* in circles. Admission *costs* about $3 a person, an amount that *makes* mazes cheaper than movies. Mazes also *last* longer than roller coaster rides. One Japanese businessperson, first dragged there by his wife, *says* that he *enjoys* it because it *keeps* him so busy that he *forgets* all his other worries. Some people *like* to amble in a leisurely way through the maze and *let* time pass them by, but most maze players *try* to get out in the shortest time possible. At the entrance, a machine *gives* people a ticket stamped with the time they *enter*. Some people *quit* in the middle and *head* for an emergency exit or *ask* a guard for help. But most *rise* to the challenge and *keep* going until they *emerge* at the other end, hoping to claim a prize.

1∂ Verb Voice

Verb voice tells whether the verb is in the active or passive voice. In the active voice, the subject (the word or words that answer who or what for the verb) performs the action of the verb. In the passive voice, the subject receives the action. The doer of the action in the passive voice may either appear in a "by the _____" phrase or be omitted.

Active: The dog bit the boy.

Passive: The boy was bitten by the dog. (The subject of this sentence is the boy, but he was not doing the action of biting.)

1f
v

> **HINT:** In the passive voice the verb phrase always includes a form of the *to be* verb, such as *is, are, was, is being*, and so on. Also, if the doer of the action is named, it is in a phrase "by the _____."

1e Verb Mood

The **mood of a verb** tells whether it expresses a fact (**declarative**), expresses some doubt or something contrary to fact (**subjunctive**), or expresses a command (**imperative**).

Tanya **giggles** loudly. (expresses a fact)
If she **were** only three inches taller, she **could** see over the counter. (expresses some condition contrary to fact)
Bring your guitar. (expresses a command)

1f Modal Verbs

Modals are helping verbs that express ability, a request, or an attitude, such as interest, expectation, possibility, or obligation.

The following list includes the more common modal verbs:

Shall, should express intent to do something, advisability:

You **should** try to exercise more often.

Will, would express strong intent:

I **will** return those books to the library tomorrow.

Can, could express capability, possibility, request:

I **can** loan you my tape of that concert.

May, might express possibility or permission, request.

She **may** buy a new computer.

Must, ought to express obligation or need:

I **ought to** fill the gas tank before we drive into town.

1g *Phrasal Verbs*

Phrasal verbs are verbs which have a following word that helps to indicate the meaning. Because the second word often changes the meaning, phrasal verbs are idioms (see Chapter 50e).

look **over** (examine)

Example: He suggested that she look **over** the terms of the contract.

look up (search)

Example: I need to look **up** that phone number in the directory.

People learning English as a second language must learn long lists of phrasal verbs (and their different meanings). In some cases, a noun or pronoun can be inserted so that the verb is separated from its additional word or words. In other cases, there can be no separation:

Separable: count in (include)

Jeremy told the team to **count** him **in.**

Inseparable: count on (rely)

Jeremy told the team they could **count on** him to help.

The following list includes some commonly used phrasal verbs and their meanings. Check a dictionary for other phrasal verbs.

Separable

add up: add
break down: analzye
bring on: cause
bring to: revive
bring up: raise
burn down: destroy by burning
burn up: consumed
    by fire or anger
call off: cancel, order away
call up: telephone
carry on: continue
carry out: fulfill, complete,
    accomplish, perform
cross out: eliminate
cut down: reduce in quantity

cut off: interrupt, sever
cut out: eliminate, delete
cut up: cut into small pieces
give out: distribute
give up: surrender
hand in: submit
keep up: maintain
leave out: omit
make up: invent, prepare
put off: postpone
put on: dress
take off: remove, undress
take up: discuss
try out: test
use up: consume

Inseparable

back out of: desert
call for: require
come across: find accidentally
come back: return
come over: visit
come to: regain consciousness
do without: deprive oneself of
fall behind: lag
get around: evade
get by: succeed with
    minimum effort
get out of: escape, evade
get through: finish
go over: review
keep on: continue

look for: seek
look into: investigate
look like: resemble
look out for: beware of
look over: examine
look up: search for
pass out: distribute, faint
pick out: choose
put out: extinguish
run across: discover by chance
run into: meet by chance
run over: hit by a car
show off: display
show up: appear

1h Verbs with -ing and to + Verb Forms

Some verbs combine only with the *-ing* form of the verb (gerund); some combine only with the to + verb form (infinitive); some verbs can be followed by either form.

Verbs followed only by -ing forms (gerunds):

admit	keep on
appreciate	postpone
avoid	practice
consider	recall
deny	regret
enjoy	risk
finish	stop
fond of	suggest
keep	

Example: He <u>admits</u> <u>spending</u> that money.
　　　　　　(verb) + (gerund)
Wrong:　　I recall to read that book.
Revised:　 I recall reading that book.

Verbs followed only by to + verb forms (infinitives):

agree	need
ask	plan
decide	promise
expect	want
hope	

Example: We <u>agree</u> <u>to send</u> an answer by tomorrow.
　　　　　　(verb) + (infinitive)
Wrong:　　I want hearing more about your proposal.
Revised:　 I want to hear more about your proposal.

Verbs that can be followed by either form:

begin	love
continue	prefer
hate	start
like	try

Example: They begin to sing.

or

They begin singing.

Exercise 1.5: Proofreading Practice

In the following paragraph underline verb phrases in each sentence and indicate the voice of the verb by writing "active" or "passive." Ask yourself the following questions:

- Is the subject receiving any action? If so, it's passive. If not, it's active.

- Is there a doer named in the "by the _____ " phrase? If so, it's passive.

The mood of most of the verbs is factual (declarative). If you find any that state something contrary to fact (subjunctive), write subjunctive. If you spot a command, write command.

(1) America <u>is</u> such a youth-oriented nation that roughly $3
    active

billion <u>is spent</u> every year by consumers who <u>want to eliminate</u>
      passive   active

wrinkles. (2) Between $1 and $2 billion of this is spent on cos-

metic surgery. (3) Now a new drug may offer a better answer. (4)

The drug, retinoic acid, was originally marketed as an acne

cream and is now being advertised as a treatment to improve

skin tone and erase wrinkles. (5) "Buy a facelift in a tube" could

be the advertising slogan for this drug, which may reverse the

process of aging.

Exercise 1.6: Sentence Practice

Combine the short sentences in the following paragraph into longer ones. Underline all the verb phrases in your revised sentences and label them as active or passive. Try to use mostly active verbs, but you will find that some passive verbs are also useful.

Retinoic acid is a new drug. It is promising. It is being prescribed by doctors as a wrinkle cream. A company owns it. They call it a wonder drug. Retinoic acid was approved by the Food and Drug Administration (FDA). The FDA approved it as an acne cream. This was done in 1971. Some users over thirty-five told doctors side effects were produced. One side effect for some people was smoother, younger-looking skin. The skin was reported by these people to have less wrinkles. Other users said their skin was irritated by the drug. The drug was not evaluated by the FDA as a wrinkle fighter. The drug is being tested now for its ability to make skin look younger. But the drug can be prescribed by doctors for its side effects. The appropriate use of the drug can be decided by doctors. They can recommend it for uses not yet approved by the FDA.

2 *Nouns and Pronouns*

2a *Nouns* (n)

A **noun** is a word that names a person, place, thing, or idea.

The following is a list of nouns:

Marilyn Monroe	Des Moines	peace
Henry	light bulb	justice
forest	Bobby	French
pictures		

2a
n

(1) Proper and Common Nouns

A **proper noun** begins with a capital letter and names a specific place, person, or thing.

A **common noun** does not begin with a capital letter and names a general category rather than some specific thing.

Proper nouns	*Common nouns*
Lake Michigan	lake
Joe Montana	football player
Coca-Cola	cola drink
Rembrandt	painter
Swedish	language

HINT: When deciding whether or not to capitalize a noun, imagine that you are filling out a form and you come to a section that asks for a name. Is the noun in question a name that could be put on the line asking for the specific name of someone or something? For example, you may be wondering whether *sociology department* is a proper noun that needs capital letters. Note the difference in the following two sentences:

Courses for social workers are often taught in a sociology department.

(Here *sociology department* is a general term, not the specific name you would fill in on any usual form.)

I signed up for a course on Indian culture taught by Professor Benton in the Sociology Department at Orton State University.

(Here *Sociology Department* names a specific department at a specific college. When Professor Benton fills out forms asking for her place of employment, she specifies the name of her department. At other colleges the name might be Sociology and Anthropology Department or Department of Sociological Science.)

(2) Singular, Plural, and Collective Nouns

A **singular noun** refers to one person, place, or thing and is the form you would look up in the dictionary.
A **plural noun** is the form that refers to more than one person, place, or thing.
A **collective noun** refers to a group acting as a unit, such as a committee, a herd, or a jury.
Exceptions: Some nouns do not fall in these categories because they refer to abstract or general concepts that cannot be counted and do not have plural forms. Examples are homework, peace, furniture, and knowledge.

Singular nouns	Plural nouns	Collective nouns
box	boxes	family
child	children	senate

(3) Noun Endings

Nouns have endings that show plural and possession.

Plurals

Some nouns add -s or -es, the most common markers at the end of a noun to indicate the plural.

Singular	Plural
one cup	many cups
one hand	a pair of hands
a box	two boxes
one kiss	several kisses

Some nouns change form.

Singular	Plural
one child	three children
one man	some men
one woman	several women
a mouse	two mice

Many nouns that end in *-f* or *-fe* form their plurals by changing the *f* to *v* and adding *es.*

Singular	Plural
one half	two halves
one life	nine lives
the leaf	the leaves

However, there are exceptions:

one roof	several roofs

Some nouns have other plural forms.

Singular	Plural
one ox	a pair of oxen
a stimulus	some stimuli
the medium	all the media

Some nouns do not change.

Singular	Plural
a deer	several deer
one sheep	two sheep

There are other ways to mark plurals. For more discussion of the spelling of plurals, see Chapter 45, and check your dictionary.

HINT 1: Nouns ending with *-s* can be confusing because the possessive marker is also an *-s.* Some writers make the mistake of putting an apostrophe in plural nouns:

Wrong: There was a sale on potato chip's.
Revised: There was a sale on potato chips.

HINT 2: Some writers do not use—or hear—the plural forms in their speech, but standard English requires the plural endings in writing. If you notice a tendency to omit written plurals, proofread your last drafts. To help your eye see the end of the word, point to the end of the noun with your pen or finger to be sure that you see the plural ending. Some writers need repeated practice to notice the missing plural endings.

HINT 3: Although the *-s* marks the plural at the end of many nouns, it is also used at the end of singular verbs with he, she, it, or a singular noun as the subject.

He walks.

The shoe fits.

Thus, when the plural subject noun has an *-s* or a different marker at the end, the verb cannot have an *-s* added at the end to mark the singular. For the same reason, a verb with a singular *-s* marker cannot have a subject noun with an *-s* plural ending. So, when proofing, check for *-s* endings, which may be needed at the end of the noun or the verb, but not both.

Possession

The possessive form shows possession, ownership, or a close relationship. This is clear when we write "Mary's hat" as Mary owns or possesses the hat, but the possessive is less apparent when we write "journey's end" or "yesterday's news." It may be more helpful to think about the "of" relationship between two nouns that exists in the possessive form:

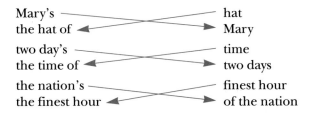

The possessive marker is either an *'s* or *'*. If the plural marker *-s* or *-es* is added to the noun, only an apostrophe is added after the plural. For singular nouns ending in *-s*, such as "grass," the *-s* after the apostrophe is optional. It can be added if it doesn't make pronouncing the word more difficult. (See Chapter 24.)

Singular	*Plural*
Miriam's hat	the girls' hats
the glass's edge	all the glasses' edges

**2a
n**

James' story (or) James's story
Aldez' zip code (Adding an *'s* here would make the pronunciation
  difficult.)

HINT: Remember that everything to the left of the apostrophe is the word and its plural. A proofreading strategy is to check the order of what is written. First, write the word, then add any plural markers, and finally, add the possessive markers afterward.

---

(4) Count and Noncount Nouns

A **count noun** names something that can be counted because it can be divided into units that are separate and distinct from each other. Count nouns, which have plurals, usually refer to things that can be seen or heard.

A **noncount noun** names something that cannot be counted because it is an abstraction or substance that is thought of as a whole or that cannot be cut into parts. Noncount nouns, which do not have plurals, have a collective meaning.

Count nouns	*Noncount nouns*
chair	furniture
word	weather
finger	humor
apple	oil
child	milk
page	air

HINT: Some nouns in English have both a count and a noncount meaning. The count meaning is specific, and the noncount meaning is abstract and general:

Count: The **exercises** were difficult to do.
Noncount: **Exercise** is good for our health.
Count: There were bright **lights** in the sky.
Noncount: **Light** is important for plants.

The names of many foods are noncount nouns:

bread	spaghetti
coffee	spinach
corn	tofu

To indicate an amount for a noncount noun, use a count noun first:

a pound of coffee	a loaf of bread
an ear of corn	a gallon of milk

2b
pr

....

HINT: Knowing whether a noun is a count or noncount noun is important in determining whether or not to use *a, an,* or *the.* (See Section 4b.)

- Singular count nouns need an article:

  She returned **the** book.
  The store offered **a** discount.

- Noncount nouns generally do not need an article:

  Plants need water.
  He enjoys **tennis.**

....

2b *Pronouns* (pr)

A **pronoun** takes the place of a noun.

If we had only nouns and no pronouns in English, we would have to write the following sentences:

Without Pronouns: (1) LeeAnn lost LeeAnn's car keys.

(2) When Michael went to the library, Michael found some useful references for Michael's paper.

Several useful categories of pronouns are shown next.

(1) Personal Pronouns

Personal Pronouns refer to people or things:

Subject case	Object case	Possessive case	
I	me	my	mine
you	you	your	yours
he	him	his	his
she	her	her	hers
it	it	its	its
we	us	our	ours
they	them	their	theirs

(2) Demonstrative Pronouns

Demonstrative Pronouns refer to things:

this
that   *This* cup of coffee is mine.
these
those

(3) Relative Pronouns

Relative Pronouns show the relationship of a dependent clause (see Chapter 8b) to a noun in the sentence:

that
which
who   Mrs. Bloom is the friend *who* helped me.
whom
whose

Sometimes relative pronouns can be omitted when they are understood.

This isn't the sandwich *that* I ordered.
This isn't the sandwich I ordered.

(4) Interrogative Pronouns

Interrogative Pronouns are used in questions:

who
whose
whom   *Which* movie do you want to see?
which
that

(5) Indefinite Pronouns

Indefinite Pronouns make indefinite reference to nouns:

anyone/anybody
either
everyone/everybody   Is *someone* going to move that car
everything   out of my way?
nothing
one
someone/somebody

....

HINT: Indefinite pronouns are usually singular and require a singular verb.

Everyone is going to the game.

However, some indefinite pronouns, such as *both, few,* and *many* require a plural verb. Other indefinite pronouns, such as *all, any, more, most, none,* and *some* may be either singular or plural, depending on the meaning of the sentence.

Singular: Some of my homework is done.
(Here some refers to a portion or a part of the homework. Because a "portion" or a "part" is thought of as a single entity, the verb is singular.)
Plural: Some of these plates are chipped.
(Here some refers to at least several plates. Because several is thought of as plural, the verb is plural.)
Singular: All the coffee is brewed.
Plural: All the customers are pleased.
....

(6) Possessive Pronouns

Possessive Pronouns do not take an apostrophe:

its nose	(not: it's nose)
that dog of hers	(not: that dog of her's)
the house is theirs	(not: the house is theirs')

Some writers confuse the possessive pronouns with contractions:

It's a warm day	= **It is** a warm day
There's a shooting star	= **There is** a shooting star

See Chapter 24 on apostrophes.

Exercise 2.1: Proofreading Exercise

Read the following paragraph and underline all the -s and -es endings that mark plural nouns and circle all the 's, s', and ' possessive markers.

It is a sad fact of life that what some people call the "everyday courtesies of life" are disappearing faster than finger bowls and engineers' slide rules. People in movie theaters carry on loud conversations, older people on buses rarely have anyone get up and offer them a seat, and few bother to offer thanks to a helpful salesperson. Some people say that courteous ways seem to have lingered longer in small towns than in big cities and that some regions—notably the South—cling more than others to some remaining signs of polite behavior. But more often we hear complaints that courtesy is declining, dying, or dead. Says one New York executive: "There's no such thing as umbrella courtesy. Everybody's umbrella is aimed at my eye level." And a store owner in another city says that short-tempered waiters in restaurants and impatient salesclerks in stores make her feel as if she's bothering them by asking for service. Common courtesy may be a thing of the past.

Exercise 2.2: Proofreading Practice

In the following paragraph there are some missing -s and -es plural noun endings and missing possessive markers. Add any that are missing.

Among the people who are most aware of the current lack of everyday politeness are airline flight attendant and newspaper advice columnist. Says one flight attendant: "Courtesy is almost zero. People think you're supposed to carry all their bag on and off the flight, even when you have dozen of other passenger to attend to." One syndicated advice columnist notes that courtesy is so rare these day that when someone is kind, helpful, or generous, it is an event worth writing about to an advice columnist. Some teacher blame televisions poor example, especially the many rude detective who shove people around, bang down all those door, and yell in peoples face. Too many of our current movie hero are not particularly gallant, thoughtful, or polite. As a psychologist recently noted, it is hard to explain to children what good manner are when they don't see such behavior on their television or movie screen.

Exercise 2.3: Pattern Practice

In the following paragraph there are many singular nouns. Where it is appropriate, change the singular nouns to plural, add the appropriate noun endings, and change any other words or word endings that need to be altered.

The foreign tourist who travels in the United States often notices that the American is not as polite as a person from another country. The tourist from Europe, who is used to a more formal manner, is particularly offended by the American who immediately calls the tourist by his or her first name. Impoliteness in the United States extends even to an object. An English businessperson noted that in America a public sign issues a command: "No Smoking" or "Do Not Enter." In England such a sign would be less commanding: "No Smoking Please" or "Please Do Not Enter." An American can also be rude without meaning to be. As a Japanese visitor noticed, the nurse who led him into the doctor's office said, "Come in here." In Japan, the visitor noted, a nurse would say, "Please follow me." The foreign tourist, unfortunately, has a variety of such stories to take back to his or her country.

Exercise 2.4: Proofreading Practice

In the parentheses in the following paragraph there are choices to make between count and noncount nouns. Underline the correct choice.

(1) (American/Americans) have always enjoyed drinking (coffee/coffees). (2) Now there is a new trend as (restaurant/restaurants) and (store/stores) are beginning to sell many specialty (coffee/coffees) with (flavor/flavors) such as chocolate, cinna-

mon, and almond. (3) Americans, who are used to eating (dozen/dozens) of different flavors of (ice cream/ice creams), can now decide between different types of coffee with (milk/milks) or with whipped (cream/creams). (4) This can cause (problem/problems) because customers need more (information/informations) in order to choose between flavors and types of coffee they have never tried before. (5) (Advertising/Advertisings) will surely help American coffee (drinker/drinkers) to become more familiar with specialty coffees.

Exercise 2.5 Pattern Practice

Write a sentence using each of the nouns listed here. Make the noun plural if it can be used in the plural.

1.	laughter	6.	liberty
2.	machine	7.	ice
3.	chair	8.	engineering
4.	homework	9.	key
5.	book	10.	telephone

3 Pronoun Case and Reference

3a Pronoun Case (ca)

Pronoun case refers to the form of the pronoun that is needed in a sentence.

Pronoun Cases

	Subject		Object		Possessive	
	Singular	Plural	Singular	Plural	Singular	Plural
1st:	I	we	me	us	my, mine	our, ours
2nd:	you	you	you	you	your, yours	your, yours
3rd:	he	they	him	them	his	their, theirs
	she	they	her	them	her, hers	their, theirs
	it	they	it	them	it, its	their, theirs

(1) Subject Case

Subject case refers to pronouns used as subjects. When pronouns are used as subjects or come after linking verbs such as *is*, use the subject case:

She won the lottery. *(She* is the subject case pronoun.)

Who's there? It is **I**. (In the second sentence *I* is the subject case pronoun that comes after the linking verb *is*.)

(2) Object Case

Object case refers to pronouns used as objects. When pronouns are objects of verbs (receive the action of the verb), use the object case:

I hugged **her**. (object)

When pronouns are objects of verb forms (receive the action of the verb form), use the object case:

Seeing Dan and **me**, she waved. (object)

When pronouns are indirect objects of verbs (explain for whom or to whom something is done), use the object case:

I gave **her** the glass. (indirect object)

The indirect object can often be changed into a *to + object pronoun* phrase:

I gave the glass **to her**.

Use the object case when pronouns are used as objects of prepositions (complete the meaning of the preposition):

Al gave the money to **them**. (object)

....

HINT 1: Remember that *between, except,* and *with* are prepositions and take the object case.

Wrong: between you and **I**
Revised: between you and **me**

Wrong: except Fran and **I**
Revised: except Fran and **me**

Wrong: with **he** and **I**
Revised: with **him** and **me**

HINT 2: Don't use *them* as a pointing pronoun in place of *these* or *those*. Use *them* only as the object by itself.

Wrong: He liked **them** socks.
Revised: He liked **those** socks. (or) He liked **them**.

(3) Possessive Case
Possessive case refers to pronouns used as possessives.

Is this **her** hat?

-or-

Is this **hers**?

We gave him **our** money.

-or-

We gave him **ours**.

HINT 1: The possessive case pronouns never take apostrophes.

Wrong: The insect spread **it's** wings.
Revised: The insect spread **its** wings.

HINT 2: Use possessive case before *-ing* verb forms.

Wrong: The crowd cheered **him** making a three-point basket.
Revised: The crowd cheered **his** making a three-point basket.

(4) Pronouns in Compound Constructions
When your sentence has two pronouns or a noun and a pronoun, you can find the right case by temporarily eliminating the noun or one of the pronouns as you read it to yourself. You'll hear the case that is needed.

Wrong: John and **him** went to the store.
(If *John* is eliminated, the sentence would be *"Him* went to the store." It's easier to notice the wrong pronoun case here.
Revised: John and **he** went to the store.

When in doubt as to which pronoun case to use, some writers make the mistake of choosing the subject case because it sounds more formal or "correct."

**3a
ca**

Wrong: Mrs. Wagner gave the tickets to **Lutecia** and **I**.

> Once again, try the strategy of dropping the noun, *Lutecia*. You'll be able to hear that the sentence sounds wrong.

>> **Wrong:** Mrs. Wagner gave the tickets to **I**. Because *to* is a preposition, the noun or pronoun that follows is the object of the preposition and should be in the object case.

Revised: Mrs. Wagner gave the tickets to **Lutecia** and **me**.

When a pronoun and noun are used together, you can use the same strategy of dropping the noun to hear whether the case of the pronoun sounds wrong.

Wrong: Us players gave the coach a rousing cheer.

> When you drop the noun *players*, the sentence is as follows:

>> **Wrong: Us** gave the coach a rousing cheer.

Revised: We players gave the coach a rousing cheer.

Wrong: The lecturer told **we students** to quiet down.

> **We students** is the object of the verb and needs the object case pronoun.

Revised: The lecturer told **us students** to quiet down.

Wrong: The newest members of the club, **Marni** and **me**, were asked to pay our dues promptly.

> Since the phrase *Marni and me* explains the noun *members* (the subject of the sentence), the subject case of the pronoun is needed here.

Revised: The newest members of the club, **Marni and I**, were asked to pay our dues promptly.

Wrong: The usher had to find more programs for the latecomers, **Jeff** and **I**.

> Because the phrase *Jeff and I* explains the noun *latecomers* (the object of the preposition *for*), the pronoun has to be in the object case.

Revised: The usher had to find more programs for the latecomers, **Jeff** and **me**.

(5) Who/Whom

In informal speech some people may not distinguish between *who* and *whom*. But for formal writing, the cases are as follows:

Subject	*Object*	*Possessive*
who	whom	whose
whoever	whomever	

Subject Case: Who is going to the concert tonight?
(*Who* is the subject of the sentence.)

Object Case: To **whom** should I give this ticket?
(*Whom* is the object of the preposition *to*.)

Possessive Case: No one was sure **whose** voice that was.

When *who* introduces a dependent clause after a preposition, use the subject case:

Give this to **whoever** wants it.

....

HINT: If you aren't sure whether to use *who* or *whom*, turn a question into a statement or rearrange the order of the phrase:

Question: Who/whom are you looking for?
Statement: You are looking for **whom**.
    (object of the preposition)

Sentence: She is someone **who/whom** I know well.
Rearranged Order: I know **whom** well.
    (direct object)

....

(6) Omitted Words in Comparisons

In comparisons using *than* and *as*, choose the correct pronoun case by recalling the words that are omitted:

Example: He is taller than **I/me**.
    The omitted words here are "am tall."
    He is taller than **I** (am tall)
Revised: He is taller than *I*.

Example: Our cat likes my sister more than **I/me**.
    The omitted words here are "it likes."
    Our cat likes my sister more than (it likes) **me**.
Revised: Our cat likes my sister more than **me**.

3a
ca

Exercise 3.1: Proofreading Practice
In the following paragraph there are some errors in pronoun case.
Underline the incorrect pronoun forms and write the correct form above
the underlined word.

Have you ever wondered how people in the entertainment
industry choose what you and me will see on television, read in
books, and hear on records? Some producers and publishers say
that the executives in their companies and them rely on instinct
and an ability to forecast trends in taste. But we consumers cannot be relied on to be consistent from one month to the next.
So, market researchers constantly keep seeking our opinions.
For example, they ask we moviegoers to preview movies and to
fill out questionnaires. Reactions from we and our friends are
then studied closely. Sometimes, the market researchers merely
forecast from previous experience what you and me are likely to
prefer. Still, some movies fail for reasons that the market
researchers cannot understand. When that happens, who does
the movie studio blame? The producer will say that the director
and him did all they could but that the leading actor failed to
attract an audience. Sometimes, though, us moviegoers simply
get tired of some types of movies and want more variety.

Exercise 3.2: Pattern Practice
Using the patterns given here, write a similar sentence of your own for
each pattern.

Pattern A: a sentence with an object case pronoun after the
             preposition *between, except,* or *with*

Everyone was able to hear the bird call **except her**.

Pattern B: a sentence with a compound object that includes a pronoun in the object case.

The newspaper article listed Arthur and **him** as the winners of the contest.

Pattern C: a sentence with a comparison that includes a subject case pronoun

Everyone in the room was dressed more warmly than **I**.

Pattern D: a sentence with a comparison that includes an object case pronoun

The bird was more frightened of the dog than **me**.

Pattern E: a sentence with a compound subject that includes a subject case pronoun

During the festival the announcer and **she** took turns thanking all the people who had helped to organize the events.

3b *Pronoun Reference* (ref)

Pronoun reference is the relationship between the pronoun and the noun (*antecedent*) for which it is substituting.

Pronouns are substitutes for nouns. To help your reader see this relationship clearly:

- Pronouns should indicate to which nouns they are referring.

- Pronouns should be reasonably close to their nouns.

  Unclear Reference: Gina told Michelle that **she** took **her** bike to the library.

  (Did Gina take Michelle's bike or her own bike to the library?)

  Revised: When Gina took Michelle's bike to the library, she told Michelle she was borrowing it.

Be sure that your pronouns refer to a noun that has been mentioned on the page and not merely implied. Also, watch out for the vague *they* that doesn't refer to any specific group or the vague *this* or *it* that doesn't refer back to any specific word or phrase.

Unclear Reference: In Hollywood **they** don't know what the American public really wants in movies.

(Who are the *they* referred to here?)

Revised: In Hollywood the screenwriters and producers don't know what the American public really wants in movies.

Unclear Reference: When the town board inquired about the cost of the next political campaign, the board was assured that **they** would pay for **their** own campaigns.

(Who does *they* and *their* refer to? Most likely *they* refers to the politicians who will be campaigning, but the word "politician" is only inferred.)

Revised: When the town board inquired about the cost of the next political campaign, the board was assured that the politicians would pay for their own campaigns.

Unclear Reference: Martina worked in a national forest last summer, and **this** may be her career choice.

(What does *this* refer to? Because there is no word or phrase in the first part of the sentence to which the pronoun refers, the revised version has only one among several possible answers.)

Revised: Martina worked in a national forest last summer, and serving as a forest ranger may be her career choice.

(1) Pronoun Number

For collective nouns, such as *group, committee,* and *family,* use either a singular or plural pronoun, depending on whether or not the group is seen to be acting as a unit or acting separately as many individuals within the unit.

The committee reached its decision before the end of the meeting.

(Here the committee acted as a unit.)

The committee relied on their own consciences to reach a decision.

(Here everyone relied separately on his or her own conscience.)

Remember to be consistent in pronoun number. Don't shift from singular to plural or plural to singular.

Wrong: After <u>someone</u> studies music for awhile, <u>she</u> may decide to try playing
                Singular   Singular
another instrument. Then, <u>they</u> can compare and decide which instrument <u>they</u>
                Plural   Plural
like better.

Revised: After people study music for awhile, <u>they</u> may decide to try to play
                                                    Plural
another instrument. Then, <u>they</u> can compare and decide which instrument <u>they</u>
                          Plural   Plural
like better.

(2) Compound Subjects

Compound subjects with *and* take the plural pronoun.

The **table** and **chair** were delivered promptly, but **they** were not the style I had
ordered.

For compound subjects with *or* or *nor*, the pronoun agrees with
the subject word closer to it:

The restaurant offered either regular *patrons* or each new *customer* a free cup
of coffee with **his** or **her** dinner.

Neither this **house** nor the **others** had **their** shutters closed.

(3) Who/Which/That

When *who, which,* or *that* begins a dependent clause, use as follows:

* *Who* is used for people (and sometimes animals).

  He is a person **who** can help you.

* *Which* is used most often for non-essential clauses though
  some writers also use it for essential clauses (see Chapter 9).

  The catalogue, **which** I sent for last month, had some unusual merchandise.
  (The *which* clause here is non-essential.)

* *That* is used most often for essential clauses.

  When I finished the book **that** she lent me, I was able to write my paper.
  (The *that* clause here is essential.)

(4) Indefinite Words

Indefinite words such as *any* and *each* usually take the singular
pronoun.

Each of the boys handed in **his** uniform.

(5) Indefinite Pronouns

He was traditionally used to refer to indefinite pronouns ending in *-body* and *-one*, as in the following example:

Everyone brought **his** own pen and paper.

To avoid the exclusive use of the male pronoun when the reference is to both males and females (a practice seen by many people as sexist; see Chapter 48 on sexist language), there are several solutions.

- Use both the male and female pronoun.

  Everyone has **his** or **her** coat.
  (Some people view this as very wordy.)

- Switch to the plural subject and pronoun.

  All the people have **their** coats.

- Use the plural pronoun.

  Everyone has **their** coat.
  (Some people view this as incorrect. Others, such as the National Council of Teachers of English, accept this as a way to avoid sexist language.)

- Use *a, an,* or *the* if the meaning remains clear.

  Everyone has a coat.

Exercise 3.3: Proofreading Practice

In the following sentences each pronoun should clearly and correctly refer back to a noun in the sentence. If the reference is clear and correct, write a C before the sentence number. If there is a problem with pronoun reference, write an X before the number.

1. Whenever Frisha tries to speak Spanish with Maya, she has trouble understanding her pronunciation.
2. Although jogging is still a popular means of exercise, some shoe manufacturers say that it is not as popular as it was five years ago.
3. Every person on the committee had read their copy of the report before the meeting.
4. After the coach and the players reviewed the new plays for the third time, they decided that it was enough for one evening.
5. Either George or Phil can lend you his book before the exam.

Exercise 3.4: Proofreading Practice

In the following paragraph there are some pronoun reference problems. Underline all pronouns that do not clearly refer back to nouns, and write clearer or more appropriate nouns or pronouns above the underlined words. You may find that your changes will involve changing some other words as well.

Rising insurance premiums are taking their toll on the rock and roll concert business, and it is likely to get higher before conditions improve. People who have been buying tickets for the last ten years are angry at paying five or six dollars more for his or her ticket. But insurance companies say that instances of violence and injury at rock concerts and the rising number of people who file claims are causing it. Property damage has created an additional problem and has caused claims to increase tenfold over the last ten years. Each claim is often for large sums of money, and they are usually awarded by juries sympathetic to damage caused by rock concert audiences. The situation has gotten so bad recently that some concerts have been canceled when they could not get insurance, and in one case, a particular act was cut from the show because they were considered dangerous. This may cause the number of rock concerts to decrease in the future.

4 *Adjectives and Adverbs* (ad)

4a *Adjectives and Adverbs*

Adjectives and **adverbs** describe or tell us more about other words in a sentence. The way to distinguish adjectives from adverbs is to locate the words they describe or modify. Adjectives modify nouns and pronouns. Adverbs modify verbs, verb forms, adjectives, and other adverbs.

Adjectives modifying nouns and pronouns:

red (adjective)	⎡ house (noun)	it (pronoun) ⎤	was beautiful (adjective)
cheerful (adjective)	⎣ smile (noun)		

Adverbs modifying verbs, verb forms, adjectives, and other adverbs:

danced (verb)	⎡ gracefully (adverb)	ran very (adverb) ⎤	quickly (adverb)
very (adverb)	⎣ tall (adjective)		

Many adverbs end in *-ly*:

Adjective	Adverb
rapid	rapidly
nice	nicely
happy	happily

But the *-ly* ending isn't a sure test for adverbs because some nouns have an *-ly* ending for the adjective form (*ghost* and *ghostly*), and some adverbs do not end in *-ly* (*very, fast, far*). To be sure, check your dictionary, because it will indicate whether the word is an adjective or adverb.

Some suggestions for using adjectives and adverbs correctly follow:

- Use the *-ed* adjective form where it is needed.
  One type of adjective is the *-ed* form of a verb (the past participle); it is used to describe a noun. Be sure to include the *-ed* ending.

  used clothing
  experienced drivers
  painted house

- Use adjectives following linking verbs such as *appear, seem, taste, feel,* and *look.*

  The sofa seemed comfortable.   The water tastes salty.
      (sofa = comfortable)   (water = salty)

However, some verbs used as linking verbs can also be action verbs when the meaning of the verb changes. Note the two different meanings of the verb *looked* in the following sentences:

The cat looked sleepy.

   (cat = sleepy)

The cat looked eagerly at the canary.

   (In this sentence the cat is performing the action of looking.)

- Use adverbs to modify verbs.

Wrong: He ran quick.   **Wrong:** The glass broke sudden.
Revised: He ran quickly.   **Revised:** The glass broke suddenly.

Wrong: She sang sweet.
Revised: She sang sweetly.

- Be sure to distinguish between the following adjectives and adverbs:

Adjectives	*Adverbs*
sure	surely
real	really
good	well
bad	badly

Wrong: She sure likes to dance   **Wrong:** The car runs bad.
Revised: She surely likes to dance. **Revised:** The car runs badly.

Wrong: He sings good.
Revised: He sings well.

HINT: *Well* can also be an adjective when it refers to good health.

Despite her surgery, she looks well.

   (she = well)

- When you use adverbs such as *so, such,* and *too,* be sure to complete the phrase or clause.

Incomplete: Hailey was so tired.

Revised: Hailey was so tired that she left the office early.

Incomplete: O'Malley's is such a popular restaurant.

Revised: O'Malley's is such a popular restaurant that reservations are recommended.

Incomplete: Gary's problem was that he was too proud.

Revised: Gary's problem was that he was too proud to ask for help.

Exercise 4.1: Proofreading Practice

The following paragraph has some errors in adverb and adjective forms. Rewrite the paragraph so that all the adjectives and adverbs are correct. Underline the words that you have changed.

We all know that when football players are very tired, their concern coaches call them back to the sidelines and give them pure oxygen to breathe. But new evidence indicates that these exhaust players could just as well be saving their breath. It seems clear that 100 percent oxygen doesn't particularly help athletes. In a controlled test some athletes breathed in very rapid either normal air or pure oxygen. When tested as to how quick the subject revived, there was no difference. Both groups said they felt good within about three minutes. One of the players who breathed plain air even commented on the fact that he felt so well. The biggest surprise of all was that none of the players being tested could even tell whether they had breathed real pure oxygen or just normal air.

Exercise 4.2: Pattern Practice

Using the patterns given here, write a sentence of your own for each pattern.

Pattern A: sentence with an *-ed* adjective modifying a noun

The **fertilized** plant grew quickly on my windowsill.

Pattern B: sentence with an adverb modifying another adverb

The sound echoed **very** clearly.

Pattern C: sentence with the adverb *so, such,* or *too* that is complete

It was **such** a long concert that I was tempted to leave during intermission.

Pattern D: an *-ed* adjective after a linking verb

The old man seemed **pleased** when the child said hello.

Pattern E: sentence with the adverb *well*

With some coaching, the game show contestant answered the questions very **well**.

Pattern F: sentence with the adverb *badly*

As the horse cleared the hurdle, it got caught on a bar, fell, and hurt its back leg **badly**.

4b A, An, The

Use *a* when the word following it starts with a consonant sound:

a book
a horse
a leg
a one-inch pipe
a youth
a union (use *a* when the *u* sounds like the *y* in *you*)
a PTA parent

Use *an* when the word following it starts with a vowel or an unsounded *h* (as in *honor, hour,* and *honest.*)

an egg
an ancient coin
an hour
an eagle
an SOS signal (the *S* here is sounded as *es*)

HINT: Formerly, *an* was used before unaccented syllables beginning with *h*, as in the following:

an historian
an hotel
an habitual offender

However, this is becoming less frequent, and *a* is now considered acceptable, as in the following:

a historian
a hotel
a habitual offender

A and *an* are used to identify nouns in a general or indefinite way and refer to any member of the group. *A* and *an*, which mean "one among many," are generally used with singular count nouns. (See Section 2a on count nouns.)

> She likes to read **a** book before going to sleep.
> (This sentence does not specify which book, just any book.)
> She bought **a** newspaper. (*Newspaper* is a singular count noun.)

The is used to identify a particular or specific noun in a group or a noun already identified in a previous phrase or sentence. *The* may be used with singular or plural nouns.

> She read **the** book. (This sentence identifies a specific book.)
> Give **the** coins to *the* boys. (This sentence identifies specific groups.)
> **A** new model of computer was introduced yesterday. **The** model will cost much less than **the** older model.

Use *a* or *an* to introduce a noun the first time it is mentioned, and then use *the* afterward whenever the noun is mentioned.

Other uses of *the*:

• With an essential phrase or clause following the noun:

> **The** man who is standing at the door is Charlie Johnson.
> **The** coffee in my cup is hot.

**4b
ad**

BUT no article is used with noncount nouns describing something in general:

Man is a creature of habit.
Coffee is no longer a popular breakfast drink.

- With a word referring to a class as a whole:

  The ferret is a popular pet.

- With names composed partly of common nouns:

  the British Commonwealth
  the Sahara Desert

- With names composed of common nouns plus proper names contained within *of* phrases:

  the Province of Quebec
  the University of Illinois

- With plural names:

  the Netherlands
  the Balkans

- With names of rivers, oceans, seas, points on the globe, deserts, forests, gulfs, and peninsulas:

  the Nile
  the Pacific Ocean
  the Equator
  the Persian Gulf

- With points of the compass used as names:

  the South
  the Midwest

- With points of time:

  the beginning
  the present
  the afternoon

- With superlatives:

  the best reporter

  the most expensive car

- With adjectives used as nouns:

  The homeless are in need of health care.

- With gerunds or abstract nouns followed by *of* phrases:

  The meaning of that word is not clear.

  BUT articles are not used with names of streets, cities, states, countries, continents, lakes, parks, mountains, names of languages, sports, holiday, universities, and colleges without *of* in the name, and academic subjects:

  He traveled to Africa.

  Sutherland's store is on Fifth Avenue.

  Camping equipment is sold in most towns along Lake Michigan.

  She is studying Chinese.

  He prefers to watch volleyball.

  My major is political science.

  They celebrated Thanksgiving together.

  She applied to Brandeis University.

Exercise 4.3: Proofreading Practice

In the following paragraph choose either a or an to complete the sentences correctly.

Maintaining (1. a, an) clear complexion, salvaging (2. a, an) usually bad semester, and decorating (3. a, an) dorm room are among the topics treated in one of the magazine world's fastest-growing segments, magazines for college students. This market is fueled by advertisers eager to reach (4. a, an) untapped market of twelve to thirteen million college students with (5. a, an) large disposable income and (6. a, an) earnings potential of many billions of dollars after graduation. Most college magazines are quarterlies, distributed free at (7. a, an) campus newsstand or by direct mail as (8. a, an) insert in the college paper. While profits are high, there is some criticism that these magazines are merely

(9. a, an) advertising vehicle and do not focus on substantive issues, such as (10. a, an) close look at student loan programs or (11. a, an) honest appraisal of racism on campus.

Exercise 4.4: Proofreading Practice

In the following paragraph add "a," "an," or "the" where these words are needed.

One of most interesting physicists of this century was Richard Feynman. He wrote best-selling book about his own life, but he became even more famous on television as man who was member of team that investigated after accident happened to *Challenger*, space shuttle that crashed in 1986. People watched on television as he demonstrated that faulty part in space shuttle probably caused accident. Feynman's greatest achievement in science was theory of quantum electrodynamics, which described behavior of subatomic particles, atoms, light, electricity, and magnetism. Field of computer science also owes much to work of Feynman. Many scientists consider Feynman to be one of geniuses of twentieth century.

Exercise 4.5: Pattern Practice

Write a sentence using the suggested nouns and also using "a," "an," or "the" before these nouns.

Example: egg, piece of toast, cup

Sentence: For breakfast, I ordered an egg, a piece of toast, and a cup of coffee.

1. used car, salesperson, honest
2. train, hour, Amtrak
3. yeast, bread, oven, cookbook
4. A's, F's (as letter grades in a college course), grade book
5. old barn, young chickens, wire fence

4c Some/Any, Much/Many, Little/Few, Less/Fewer, Enough, No

Some/Any: Both modify count and noncount nouns (see Chapter 2a).

> She brought **some** fresh flowers.
> There is **some** water on the floor.

> Do you have **any** erasers?
> Do you have **any** food?

Some is used in positive statements.

> They ate **some** fruit.

Any is used in negative statements and in questions.

> They did not eat **any** fruit.
> Did they eat **any** fruit?

Much/Many: *Much* modifies only noncount nouns. *Many* modifies only count nouns.

> They have **much** money in the bank.
> **Many** Americans travel to Europe.

Little/Few: *Little* modifies only noncount nouns. *Few* modifies only count nouns.

> He had **little** food in the house.
> There are a **few** doctors in the town.

Less/Fewer: *Less* modifies only noncount nouns. *Fewer* modifies only count nouns.

> Use **less** oil in the mixture.
> We ordered **fewer** magazine subscriptions than we did last year.

Enough: Modifies both count and noncount nouns.

> I have **enough** glasses for everyone.
> There is **enough** money to buy a car.

No: Modifies both count and noncount nouns.

There are **no** squirrels in the park.
There is **no** time to finish now.

4d Comparisons

Adverbs and adjectives are often used to show comparison, and the degree of comparison is indicated in their forms.

In comparisons, most adjectives and adverbs add *-er* and *-est* as endings or combine with the words *more* and *most* or *less* and *least.*

Positive form is used when no comparison is made:

a large box
an acceptable offer

Comparative form is used when two things are being compared (with *-er, more, less* or *least*):

the larger of the two boxes
the more (or less) acceptable of the two offers

Superlative form is used when three or more things are being compared (with *-est* or *most*):

the largest of the six boxes
the most (or least) acceptable of all the offers

Positive	*Comparative*	*Superlative*
(for one)	(for two)	(for three or more)
tall	taller	tallest
pretty	prettier	prettiest
cheerful	more cheerful	most cheerful
selfish	less selfish	least selfish

Curtis is tall.
Curtis is taller than Rachel.
Curtis is the tallest player on the team.

Some guidelines for choosing between *-er* and *-est* or *more* and *most* (or *less* and *least*) are as follows:

- With one-syllable words, the *-er* and *-est* endings are commonly used.

  quick   quicker   quickest

- With two-syllable words, some adjectives take *-er* and *-est,* and some use *more* and *most* (or *less* and *least*). Check the dictionary to be sure.

  happy   happier   happiest
  thoughtful   more thoughtful most thoughtful

- For adverbs, *more* and *most* or *less* and *least* are commonly used.

  smoothly   more smoothly   most smoothly

- For words with three or more syllables, use *more* and *most* or *less* and *least*.

  generous   more generous   most generous

Irregular forms of comparisons are as follows:

Positive	*Comparative*	*Superlative*
(for one)	(for two)	(for three or more)
good	better	best
well	better	best
little	less	least
some	more	most
much	more	most
many	more	most
bad, badly	worse	worst

....

HINT 1: Be sure to avoid double comparisons in which both the *-er* and *more* (or *-est* and *most*) are used.

Wrong: the most farthest
Revised: the farthest
Wrong: more quicker
Revised: quicker

HINT 2: Be sure to complete your comparisons by using all the words that are needed.

Incomplete: Driving down Hill Street is slower than Western Avenue.

> (It is the act of driving down one street that is being compared to driving down another street. The streets themselves are not being compared.)

Revised: Driving down Hill Street is slower than **driving down** Western Avenue.

Incomplete: The weather here is as warm as Phoenix.

Revised: The weather here is as warm as **it is in** Phoenix.

Incomplete: The results of the second medical test were more puzzling than the first test.

Revised: The results of the second medical test were more puzzling than **those of** the first test.

HINT 3: Remember to choose the correct pronoun in comparisons with omitted words. (See Chapter 3a.)

Terry jumps higher than I (do).

Terry likes Julie more than (he likes) **me**.

Exercise 4.6: Proofreading Practice

In the following paragraph there are a number of errors in the words used to show comparisons. Revise the paragraph to correct these errors.

(1) A new sport, already popular in Canada and sweeping across the United States, is indoor box lacrosse. (2) It is more faster, furiouser, and often a more brutal version of the field game of lacrosse. (3) Box lacrosse is indeed an exciting game as it is more speedy and more rougher than ice hockey but requires the kind of teamwork needed in basketball. (4) Scores for box lacrosse are more high than field lacrosse because the indoor game has a more smaller playing area with the most opportunities for scoring. (5) The team in box lacrosse is also more smaller than field lacrosse as there are only six people on a side in the indoor game and ten people on conventional field lacrosse teams. (6) In addition, box lacrosse is played on artificial turf in ice-hockey rinks, and the sticks are more short and more thinner than conventional field lacrosse sticks. (7) In indoor lacrosse almost anything goes—and usually does in this rough-and-tumble sport.

Exercise 4.7: Pattern Practice

Listed here is some information to use in sentences of your own. Try to include as many comparisons as you can in your sentence.

Example: Write a sentence comparing the cost of the items listed here. Use the word *expensive* in your sentence.

bananas:	$.25/pound
apples:	$.49/pound
pears:	$.60/pound

Sample Sentence: At the First Street Fruit Market, apples are more expensive than bananas, but bananas are less expensive than pears, which are the most expensive of these three fruits.

1. Write a sentence of your own about the magazines described here, and use the word *interesting*.

   Today's Trends is very dull.
   Home Magazine is somewhat interesting.
   Now! is very interesting.

2. Write a sentence of your own about the ages of the three teenagers described here, and use the words *old* and *young*.

   Chip is twelve years old.
   Michelle is fifteen years old.
   Ethan is eighteen years old.

3. Write a sentence of your own about the movies described here, and use the word *scary*.

   Terror at Night is not a very scary movie.
   Teen Horror is a somewhat scary movie.
   Night of the Avengers is a very scary movie.

4. Write a sentence of your own about the car engines described here, and use the word *powerful*.

   The Hyundai engine is not very powerful.
   The Ford engine is fairly powerful.
   The Ferrari engine is very powerful.

5. Write a sentence of your own about the professors described here, and use the word *clear*.

Professor Titschler's lectures are not very clear.

Professor Hensen's lectures are somewhat clear.

Professor Gottner's lectures are very clear.

5 *Prepositions* (prep)

Prepositions connect nouns and pronouns to another word or words in a sentence.

They left **in** the morning.
  (The preposition *in* connects *morning* with the verb *left*.)

5a *Idiomatic Prepositions*

Choosing the right preposition to follow a particular word can be difficult. When it is, look up the particular word (not the preposition) in the dictionary. Some troublesome combinations include the following:

Wrong	*Revised*
apologize about	apologize for
bored of	bored with
capable to	capable of
concerned to, on	concerned about, over, with
in search for	in search of
independent from	independent of
interested about	interested in, by
outlook of life	outlook on life
puzzled on	puzzled at, by
similar with	similar to

Selecting other prepositions can also be difficult. See the Glossary of Usage at the back of this book for help with the following:

among/between	different from/different than
compared to/compared with	off of
could of	should of

HINT: In formal writing, avoid putting a preposition at the end of a sentence, if possible.

Informal: This is the argument he disagreed **with**.

Formal: This is the argument **with** which he disagreed.

Some prepositions, however, cannot be rearranged.

He wants to go **in**.

The mayor was well thought **of**.

The results may not be worth worrying **about**.

5b *On/At/In*

For students learning English as another language, the following is a guide to help select the right preposition to indicate time or place.

Prepositions of time:

On Use with days (*on* Monday).

At Use with hours of the day (*at* 9 P.M.) and with noon, night, midnight, and dawn (*at* midnight).

In Use with other parts of the day: morning, afternoon, evening (*in* the morning); use with months, years, seasons (*in* the winter).

They are getting married **on** Sunday at **four** o'clock **in** the afternoon.

Prepositions of place:

On Indicates a surface on which something rests.

The car is **on** the street.

She put curtains **on** the windows.

At Indicates a point in relation to another object.

My sister is **at** home.

I'll meet you **at** Second Avenue and Main Street.

In Indicates that an object is inside the boundaries of an area or volume.

The sample is **in** the bottle.

She is **in** the bank.

Exercise 5.1: Proofreading Practice

In the following paragraph, underline the prepositions that are incorrectly used, and then write in the correct words.

The mail carrier knew she should of stayed away from the dog barking on the porch, but it was her first day on a new job. She was concerned on delivering all the mail she had in her bag and did not want to have to report any problems. Her co-workers had warned her on the animals along her route, especially that dog at Mayfield Street. Between all the problems she seemed to be having, she did not want to let her co-workers know that she was afraid about animals. But when she tried to put the mail at the mailbox, the dog jumped up and grabbed all of it in his mouth. No one had told her the dog was trained to collect the mail and bring it inside the house.

Exercise 5.2: Pattern Practice

Listed here is some information to use in sentences of your own.

Example: Write a sentence using **on** as a preposition of time and **in** as a preposition of place.

Sample Sentence: On Saturday all the stores **in** the mall are open late.

1. Write a sentence using *in* as a preposition of time and *on* as a preposition of place.
2. Write a sentence using *at* as a preposition of time and *in* as a preposition of place.
3. Write a sentence using *on* as a preposition of time and *on* as a preposition of place.
4. Write a sentence using *in* as a preposition of time and *at* as a preposition of place.
5. Write a sentence using *at* as a preposition of time and *in* as a preposition of place.

6 *Subjects* (sub)

A **subject** is the word or words that indicate who or what is doing the action of active verbs. The subject of a passive verb is acted upon by the verb.

HINT: To find the subject, look first for the verb (see Chapter 1) and then ask *who* or *what* is doing the action for active verbs. Ask *who* or *what* is acted on for passive verbs.

Annie worked as an underpaid lifeguard last summer.

1. Locate the verb: *worked* (active)
2. Ask: Who or what *worked*?
3. The answer is "Annie worked," so *Annie* is the subject.

Annie was paid less than minimum wage by the swimming pool manager.

1. Locate the verb: *was paid* (passive)
2. Ask: Who or what *was paid*?
3. The answer is "Annie was paid," so *Annie* is the subject.

There are several complications to remember when finding subjects. Some subjects have more than one word.

John and Bill **realized** that despite being roommates they really liked each other.

1. Who *realized*? John and Bill.
2. The subject is *John and Bill.*

That roommates occasionally disagree **is** well known.

1. What *is* well known? That roommates occasionally disagree.
2. The subject is *That roommates occasionally disagree.*

The subject word may have other words describing it both before and after the subject word. The subject may thus be buried among describing words.

The major **problem** with today's parents **is** their tendency to avoid being like their parents.

Almost **all** his records **are** now available on compact disks.

Too many **farmers** in that area of the state **planted** soybeans last year.

Subjects in commands are not expressed in words because the person being addressed is the reader (*you*). "Turn the page" really means that you, the reader, should turn the page. *You* as the subject is said to be indefinite or understood and therefore not mentioned in words.

**6
sub**

Close the door.

   (Who is being told to close the door? *You are.*)

Mix the eggs thoroughly before adding milk.

   (Who is being told to mix the eggs? *You are.*)

Most subjects come before the verb, but some come in the middle of or after the verb. For questions, the subject comes in the middle of or after the verb.

When (is) the <u>band</u> (going) to start?
       verb

Are <u>they</u> here yet?
verb

For sentences that begin with *there is, there are,* or *it is,* the subject comes after the verb.

There is a buzzing *sound* in my left ear.

Now there are buzzing *sounds* in both ears.

It is *one* of those medical mysteries, I guess.

When verbs are in the passive voice, the doer of the action is expressed in a phrase beginning with the word *by,* and the subject receives the action. Sometimes, when we are not interested in who is doing the action or when it is obvious who did it, the *by* phrase is omitted.

                                 doer
The **ball** (was hit) by the boy.

   -or-

The **ball** (was hit.)

                                          doers
The **experiment** (was performed) by several assistants.

   -or-

The **experiment** (was performed.)

In some languages the subject can be omitted, but in English the subject is left out only when expressing a command (see Chapter 1e).

Omitted Subject: All the children laughed when were watching the cartoon.
   (This sentence has no subject for the verb *were watching.*)
Revised: All the children laughed when *they* were watching the cartoon.

Omitted Subject: She asked the computer consultant was in the lab to look at her program.

(This sentence has no subject for the verb *was*.)

Revised: She asked the computer consultant *who* was in the lab to look at her program.

In some languages, the subject can be repeated as a pronoun before the verb. In English the subject is included only once.

Repeated Subject: Bones in the body they become brittle when people grow older.

(In this sentence both *bones* and *they* are the subject of the verb *become*.

Revised: Bones in the body become brittle when people grow older.

Repeated Subject: The plane that was ready for take-off it stopped on the runway to wait for another passenger.

(In this sentence both *plane* and *it* are the subject of the verb *stopped*.)

Revised: The plane which was ready for take-off stopped on the runway to wait for another passenger.

Exercise 6.1: Proofreading Practice

Underline the subjects of all the verbs in the following sentences. Remember, it's easier to start by finding the verb and then asking who? or what? As an example, the first sentence is already marked.

(1) <u>Humans</u> are unique in preferring to use the right hand. (2) Among other animals, each individual favors one hand or another, but in every species other than humans, the split between the right and the left hand is even. (3) Only humans seem to favor the right hand. (4) Even in studies of prehistoric people, anthropologists have found this preference among humans. (5) For example, in ancient drawings over five thousand years old, most people are shown using their right hand. (6) This evidence suggests that it is not a matter of cultural pressures but perhaps of some genetic difference. (7) However, since left-handedness seems to run in families, it is not clear how hand preference is passed from one generation to the next.

Exercise 6.2: Pattern Practice

In the blanks write in a subject word or words that could fit the sentence. Try to add a word or phrase describing the subject.

(1) Almost every week of the year <u>drunken teenagers</u> cause highway accidents that could have been avoided. (2) These _____ usually say that they thought they were in control, but the _____ they were driving still get away from them and cause damage. (3) Worst of all, _____ are the real victims of these accidents because they are just as likely to get hurt. (4) Maybe _____ are right when they say that _____ should not have drivers' licenses. (5) There is _____ of wisdom in that statement.

7 *Phrases* (phr)

A **phrase** is a group of related words that does not have its own subject and complete verb. In phrases, the words can work together as the subject or verb in a sentence, or they can add information to other parts of the sentence.

Note how the related words in these phrases work together to offer information:

A major earthquake hit the area last night.
(This phrase is the subject of the sentence.)

Listening to music is one form of relaxation.
(This phrase is the subject of the sentence.)

Dr. Smalley, **a famous brain surgeon**, will be on television this evening.
(This phrase tells us more about the subject, Dr. Smalley.)

The bike **leaning on its side** fell over during the rainstorm.
(This phrase also tells us more about the subject.)

They **may have been eating** when I called.
(This phrase is the verb phrase.)

He always walks **with his toes pointed out**.
(This phrase gives added information about the verb.)

Her favorite pastime is **visiting museums**.
(This phrase, which comes after a linking verb, completes the subject.)

Jenny looks like Crazy Edna, **a second cousin of mine**.
(This phrase gives added information about another element in the sentence.)

Exercise 7.1: Proofreading Practice

In the following paragraph some of the phrases have been underlined. Each one of those underlined phrases performs one of the six functions listed. Identify the function of the phrase by the appropriate number. The first sentence has been done as an example.

1. The phrase acts as the subject.
2. It tells something more about the subject.
3. It acts as the verb.
4. It tells something more about the verb.
5. It completes the subject of a linking verb.
6. It tells something more about another element in the sentence.

(1) <u>Finding a place for our garbage</u> is a problem as old as
     1
human beings. (2) On the Pacific coast there are <u>large, round</u>
<u>shell-mounds</u> where for centuries Indians <u>had been discarding</u>
the bones and clamshells that constituted their garbage. (3)
When people gathered together <u>in cities</u>, they hauled their waste
to the outskirts of town or dumped it <u>into nearby rivers.</u> (4) In
the United States the first municipal refuse system was instituted
in Philadelphia, <u>a well-organized city</u>. (5) Here slaves were
forced to wade <u>into the Delaware River</u> and toss bales of trash
into the current. (6) Eventually <u>this dumping into rivers</u> was out-
lawed, and people looked for new solutions to the garbage problem. (7) Municipal dump sites, <u>unused plots of land far away</u>
<u>from houses</u>, were <u>a frequent answer</u>. (8) But landfill sites <u>are</u>
<u>decreasing</u> as many are closed because of health hazards or

because of cost. (9) America, <u>a land of throwaway containers and fancy packaging</u>, clearly faces a garbage problem, <u>a problem without any apparent answers</u>.

Exercise 7.2: Pattern Practice

In each of the following sentences one of the phrases has been underlined. Describe the function of that phrase, and then make up your own sentence that has a phrase performing the same function. The first sentence has been done as an example.

1. America <u>is facing</u> a garbage crisis that gets worse each year.

verb phrase
   They <u>have lived</u> in Chicago for almost two years.

verb phrase

2. In 1960 <u>the average American</u> sent 2.2 pounds of trash to the dumps each day, but now it's 5.1 pounds a day.

3. We need new dump sites, but they are <u>hard to find</u> because no one wants a landfill next door.

4. Some cities, <u>the ones without potential new landfill space,</u> have given up looking for nearby sites.

5. These cities <u>have started</u> a new practice, exporting their garbage to other states.

6. For example, in Ohio, trash arrives <u>from New Jersey.</u>

7. Exporting garbage is an answer, <u>a temporary one,</u> until other states start refusing to accept someone else's trash.

8 *Clauses* (cl)

A **clause** is a group of related words that (unlike a phrase) has both a subject and a complete verb. A sentence may have one or more than one clause.

A sentence with one clause:

> Some <u>students</u> <u>see</u> themselves working in office environments and wearing
>   subject verb
> formal business clothes.

A sentence with two clauses:

> Although <u>it</u> <u>becomes</u> expensive to buy a wardrobe of business clothes, such
>   subject 1   verb 1
> <u>people</u> <u>enjoy</u> the daily opportunities to dress well.
>   subject 2 verb 2

A sentence with one clause embedded in the middle of another clause:

> <u>Students</u>   <u>who</u>   <u>seek</u>   well-paying jobs often <u>think</u> of careers in busi-
>   subject 1   subject 2   verb 1   verb 2
> ness and finance.

8a *Independent Clauses* (in cl)

An **independent clause** is a clause that can stand alone as a complete sentence because, as the term *independent* suggests, it doesn't depend on anything else to complete the thought.

The characteristics of an independent clause are as follows:

It has a complete verb and subject.

> <u>No one</u> <u>could understand</u> the message written on the blackboard.
>   subject   complete verb

It expresses a complete thought and can stand alone as a sentence.

> He never wanted to lend any of his cassette tapes.

Two different groups of connecting words can be used at the beginning of an independent clause:

1. *And, but, for, or, nor, so, yet*
   (For use of the comma with these connectors, see Chapters 11 and 23a.)

> Detasseling corn is exhausting work, but she needed the money.

2. *Therefore, moreover, thus, consequently,* etc.
   (For the use of the semicolon with these connectors, see Chapters 11 and 25a.)

> Detasseling the corn is exhausting work; however, she needed the money.

An independent clause can be combined with a dependent clause or with another independent clause to form a sentence. (See Chapter 10.)

An independent clause can be its own sentence:

> The popularity of some cartoon characters lasts for years.

Two independent clauses can form one sentence:

> Mickey Mouse, Donald Duck, and Bugs Bunny are perennial favorites, but other once-popular characters such as Jiggs and Maggie have disappeared.

An independent clause can be joined with a dependent clause:

> <u>Since Garfield the Cat and the Peanuts characters have become great</u>
> dependent clause
> <u>favorites</u>, perhaps they will last for several generations like Mickey Mouse.

Exercise 8.1: Proofreading Practice

In the following paragraph there are groups of underlined words that are numbered. Identify each group as a phrase or a clause. The first sentence has been done as an example.

(1) For years strange noises, <u>which would start in June and last</u>
clause
<u>until September</u>, filled the air around the waters of Richardson

Bay, <u>an inlet of water near Sausalito, California</u>. (2) The noise
phrase

was heard in the houseboats, <u>especially those with fiberglass

hulls</u>, moored along the southwestern shore of the bay. (3) <u>The

noise was usually described as a deep hum like an electric

foghorn or an airplane motor</u>. (4) The noise, <u>which would start

in late evening</u>, would stop by morning, <u>ruining people's sleep</u>.

(5) <u>During the summer of 1984 the hum was unusually loud and

stirred investigations</u>. (6) Originally, suspicion centered on a

nearby sewage plant, <u>which was suspected of dumping sewage at

night when no one would notice</u>. (7) Some others thought there

were <u>secret Navy experiments going on</u>. (8) An acoustical engi-

neer, <u>studying the mystery sound for months</u>, kept thinking he

would find the answer, <u>but he didn't</u>. (9) Finally, a marine ecolo-

gist identified the source of the hum as the sound of the plainfin

midshipman, <u>a fish also known as the singing toad</u>. (10) <u>The

male's singing</u> was the sound everyone heard, he said, <u>though

some people still suspect the sewage plant</u>.

**8a
in cl**

Exercise 8.2: Pattern Practice

*In this paragraph on visual pollution notice the patterns of clauses that
are present:*

1. Some sentences have one clause.
2. Some have two clauses separated by punctuation.
3. Some have one clause in the middle of another.

Each sentence in the paragraph follows one of these patterns. Identify that pattern by its number, and then write your own paragraph of five or more sentences. Identify the pattern of clauses in each of your sentences by using these same numbers. As a subject for your paragraph, you may want to describe other types of pollution, such as noise pollution caused by dual-exhaust cars, air pollution caused by cigarette smoke or overpowering perfumes, or visual pollution caused by litter.

(1) One type of pollution that the government has tried to eliminate is the visual pollution of billboards along our highways. (2) In 1965 Congress passed the Highway Beautification Act to outlaw those ugly signs, but the act didn't work. (3) While the federal government paid for the removal of 2235 old billboards in 1983, the billboard industry was busy putting up 18,000 new signs in the same year. (4) Since then the situation has gotten worse. (5) The 1965 act had all kinds of loopholes; however, the real problem is a requirement in the act to pay billboard companies for removing the signs. (6) Since some communities don't have the funds for this, too many old signs are still standing, along with all the new ones going up.

8b Dependent Clauses (dep cl)

A **dependent clause** is a clause that cannot stand alone as a complete sentence. As the term *dependent* suggests, a dependent clause depends on another clause in the sentence to complete the thought.

....

HINT 1: Dependent clauses have marker words at the beginning of the clause. (See the explanation of adverb clauses in the box in this Chapter.)

HINT 2: If you say the dependent clause aloud, you may be able to hear that you need to add more information.

"When I got up this morning…"
    (Are you waiting for more information?)

HINT 3: To locate dependent clauses punctuated as sentences, try proofreading your papers backward from the last sentence to the first.

There are two kinds of dependent clauses: adjective and adverb clauses.

(1) Adjective Clauses (the *who/which/that* clauses)

An **adjective clause** tells us more about a noun or pronoun in the sentence and starts with one of the following words: *who, which, that, whose, whom.*

The female singer, **who used to play lead guitar**, now lets the other band members play while she sings.

The group tried a concert tour, **which was a financial disaster**.

The rumor **that the poor ticket sales were due to mismanagement** never appeared in print.

(2) Adverb Clauses (the *because/if/when* clauses)

An **adverb clause** tells us more about other verbs, adjectives, or adverbs in a sentence or another whole clause. The marker word that starts adverb clauses is one of a long list, including the following more common ones:

after	before	though	when
although	even if	unless	whenever
as	even though	until	whether
as if	if	what	while
because	since	whatever	

HINT: You can recognize adverb clauses by the marker words at the beginning. Because of the meaning of these marker words, they create the need for another clause to complete the thought. Try to set up an equation such as the following:

After X, Y.
Because X, Y.
If X, Y.

After I eat lunch tomorrow… (What will happen?)
After I eat lunch tomorrow, I will call you.

Because it was so dark out… (What happened?)
Because it was so dark out, she tripped on the steps.

If I win the lottery… (What will happen?)
If I win the lottery, I'll quit my job and retire.

When it began to rain… (What happened?)
When it began to rain, the game was canceled.

Dependent clauses may appear first in a sentence, before the independent clause, or they may appear at the end of the sentence where they are harder to recognize:

I will call you **after I eat lunch tomorrow.**
She tripped on the steps **because it was so dark out.**
The game was canceled **when it began to rain.**

HINT: Remember this punctuation rule for dependent clauses: When the adverb clause appears at the beginning of a sentence, it is followed by a comma. When the independent clause begins the sentence, no punctuation is needed before the adverb clause. (See Chapter 23b.)

Until gas prices are lowered, I will continue to buy compact cars.
(adverb clause first)

I will continue to buy compact cars **until gas prices are lowered**.
(adverb clause last)

Exercise 8.3: Proofreading Practice

Identify the dependent clauses in the following paragraph by underlining and labeling them either as adjective or adverb clauses.

8b
dep cl

(1) The tiny lichen is an amazing plant. (2) It can survive in an incredibly difficult environment because it can do things no other plant can do. (3) The lichen, which can anchor itself on a bare rock by etching the rock's surface with powerful acids, grows into the pits that it burns out. (4) Since lichens grow in cold climates above the tree line, they are often frozen or covered by snow most of the year. (5) Unlike the cactus in the desert, the lichen has no way of retaining moisture. (6) Because of this, the sun dries lichens into waterless crusts during the day. (7) When there is a drought, lichens may dry out completely for several months. (8) Even under ideal conditions their total daily growing period may last only for an hour or two while they are still wet with morning dew. (9) The lichen, which may take twenty-five years to grow to a diameter of one inch, can live for several thousand years. (10) These amazing plants are able to live in all sorts of difficult places, but not in cities because the pollution kills them.

Exercise 8.4: Pattern Practice

Write your own paragraph with sentences that include dependent clauses. As in Exercise 8.3, identify the dependent clauses by underlining and labeling them either as adjective or adverb clauses. If possible, use the sentences in Exercise 8.3 as patterns. As a subject for your paragraph, you may wish to describe an animal, a person, or another plant like the lichen that manages to survive under difficult conditions.

Exercise 8.5: Proofreading Practice

Identify the independent clauses in this paragraph by underlining them. If an independent clause is interrupted by a dependent clause, put parentheses around the dependent clause. The first sentence has been done as an example.

(1) In 1976 Sony, (which is one of Japan's leading electronic companies,) introduced the first consumer videocassette recorder, the VCR. (2) Within a decade, more than one-third of all homes in the United States had VCRs because people have found them such a convenient source of entertainment. (3) When people want to go out in the evening, they can record their favorite programs and watch them at a different time. (4) In addition, families can produce video histories of weddings, anniversaries, and bar mitzvahs, or they can watch sporting events and see replays whenever they want. (5) The price of a VCR, which fell about 80 percent in the first decade, is another factor in making this new electronic gadget so popular, and videotapes can be rented everywhere, from service stations and supermarkets to public libraries. (6) Because it is reasonably cheap, is convenient, and is a good source of entertainment, the VCR will continue to be a visible part of the American scene.

Exercise 8.6: Pattern Practice

Read the following paragraph and identify the sentence patterns by the kinds of clauses in each. Choose the most appropriate of the following numbers and write that number above the sentence:

1. Independent clause as its own sentence
2. Two independent clauses joined into one sentence
3. One independent clause with a dependent clause
4. Two independent clauses and a dependent clause

The first sentence has been done as an example. Write your own paragraph using these sentence patterns. You may want to write about some other electronic equipment that you like, such as stereos or portable tape cassette players, or you may want to write about another recent addition to the American scene, such as music videos or unusual clothing fashions.

3
(1) In addition to its popularity as home entertainment, the VCR has many commercial and educational uses because it can display both pictures and sound so easily. (2) Videotapes are useful as sales promoters, and they have successfully been introduced into supermarkets to show shoppers how to prepare kiwi fruits and how to cook bok choy. (3) In sporting goods stores videotape pitches showing the success of body-building equipment have resulted in greatly increased sales. (4) Moreover,

banks have found videotaping useful for security, and supermarkets now routinely videotape customers as they cash checks. (5) Although these commercial uses of VCRs have just recently begun to appear, educational videotapes have been widely used for a long time in classrooms at all levels from primary school to university classes. (6) Self-improvement videos that help people learn aerobic dancing, tennis, golf, cooking, and Spanish are consistently among the best-selling video tapes. (7) The VCR has become a useful commercial and educational tool.

9 *Essential and Nonessential Clauses and Phrases*

9a *Essential Clauses and Phrases* (es)

> An **essential clause** or **phrase** (also called a *restrictive*, or *necessary*, clause or phrase) appears after a noun and is essential in the sentence to complete the meaning. An essential clause or phrase cannot be moved to another sentence because if it is taken out, the meaning of the sentence is changed.

Compare the meaning of the following two sentences with and without the clause after the noun *people*:

People **who can speak more than one language** are called multilingual.

People are called multilingual.

The second sentence seems odd because not all people are called multilingual. Because we need the *who* clause in the first sentence to understand the meaning, it is an essential clause.

Please repair all the windows **that are broken**.

> (If the *that* clause is taken out, the sentence is a request to repair all the windows, not just those that are broken. Since the meaning of the sentence is changed when the *that* clause is removed, the *that* clause is essential to the sentence.)

Sylvester Stallone's movie **Rambo II** will be on TV tonight.

(The movie title *Rambo II* is necessary because Sylvester Stallone has appeared in many movies. If the phrase *Rambo II* is taken out of the sentence, it then says that Stallone's only movie will be on TV.)

....

HINT 1: Essential clauses and phrases are not set off by commas.

HINT 2: Clauses starting with *that* are almost always essential.

....

9b Nonessential Clauses and Phrases (non es)

A **nonessential clause** or **phrase** (also called a *nonrestrictive* or *unnecessary* clause or phrase) adds extra information but can be removed from a sentence without disturbing the meaning. The information can be put in another sentence.

Compare the following two sentences to see if the primary meaning of the sentence remains the same after the clause is removed:

My cousin Jim, **who lives in Denver**, is coming for a visit over Thanksgiving vacation.

My cousin Jim is coming for a visit over Thanksgiving vacation.

The *who* clause adds some information about where Jim lives, but it is not necessary. Because this *who* clause is nonessential, it can be moved to another sentence without changing the meaning of the main clause. (The assumption here is that the writer has only one cousin named Jim. If the writer had two cousins named Jim, one who lives in Denver and another one who lives in St. Louis, then the clause *who lives in Denver* would be necessary to identify to which cousin Jim the reference is made.)

Sandwich Supreme, **one of the first of a new chain of gourmet sandwich shops**, serves six different types of cheese sandwiches with a choice of three different types of bread.

(If the phrase describing Sandwich Supreme as a part of a chain of gourmet shops is removed from the sentence, the meaning of the main clause remains intact. The phrase is therefore not essential.)

Rambo II, **starring Sylvester Stallone**, will be on TV tonight.
(In this sentence, the phrase noting who stars in the movie can be removed because it merely adds information about the name of one of the actors. Compare this sentence with the example of *Rambo II* as an essential clause in Section 8a.)

....

HINT: Nonessential clauses and phrases are set off by a pair of commas when they appear within a sentence. Only one comma is needed when they appear at the end of a sentence. (See Chapter 23c.)

The compact disk, a revolutionary advance in high-fidelity recording, is making records and tape cassettes obsolete.
(Here the non-essential phrase appears in the middle of the sentence and needs two commas.)

Consumers are spending millions of dollars now on compact disks, a revolutionary advance in high-fidelity recording.
(Here the nonessential phrase appears at the end of the sentence and needs only one comma.)

....

Some sentences will be punctuated differently depending on the meaning to be conveyed. A few examples follow.

Phil's son Steve is playing in the soccer match.
(This sentence states that Phil has more than one son, and a son named Steve is playing in the soccer match.)

Phil's son, Steve, is playing in the soccer match.
(This sentence states that Phil has only one son, and an extra bit of information is that his name is Steve.)

The bank offered loans to the farmers, who were going to plant soybeans.
(This sentence states that all farmers received loans.)

The bank offered loans to the farmers who were going to plant soybeans.
(This sentence states that the bank offered loans only to the farmers planting soybeans, not to those planting other crops.)

Exercise 9.1: Proofreading Practice

In the following paragraph there are underlined phrases. Identify these as either essential or nonessential phrases by writing an E (for essential) or N (for nonessential) above each underlined phrase.

(1) Art fraud, <u>a widespread problem</u>, is probably as old as art itself. (2) Fourteenth-century Italian stonecarvers <u>who wanted to deceive their buyers</u> copied Greek and Roman statues and then purposely chipped their works so they could peddle them as antiquities. (3) Today forgers, <u>who have become specialists in different kinds of fraud</u>, produce piles of moderately priced prints, paintings, statues, and pottery. (4) The people <u>whom they defraud</u> are usually beginning or less knowledgeable collectors. (5) These people, <u>who usually can afford to spend only a few thousand dollars at most for a work of art</u>, have not developed a skilled eye for detecting fraud.

Exercise 9.2: Pattern Practice

In the following paragraph there are some underlined clauses and phrases, both essential and nonessential. Practice using clauses and phrases like these in your writing by composing your own sentences in the same patterns as the following sentences. As your topic, you may want to describe another common kind of fraud or deception that exists today.

(1) Thomas Hoving, <u>the former director of the Metropolitan Museum of Art</u>, estimates that 40 percent of the art <u>that is on the market today</u> is fake. (2) However, much of this fraudulent art is not detected because even buyers <u>who suspect fraud</u> find it difficult to prove that the seller knowingly unloaded a fake on them. (3) Thus collectors <u>who get stuck with dubious pieces of art</u> usually don't go to court. (4) Instead, they attempt to return the piece to the person <u>from whom they bought it</u>. (5) If that isn't possible, some collectors, <u>particularly the less honest ones</u>, pass the piece of art on to another unsuspecting buyer.

10 Sentences (sent)

A **sentence** is a group of words that has at least one independent clause and expresses a relatively complete thought.

Some writers have difficulty distinguishing between a sentence and a fragment (an incomplete sentence). The following are characteristics of sentences that should help.

Although sentences are said to express "a complete thought," sentences normally occur in the context of other sentences that explain more fully. A sentence may therefore seem to need more information because it will refer to other sentences.

He was able to do it.

> (This is a complete sentence because it is an independent clause. We don't know who "he" is or what he is able to do, but when this sentence appears with others, more explanation will make this clear.)

Sentences can start with any word.

- *And* and *but* are connecting words that can start an independent clause.

  But the dog did not bark.

  > (This sentence may not seem "complete" because it needs a context of other sentences to explain the whole situation.)

- *Because, since,* and other markers that begin adverbial clauses can open a sentence as long as an independent clause follows.

  Because she did not lock her bike, it was stolen.

  > (dependent clause first, then an independent clause)

- Dependent clauses and phrases can start a sentence as subjects.

  That it was hot did not bother the athletes.

  > (dependent clause as subject)

- Transition words and phrases, such as *first, to sum up,* and *meanwhile,* can begin a sentence.

  Next, she lifted the window.

(We don't know what "she" did first, but again, the context of other sentences will help.)

Sentences can have pronouns as subjects.

He was proud of his accomplishments.

Sentences don't have to have any specified length. They can have only a few or many words.

Go away! (short complete sentence)

> Whenever it is time to put away my winter clothing after a long, cold winter season, I always have a deep feeling of relief as if I am forcing the cold air to stay away until next year. (long complete sentence)

The complete verb in a sentence may be in a contraction.

He**'s** here.

> (The verb *is* is less obvious because it is contracted.)

Punctuation errors and other problems in a sentence may occur, but these errors do not make a sentence a fragment.

The current interest in healthful foods has not diminished the sale of fast food, high-fat hamburgers and hot dogs continue to sell well.

> (This sentence is incorrectly punctuated with a comma, but it is still a sentence. See Chapter 11a.)

....

HINT: To punctuate a sentence, remember these patterns:

A. | Independent clause | .

B. | Independent clause | , and | independent clause | .
          but
          for
          or
          nor
          so
          yet

C. | Independent clause | ; | independent clause | .

D. | Independent clause | ;   therefore, | independent clause | .
                             moreover,
                             consequently,
                             thus,
                             (and so on)

E. | Dependent clause | , | independent clause | .

F. | Independent clause | | Dependent clause | .

G. | First part of an independent clause | , | non-essential | ,
   } rest of the clause | .

H. | First part of an independent clause | | essential |
   } rest of the clause | .

For a more complete explanation of sentence punctuation, see Chapters 23 and 25.

There are four types of sentences:

10a Simple Sentences

Simple sentences have one independent clause.

| Independent clause |

Doctors and researchers are concerned about the growing death rate from asthma.

10b Compound Sentences

Compound sentences have two or more independent clauses.

Independent clause	+	independent clause

Doctors and researchers are concerned about the growing death rate from asthma, but they don't know the reason for it.

10c *Complex Sentences*

Complex sentences have at least one independent clause and at least one dependent clause (in any order).

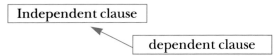

Independent clause

dependent clause

Doctors and researchers are concerned about the growing death rate from asthma because it is a common, treatable illness.

10d *Compound-Complex Sentences*

Compound-Complex sentences have at least two independent clauses and at least one dependent clause (in any order).

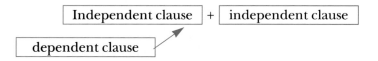

Independent clause	+	independent clause

dependent clause

Doctors and researchers are concerned about the growing death rate from asthma because it is a common, treatable illness, but they don't know the reason for the 23 percent increase in the last five years.

Exercise 10.1: Proofreading Practice

Identify each of the numbered groups of words with the appropriate letter(s) from this group:

    I   =   incomplete sentence
    S   =   simple sentence
   CP   =   compound sentence
   CX   =   complex sentence
CP-CX   =   compound-complex sentence

(1) When we have a romantic relationship with another person, we want to know how the other person feels about us. (2) But, as psychologists have found out from their studies, we rarely resort to asking about the other person's feelings. (3) Some people do this, but most people tend to use indirect means. (4) Such as asking a third person's opinion or using some more indirect means of inquiry. (5) A recent study of college students confirmed the tendency among students to use indirect means; moreover, in the study two psychologists learned students' most-often-used indirect tactic, which was to make the other person choose between alternatives, for example, asking the other person to choose their relationship over something else such as an opportunity to go off for a weekend of skiing. (6) Another way described by the students was testing the other person's limits of endurance in terms of behavior. (7) For example, the student would do something just to see if the other person would put up with it. (8) Yet another kind of testing of relationships was trying to make the other person jealous, and about one-third of the students being studied cited this as a kind of test of the other person's love. (9) The psychologists, who were also looking for instances of people who directly ask the other person about their feelings, found very few examples. (10) Asking the other person directly was reported to be a very difficult thing to do.

Exercise 10.2: Pattern Practice

Practice the sentence patterns in the following paragraph by writing your own simple, compound, complex, and compound-complex sentences. Follow the patterns used by these sentences. For your subject matter, you may write about a form of exercise you prefer.

(1) Many people who have suffered the sprains and aches of aerobic exercising now prefer an alternate form called non-impact aerobics. (2) This involves ways to exercise without causing stress to the body, and it requires strength, endurance, flexibility, and balance. (3) Nonimpact exercises involve larger

arm motions and leg motions that keep one foot on the floor to reduce bouncing and jumping. (4) Because some people want more upper-body exercise, some low-impact aerobics also include the use of wristweights. (5) It's not entirely clear that low-impact aerobics deliver the same aerobic benefit as traditional programs, but for those who want to avoid injury or cannot follow the more strenuous routines, it does provide benefit. (6) However, for both traditional aerobics and the nonimpact variety, the main cause of injury is still bad shoes, bad floors, bad stretches, and bad instruction.

Answer Key for Exercises in Part 1

Exercise 1.1

(1) For a long time psychologists have wondered what memories are and where they are stored in the human brain. (2) Because it is the basis of human intellect, memory has been studied intensely. (3) According to one psychologist, memory is an umbrella term for a whole range of processes that occur in our brains. (4) In particular, psychologists have identified two types of memory. (5) One type is called declarative memory, and it includes memories of facts such as names, places, dates, even baseball scores. (6) It is called declarative because we use it to declare things. (7) For example, a person can declare that his or her favorite food is fried bean sprouts. (8) The other type is called procedural memory. (9) It is the type of memory acquired by repetitive practice or conditioning, and it includes skills such

as riding a bike or typing. (10) We <u>need</u> both types of memory in our daily living because we <u>need</u> facts and <u>use</u> a variety of skills.

Exercise 1.2

(1) To learn more about memory, a psychologist <u>studied</u> visual memory by watching monkeys. (2) To do this, he <u>used</u> a game that <u>required</u> the monkey to pick up a block in order to find the food in a pail underneath. (3) After a brief delay the monkey again <u>saw</u> the old block on top of a pail and also <u>saw</u> a new block with a pail underneath it. (4) Only the new block now <u>covered</u> a pail with bananas in it. (5) The monkey quickly <u>learned</u> each time to pick up the new block in order to find food. (6) This <u>demonstrated</u> that the monkey <u>remembered</u> what the old block <u>looked</u> like and also what <u>distinguished</u> the new block. (7) The psychologist <u>concluded</u> that visual memory <u>was</u> at work.

Exercise 1.3

1. learn
2. begin
3. are
4. become
5. has studied
6. may represent
7. took
8. hopped
9. was going
10. concludes
11. sees
12. would not see
13. would conclude
14. failed

Exercise 1.4

Last year, one of the most popular new attractions in Japanese recreation parks *was* a maze for people to walk through. For some people this *could be* twenty minutes of pleasant exercise, but others *took* an hour or two because they *ran* in circles. Admission *cost* about three dollars a person, an amount that *made* mazes cheaper than movies. Mazes also *lasted* longer than roller coaster rides. One Japanese businessperson, first dragged there by his wife, *said* that he *enjoyed* it because it *kept* him so busy that he *forgot* all his other worries. Some people *liked* to amble in a leisurely way through the maze and *let* time pass by, but most maze players *tried* to get out in the shortest time possible. At the entrance, a machine *gave* people a ticket stamped with the time they *entered*.

Some people *quit* in the middle and *headed* for an emergency exit or *asked* a guard for help. But most *rose* to the challenge and *kept* going until they *emerged* at the other end, hoping to claim a prize.

Exercise 1.5

1. is (active)
   is spent (passive)
   want to eliminate (active)
2. is spent (passive)
3. may offer (active) (subjunctive)
4. was marketed (passive)
   is being advertised (passive)
5. buy (active) (command)
   could be (active) (subjunctive)
   may reverse (active) (subjunctive)

Exercise 1.6

Retinoic acid <u>is</u> a promising new drug that <u>is being prescribed</u>
     active   passive
by doctors as a wrinkle cream. A company that <u>owns</u> it <u>calls</u> it a
                                             active   active
wonder drug. Although the Food and Drug Administration

(FDA) <u>approved</u> it in 1971 as an acne cream, some users over
         active
thirty-five <u>told</u> doctors that it <u>produced</u> side effects such
         active   active
as smoother, younger-looking skin. These people <u>reported</u>
                                     active
that their skin <u>had</u> less wrinkles, but other users <u>said</u> the drug
             active   active
<u>irritated</u> their skin. Because the FDA <u>did</u> not <u>evaluate</u> the drug
 active   active
as a wrinkle fighter, they <u>are</u> now <u>testing</u> it for its ability to make
                              active
skin look younger. Since doctors <u>can decide</u> the appropriate
                                  active
use of the drug, they <u>can</u> prescribe it for its side effects and
                        active
<u>recommend</u> it for uses not yet approved by the FDA.
   active

Exercise 2.1

It is a sad fact of life that what some people call the "everyday courtes<u>ies</u> of life" are disappearing faster than finger bowl<u>s</u> and engineer<u>s</u> slide rulers. People in movie theater<u>s</u> carry on loud conversation<u>s</u>, older people on bus<u>es</u> rarely have anyone get up and offer them a seat, and few bother to offer thank<u>s</u> to a helpful salesperson. Some people say that courteous way<u>s</u> seem to have lingered longer in small town<u>s</u> than in big cit<u>ies</u> and that some region<u>s</u>—notably the South—cling more than other<u>s</u> to some remaining sign<u>s</u> of polite behavior. But more often we hear complaint<u>s</u> that courtesy is declining, dying, or dead. Says one New York executive: "There's no such thing as umbrella courtesy. Everybody<u>(s)</u> umbrella is aimed at my eye level." And a store owner in another city says that short-tempered waiter<u>s</u> in restaurant<u>s</u> and impatient salesclerk<u>s</u> in stor<u>es</u> make her feel as if she's bothering them by asking for service. Common courtesy may be a thing of the past.

Exercise 2.2

Among the people who are most aware of the current lack of everyday politeness are airline flight attendants and newspaper advice columnists. Says one flight attendant: "Courtesy is almost zero. People think you're supposed to carry all their bags on and off the flight, even when you have dozens of other passengers to attend to." One syndicated advice columnist notes that courtesy is so rare these day that when someone is kind, helpful, or generous, it is an event worth writing about to an advice columnist.

Some teachers blame television's poor example, especially the many rude detectives who shove people around, bang down all those doors, and yell in people's face. Too many of our current movie heroes are not particularly gallant, thoughtful, or polite. As a psychologist recently noted, it is hard to explain to children what good manners are when they don't see such behavior on their television or movie screens.

Exercise 2.3

Foreign tourists who travel in the United States often notice that Americans are not as polite as persons from other countries. Tourists from Europe, who are used to more formal manners, are particularly offended by Americans who immediately call tourists by their first names. Impoliteness in the United States extends even to objects. An English businessperson noted that in America public signs issue commands: "No Smoking" or "Do Not Enter." In England such signs would be less commanding: "No Smoking Please" or "Please Do Not Enter." Americans can also be rude without meaning to be. As a Japanese visitor noticed, the nurse who led him into the doctor's office said, "Come in here." In Japan, the visitor noted, nurses would say, "Please follow me." Foreign tourists, unfortunately, have a variety of such stories to take back to their countries.

Exercise 2.4

1. Aamericans, coffee
2. restaurants, stores, coffees, flavors
3. dozens, ice cream, milk, cream
4. problems, information
5. Advertising, drinkers

Exercise 3.1

Have you ever wondered how people in the entertainment

industry choose what you and me will see on television, read in
                                      I

books, and hear on records? Some producers and publishers say

that the executives in their companies and them rely on instinct
                                          they

and an ability to forecast trends in taste. But we consumers can-

not be relied on to be consistent from one month to the next.
So, market researchers constantly keep seeking our opinions.
For example, they ask ^us we moviegoers to preview movies and to
fill out questionnaires. Reactions from ^us we and our friends are
then studied closely. Sometimes, the market researchers merely
forecast from previous experience what you and ^I me are likely to
prefer. Still, some movies fail for reasons that the market
researchers cannot understand. When that happens, ^whom who does
the movie studio blame? The producer will say that the director
and ^he him did all they could but that the leading actor failed to
attract an audience. Sometimes, though, ^we us moviegoers simply
get tired of some types of movies and want more variety.

Exercise 3.3
1. X
2. C
3. X
4. X
5. C

Exercise 3.4

Rising insurance premiums are taking their toll on the rock
and roll concert business, and <u>it is</u> ^these premiums are likely to get higher before
conditions improve. People who have been buying tickets for
the last ten years are angry at paying five or six dollars more for
<u>his or her ticket</u> ^their tickets. But insurance companies say that instances of

violence and injury at rock concerts and the rising number of

people who file claims are causing <u>it</u>. [these higher insurance premiums] Property damage has cre-

ated an additional problem and has caused claims to increase

tenfold over the last ten years. Each claim is often for large sums

of money, and <u>they are</u> [it is] usually awarded by juries sympathetic to

damage caused by rock concert audiences. The situation has

gotten so bad recently that some concerts have been canceled

when <u>they</u> [concert organizers] could not get insurance, and in one case, a particular

act was cut from the show because <u>they were</u> [it was] considered danger-

ous. <u>This</u> [These insurance problems] may cause the number of rock concerts to decrease in

the future.

Exercise 4.1

We all know that when football players are very tired, their <u>con-</u>
<u>cerned</u> coaches call them back to the sidelines and give them
pure oxygen to breathe. But new evidence indicates that these
<u>exhausted</u> players could just as well be saving their breath. It
seems clear that 100 percent oxygen doesn't particularly help athletes. In a controlled test some athletes breathed in very <u>rapidly</u>
either normal air or pure oxygen. When tested as to how <u>quickly</u>
the subjects revived, there was no difference. Both groups said
they felt <u>well</u> within about three minutes. One of the players who
breathed plain air even commented on the fact that he felt <u>so well</u>
<u>that he was ready to play again</u>. The biggest surprise of all was that
none of the players being tested could even tell whether they had
breathed <u>really</u> pure oxygen or just normal air.

Exercise 4.3

1. a	**5.** a	**9.** an
2. an	**6.** an	**10.** a
3. a	**7.** a	**11.** an
4. an	**8.** an	

Exercise 4.4

One of <u>the</u> most interesting physicists of this century was Richard Feynman. He wrote <u>a</u> best-selling book about his own life, but he became even more famous on television as <u>the</u> man who was <u>a</u> member of <u>the</u> team that investigated after <u>an</u> accident happened to *Challenger*, <u>the</u> space shuttle that crashed in 1986. People watched on television as he demonstrated that <u>a</u> faulty part in <u>the</u> space shuttle probably caused <u>the</u> accident. Feynman's greatest achievement in science was <u>the</u> theory of quantum electrodynamics, which described <u>the</u> behavior of subatomic particles, atoms, light, electricity, and magnetism. <u>The</u> field of computer science also owes much to <u>the</u> work of Feynman. Many scientists consider Feynman to be one of <u>the</u> geniuses of <u>the</u> twentieth century.

Exercise 4.6

(1) A new sport, already popular in Canada and sweeping across the United States, is indoor box lacrosse. (2) It is faster, more furious, and often a more brutal version of the field game of lacrosse. (3) Box lacrosse is indeed an exciting game as it is speedier and rougher than ice hockey but requires the kind of teamwork needed in basketball. (4) Scores for box lacrosse are higher than those for field lacrosse because the indoor game has

a smaller playing area with more opportunities for scoring. (5) The team in box lacrosse is also smaller than that in field lacrosse as there are only six people on a side in the indoor game and ten people on conventional field lacrosse teams. (6) In addition, box lacrosse is played on artificial turf in ice-hockey rinks, and the sticks are shorter and thinner than conventional field lacrosse sticks. (7) In indoor lacrosse almost anything goes—and usually does in this rough-and-tumble sport.

Exercise 5.1

The mail carrier knew she should <u>have</u> stayed away from the dog barking on the porch, but it was her first day on a new job. She was concerned <u>about</u> delivering all the mail she had in her bag and did not want to have to report any problems. Her co-workers had warned her <u>about</u> the animals along her route, especially that dog <u>on</u> Mayfield Street. <u>Among</u> all the problems she seemed to be having, she did not want to let her co-workers know that she was afraid <u>of</u> animals. But when she tried to put the mail <u>in</u> the mailbox, the dog jumped up and grabbed all of it in his mouth. No one had told her the dog was trained to collect the mail and bring it inside the house.

Exercise 6.1

(1) <u>Humans</u> are unique in preferring to use the right hand. (2) Among other animals, each <u>individual</u> favors one hand or another, but in every species other than humans, the <u>split</u> between the right and the left hand is even. (3) Only <u>humans</u> seem to favor the right hand. (4) Even in studies of prehistoric man, <u>anthropologists</u> have found this preference among humans. (5) For example, in ancient drawings over five thousand years old, most <u>people</u> are shown using their right hand. (6) This <u>evidence</u> suggests that <u>it</u> is not a matter of cultural pressures but perhaps of some genetic difference. (7) However, since <u>left-handedness</u> seems to run in families, <u>it</u> is not clear how hand <u>preference</u> is passed from one generation to the next.

Exercise 6.2

(1) Almost every week of the year <u>drunken teenagers</u> cause highway accidents that could have been avoided. (2) These <u>drivers</u>

usually say that they thought they were in control, but the <u>cars</u> they were driving still get away from them and cause damage. (3) Worst of all, <u>innocent people in other cars</u> are the real victims of these accidents because they are just as likely to get hurt. (4) Maybe <u>legislators</u> are right when they say that <u>teenagers</u> should not have drivers' licenses. (5) There is <u>a lot</u> of wisdom in that statement.

Exercise 7.1

(1) <u>Finding a place for our garbage</u> is a problem as old as
₁
human beings. (2) On the Pacific coast there are <u>large, round</u>
₅
<u>shell-mounds</u> where for centuries Indians <u>had been discarding</u>
₃
the bones and clamshells that constituted their garbage. (3)

When people gathered together <u>in cities</u>, they hauled their waste
₄
to the outskirts of town or dumped it <u>into nearby rivers</u>. (4) In
₄
the United States the first municipal refuse system was instituted

in Philadelphia, <u>a well-organized city</u>. (5) Here slaves were
₆
forced to <u>wade into the Delaware River</u> and toss bales of trash
₄
into the current. (6) Eventually <u>this dumping into rivers</u> was out-
₁
lawed, and people looked for new solutions to the garbage prob-

lem. (7) Municipal dump sites, <u>unused plots of land far away</u>
₂
<u>from houses</u>, were <u>a frequent answer</u>. (8) But landfill sites <u>are</u>
₅
<u>decreasing</u> as many are closed because of health hazards or
₃
because of cost. (9) America, <u>a land of throwaway containers and</u>
₂
<u>fancy packaging</u>, clearly faces a garbage problem, <u>a problem</u>
₆
<u>without any apparent answers</u>.

Exercise 7.2

1. Verb phrase
2. Phrase that is the subject of the sentence
3. Phrase that comes after a linking verb and completes the subject
4. Phrase that tells more about the subject
5. Verb phrase
6. Phrase that gives added information about the verb
7. Phrase that gives added information about another element in the sentence

Exercise 8.1

(1) For years strange noises, <u>which would start in June and last</u>
clause
<u>until September</u>, filled the air around the waters of Richardson

Bay, <u>an inlet of water near Sausalito, California</u>. (2) The noise was
phrase
heard in the houseboats, <u>especially those with fiberglass hulls</u>,
phrase
moored along the southwestern shore of the bay. (3) <u>The noise</u>

<u>was usually described as a deep hum like an electric foghorn or</u>
clause
<u>an airplane motor</u>. (4) The noise, <u>which would start in late</u>
clause
<u>evening</u>, would stop by morning, <u>ruining people's sleep</u>.
phrase
(5) <u>During the summer of 1984</u> <u>the hum was unusually loud and</u>
phrase   clause
<u>stirred investigations</u>. (6) Originally, suspicion centered on a

nearby sewage plant, <u>which was suspected of dumping sewage at</u>
clause
<u>night</u> <u>when no one would notice</u>. (7) Some others thought there
clause
were <u>secret Navy experiments going on</u>. (8) An acoustical engi-
phrase
neer, <u>studying the mystery sound for months</u>, kept thinking he
phrase
would find the answer, <u>but he didn't</u>. (9) Finally, a marine ecolo-
clause

gist identified the source of the hum as the sound of the plainfin

midshipman, <u>a fish also known as the singing toad</u>. (10) <u>The</u>
phrase
<u>male's singing</u> was the sound everyone heard, he said, <u>though</u>
phrase
<u>some people still suspect the sewage plant</u>.
clause

Exercise 8.2

1. 3		**4.** 1	
2. 2		**5.** 2	
3. 2		**6.** 2	

Exercise 8.3

(1) The tiny lichen is an amazing plant. (2) It can survive in
an incredibly difficult environment <u>because it can do things no</u>
adverb clause
<u>other plant can do</u>. (3) The lichen, <u>which can anchor itself on a</u>
adjective clause
<u>bare rock by etching the rock's surface with powerful acids</u>,
grows into the pits that it burns out. (4) <u>Since lichens grow in</u>
adverb clause
<u>cold climates above the tree line</u>, they are often frozen or cov-
ered by snow most of the year. (5) Unlike the cactus in the
desert, the lichen has no way of retaining moisture. (6) Because
of this, the sun dries lichens into waterless crusts during the day.
(7) <u>When there is a drought</u>, lichens may dry out completely for
adverb clause
several months. (8) Even under ideal conditions their total daily
growing period may last only for an hour or two <u>while they are</u>
<u>still wet with morning dew</u>. (9) The lichen, <u>which may take</u>
adverb clause adjective clause

<u>twenty-five years to grow to a diameter of one inch</u>, can live for several thousand years. (10) These amazing plants are able to live in all sorts of difficult places, but not in cities <u>because the pollution kills them</u>.

adverb clause

Exercise 8.5

(1) <u>In 1976 Sony</u>, (which is one of Japan's leading electronic companies,) <u>introduced the first consumer videocassette recorder, the VCR</u>. (2) <u>Within a decade, more than one-third of all homes in the United States had VCRs</u> because people have found them such a convenient source of entertainment. (3) When people want to go out in the evening, <u>they can record their favorite programs and watch them at a different time</u>. (4) <u>In addition, families can produce video histories of weddings, anniversaries, and bar mitzvahs, or they can watch sporting events and see replays whenever they want</u>. (5) <u>The price of a VCR</u>, which fell about 80 percent in the first decade, <u>is another factor in making this new electronic gadget so popular</u>, and <u>videotapes can be rented everywhere, from service stations and supermarkets to public libraries</u>. (6) Because it is reasonably cheap, is convenient, and is a good source of entertainment, <u>the VCR will continue to be a visible part of the American scene</u>.

Exercise 8.6

1. 3		**5.** 3
2. 2		**6.** 3
3. 1		**7.** 1
4. 4		

Exercise 9.1

(1) Art fraud, <u>a widespread problem</u>, is probably as old as art
N
itself. (2) Fourteenth-century Italian stonecarvers <u>who wanted to</u>
E
<u>deceive their buyers</u> copied Greek and Roman statues and then purposely chipped their works so they could peddle them as

antiquities. (3) Today forgers, <u>who have become specialists in</u>

N

<u>different kinds of fraud</u>, produce piles of moderately priced

prints, paintings, statues, and pottery. (4) The people <u>whom they</u>

E

<u>defraud</u> are usually beginning or less knowledgeable collectors.

(5) These people, <u>who usually can afford to spend only a few</u>

N

<u>thousand dollars at most for a work of art</u>, have not developed a

skilled eye for detecting fraud.

Exercise 10.1

1. CX	6. S
2. CX	7. CX
3. CP	8. CP
4. I	9. CX
5. CP-CX	10. S

2

Revising Sentences for Accuracy, Clarity, and Variety

2

This part reviews the most frequently used rules and suggestions you should know in order to write accurate, complete, clear, and effective sentences. The topics discussed here will answer your questions about a part or all of a sentence or about words interacting within a sentence. Rules and suggestions for relationships between sentences are also included here.

To help locate the chapter in this part that you want, look through the topics listed here:

11 Comma Splices and Fused Sentences (cs/fs)

A **comma splice** and a **fused sentence** (also called a **run-on**) are punctuation problems in compound sentences (see Chapter 10 on compound sentences.)

Commas and semicolons are used as follows in compound sentences:

Independent clause,	and	independent clause.
	but	
	for	
	or	
	nor	
	so	
	yet	

Independent clause;	independent clause.

Independent clause;   however,   independent clause.
                       therefore,
                       moreover,
                       thus,
                       consequently,
                       (etc.)

Commas in Compound Sentences (See Chapter 23a)

A comma is needed when you join two independent clauses (clauses that would be sentences by themselves) with any of the following seven joining words (called "coordinating conjunctions"):

and	but
for	or
nor	so
yet	

The game was over, **but** the crowd refused to leave.

Some variations:

- If both independent clauses are very short, you may want to omit the comma.

  Kate may come or she may stay home.

- Some people prefer to use a semicolon when one of the independent clauses already has a comma.

  Every Friday, depending on the weather, Sam likes to play tennis; but sometimes he has trouble finding a partner.

....

HINT: Don't put commas before every *and* in your sentences. *And* is frequently used in ways that do not require commas.

....

Semicolons in Compound Sentences (See Chapter 25a)

If you use any connecting words other than the seven joining words listed for the comma in the compound sentence or if you don't use any connecting words, you'll need a semicolon.

The game was over; **however,** the crowd refused to leave.
The game was over; **the** crowd refused to leave.

**11
cs/fs**

The two most common errors are the comma splice and the fused or run-on sentence.

11a Comma Splices

The **comma splice** is a punctuation error.

It occurs in either of the following situations:

- When a sentence has two or more independent clauses separated by a comma but does not have one of the seven joining words (coordinating conjunctions) previously listed

  Comma Splice: In Econ 150, students meet in small groups for an extra hour each week, this gives them a chance to learn from each other.

  Revised In Econ 150, students meet in small groups for an extra hour each week, and this gives them a chance to learn from each other.

- When a comma is used instead of a semicolon

  Comma Splice: The doctor prescribed a different medication, however, it's too soon to tell if it's working.

  Revised The doctor prescribed a different medication; however, it's too soon to tell if it's working.

11b Fused or Run-on Sentences

The **fused** or **run-on sentence** is a punctuation error that occurs when there is no punctuation between the independent clauses.

Fused or Run-on Sentence: I didn't know which job I wanted I was too confused to decide.

Revised: I didn't know which job I wanted, and I was too confused to decide.

-or-

Revised: I didn't know which job I wanted; I was too confused to decide.

There are several ways to fix comma splices, fused sentences, and run-ons:

- Add one of the seven joining words listed in Chapter 23a (and be sure there is also a comma).
- Separate the independent clauses into two sentences.
- Change the comma to a semicolon. (See Chapter 25a for uses of the semicolon.)
- Make one clause dependent upon another clause. (See Chapters 8b and 19d.)

11b
cf/cs

Exercise 11.1: Proofreading Practice

In the following paragraph there are some compound sentences that require commas. Add commas where they are needed.

(1) Chocolate has been grown in the Americas for several thousand years. (2) It was considered a treasure and was cultivated by the Aztecs for centuries before the Spanish discovered it in Mexico. (3) Cocoa reached Europe even before coffee or tea and its use gradually spread from Spain and Portugal to Italy, France, and north to England. (4) In 1753 the botanist Linnaeus gave the cocoa plant its scientific name, *Theobroma cacao*, the food of the gods. (5) The tree is cacao, the bean is cocoa, and the food is chocolate but it bears no relation to coca, the source of cocaine. (6) Most cacao is grown within ten degrees of the equator. (7) In the late nineteenth century the Portuguese took the plant to some islands off Africa and it soon became an established crop in the Gold Coast, Cameroon, and Nigeria, where the temperature and humidity are ideal for it.

Exercise 11.2: Pattern Practice

Combine some of the short sentences listed here (and change a few words, if you need to) so that you have five compound sentences that follow the pattern shown here. Be sure to punctuate correctly with a comma.

	and	
	but	
Independent clause,	for	independent clause.
	or	
	nor	
	so	
	yet	

There are many varieties of chocolate.
All varieties come from the same bean.
All varieties are the product of fermentation.
Once fermented, beans must be dried before being packed for shipping.
Chocolate pods cannot be gathered when they are underripe or overripe.

Chocolate pods are usually harvested very carefully by hand.
In the processing different varieties of chocolate are produced.
Dutch chocolate has the cocoa butter pressed out and alkali added.
Swiss chocolate has milk added.
Conching is the process of rolling chocolate over and over against itself.
Conching influences the flavor of chocolate.
Chocolate is loved by millions of people all over the world.
Some people are allergic to chocolate.

12 Subject-Verb Agreement (agr)

Subject-verb agreement occurs when the subject and verb endings agree in number.

12a Singular and Plural Subjects

The subject of every sentence is either singular or plural, and that determines the ending of the verb.

(1) Singular

Singular nouns, pronouns, and nouns that cannot be counted (such as *news*, *time*, and *happiness*) all take verbs with singular endings.

I chew.

You laugh.

Water drips.
Time flies.
He sings.

(2) Plural

Plural nouns and pronouns take verbs with plural endings.

We know.
You read.
They stretch.
The stamps stick.

> **HINT:** Because many plural subjects have an *-s* at the end of the noun and because many third person singular verbs in the present tense have an *-s* at the end, a sentence won't have both a plural *-s* ending on the subject and also a singular *-s* ending on the verb. Thus, you can't have two *-s* endings at the same time, one on the subject and the other on the verb.
>
> Chimes ring.
> The boy jumps.

12b Buried Subjects

It is sometimes difficult to locate the subject word if it is buried among many other words. In that case, disregard prepositional phrases; words used as modifiers; *who, which,* and *that* clauses; and other surrounding words.

Almost **all** of Art's many friends who showed up at the party last night at
(subject)
Andy's **brought** gifts. (In this sentence, *Almost* is a modifier, *of Art's many*
(verb)
friends is a prepositional phrase, and *who showed up at the party at Andy's*

is a *who* clause that describes *friends.*)

HINT 1: Find the verb and ask *who* or *what* is the doer of the verb. Many people find it easier to locate the verb first. Remember, the verb is also the word that changes when you change the time of the sentence, from present to past or past to present.

HINT 2: Be sure to eliminate phrases starting with the following words because they are normally not part of the subject.

> including
> along with
> together with
> accompanied by
> in addition to
> as well as
> except
> with
> no less than

Everyone in our family, including my sister, *has taken* piano lessons.
  subject   verb

12c Compound Subjects

Subjects joined by *and* take a plural verb (X *and* Y = more than one, plural).

The **dog** and the **squirrel** are...

The **company** and its **subsidiary** manufacture...

Sometimes, though, the words joined by *and* really act together as a unit and are thought of as one thing. If so, use a singular verb.

Peanut butter and jelly is a popular filling for sandwiches.

12∂ Either/Or Subjects

When the subject words are joined by *either...or, neither...nor,* or *not only...but* the verb agrees with the closest subject word.

Either **Alice** or her children are...

Neither the **choir** nor the director is...

Not only the **clouds** but also the snow was...

12f
agr

12e Clauses and Phrases as Subjects

When a whole clause or phrase is the subject, use a singular verb.

What I want to know is why I can't try the test again.

Saving money is difficult to do.

To live happily seems like a worthwhile goal.

However, if the verb is a form of *be* and the noun afterward (the complement) is plural, the verb has to be plural.

What we saw were pictures of the experiment.
   (*What we saw = pictures*)

12f Indefinites as Subjects

When indefinite words with singular meanings such as *each, every,* and *any* are the subject word or when they precede the subject word, they take a singular verb.

Each has her own preference.

Each **book** is checked in by the librarian.

However, when indefinite words such as *none, some, most,* or *all* are the subject, the number of the verb depends on the meaning of the subject.

Some of the book is difficult to follow.
  (The subject of the sentence here is a portion of the book and is therefore thought of as a single unit and has a singular verb.)

Some of us are leaving now.
  (The subject of this sentence is several people and is therefore thought of as a plural subject with a plural verb.)

All she wants is to be left alone.

All my sweaters are in that drawer.

12g Collective Nouns as Subjects

Nouns that refer to a group or a collection (such as *team, family, committee,* and *group*) are called collective nouns. When a collective noun is the subject and refers to the group acting as a whole group or single unit, the verb is singular.

Our **family** has just bought a new car.

In most cases, a collective noun refers to the group acting together as a unit, but occasionally the collective noun refers to members acting individually. In that case, the verb is plural.

The **committee** are unhappy with each other's decisions.
  (The subject here is thought of as different people, not a single unit.)

12h Amounts as Subjects

When the subject names an amount, the verb is singular.

Twenty-five cents is…
Four bushels is…
More than 125 miles is…

12i *Plural Words as Singular Units*

Some words that have an -*s* plural ending, such as *civics, mathematics, measles, news,* and *economics,* are thought of as a single unit and take a singular verb.

Physics is…   The news is…

Measles is…   Modern economics shows…

12j *Words as Plural Subjects*

Some words, such as those in the following list, are treated as plural and take a plural verb, even though they refer to one thing. (In many cases, there are two parts to these things.)

Jeans are…   Eyeglasses are…

Pants cover…   Shears cut…

Scissors cut…   Thanks are…

Clippers trim…   Riches are…

Tweezers pull…

12k *Titles, Company Names, and Words as Subjects*

For titles of written works, names of companies, and words used as terms, use singular verbs.

All the King's Men is the book assigned for this week.

General Foods Incorporated is hiring people for its new plant.

Cheers is a word he often says when leaving.

12l *Linking Verbs*

Linking verbs agree with the subject rather than the word that follows (the complement).

Her **problem** is frequent injuries.

Short **stories** are my favorite reading matter.

12o agr

12m *There Is, There Are, and It*

The verb depends on the complement that follows the verb.

There is an excellent old movie on TV tonight.

There are too many old movies on TV.

However, *it* as the subject always takes the singular verb, regardless of what follows.

It was the bears in the park that knocked over the garbage cans.

12n *Who, Which, and That as Subjects*

When *who, which,* and *that* are used as a subject, the verb agrees with the previous word they refer to (the antecedent).

They are the **students who** study hard.

He is the **student who** studies the hardest.

12o *One of . . . Who, Which, or That*

In the phrase *one of those who* (or *which* or *that*) it is necessary to decide whether the *who, which,* or *that* refers only to the *one* or to the whole group. Only then can you decide whether the verb is singular or plural.

Rena is one of those shoppers who only buy things on sale.

one of (those shoppers who only buy)

(In this case, Rena is p.art of a large group, shoppers who only buy things on sale, and acts like them. Therefore, *who* takes a plural verb because it refers to *shoppers*.)

The *American Dictionary* is one of the dictionaries on that shelf that includes Latin words.

one . . . that includes

(In this case the *American Dictionary*, while part of the group of dictionaries on the shelf, is specifically one that includes Latin words. (The other dictionaries may or may not.) Therefore, *that* refers back to *one* and takes a singular verb.)

12o agr

Exercise 12.1: Proofreading Practice

In the following paragraph choose the correct verb that agrees with the subject.

How children's drawings develop (1. is, are) a fascinating subject. For example, a two-year-old and sometimes even a three-year-old (2. does not, do not) create any recognizable forms in their scribbling, and most of the children recently studied by a child psychologist (3. seem, seems) not to be aware of the notion that a line stands for the edge of an object. Typically, by the age of three, children's spontaneous scribbles along with their attempts at drawing a picture (4. become, becomes) more obviously pictorial. When they notice that they have drawn a recognizable shape, either the child or some nearby adult (5. attempt, attempts) to label the shape with a name. By the age of three or four, there (6. is, are) attempts to draw images of a human, images that look like a tadpole and consist of a circle and two lines for legs. Psychologists, especially those who (7. study, studies) the development of people's concepts of reality, (8. conclude, concludes) that young children's tadpole-like drawings (9. is, are) a result of inadequate recall of what people look like. However, Clayton Peale is one of a number of psychologists who (10. insist, insists) that young children do have adequate recall but (11. isn't, aren't) interested in realism because they prefer simplicity. Once the desire for realism (12. set, sets) in, it leads to the more complex drawings done by older children.

Exercise 12.2: Pattern Practice

Using the following patterns for correct subject-verb agreement, write two sentences of your own.

Pattern A: Compound subject joined by *and* with a plural verb

The whole flower exhibit and each display in it were carefully planned for months.

Pattern B: An amount as a subject with a singular verb

Ten dollars is a small price to pay for that.

Pattern C: A title, company name, or word with a singular verb

The Mysteries of the Universe is a new educational TV series.

Pattern D: An item that is a single unit but thought of as plural (such as pants, scissors, and jeans) with a plural verb

The scissors need sharpening.

Pattern E: Plural words (such as physics, economics, and measles) with a singular verb

The news of the election results is being broadcast live from the election board office.

Pattern F: Either...or, neither...nor, not only...but—with a verb that agrees with the nearest subject

Either Todd or his friends are capable of handling that job.

Pattern G: A whole clause as the subject with a singular verb

Whatever the Finance Committee decides to do about the subject is acceptable to the rest of us.

Pattern H: A *who, what,* or *that* clause with a verb that agrees with the correct antecedent

Psycho is one of those movies which shock viewers no matter how many times they watch re-runs.

13 *Sentence Fragments* (frag)

A **sentence fragment** is an incomplete sentence.

To recognize a fragment, recall the basic requirements of a sentence:

- A sentence is a group of words with at least one independent clause (see Chapter 8a).

  After buying some useful software for her computer, <u>Ellen splurged on sev-</u>
  independent clause
  <u>eral computer games to play</u>.

- A clause has at least one subject and a complete verb (plus object or complement if needed). (See Chapter 8.)

  During the evening, the <u>mosquitoes</u> <u>avoided</u> the camp <u>fire</u>.
                 subject   verb   object

There are three types of fragments:

1. **The fragment without a subject or verb**

   This type of fragment lacks a subject or verb.

   Fragment: The five days spent on the beach just relaxing and soaking up the sun.
   (*Days* is probably the intended subject here, but it has no verb.)

   Revised: The five <u>days</u> spent on the beach just relaxing and soaking up
                       subject
   the sun <u>was</u> the best vacation I had in years.
          verb

   Fragment: She selected a current news item as the topic of her essay. Then wondered if her choice was wise.
   (The second of these two word groups is a fragment because it has no subject for the verb *wondered*.)

   Revised: She selected a current news item as the topic of her essay. Then

   <u>she wondered</u> if her choice was wise.
   subject verb

HINT 1: When you proofread for fragments, check to see that the word group has both a subject and a complete verb. Remember that *-ing* words are not complete verbs because they need a helping verb. (See Chapter 1b.)

HINT 2: To find subjects and predicates in sentences with one-word verbs, make up a *who-what* question about the sentence. The predicate is all the words from the sentence used in the *who-what* question, and the subject is the rest:

My grandmother lived in a house built by her father.
(Who lived in a house built by her father?)

Predicate: lived in a house built by her father

Subject: My grandmother

2. **Fragments caused by a misplaced period**

   Most fragments are caused by detaching a phrase or dependent clause from the sentence to which it belongs. A period has been put in the wrong place, often because the writer thinks a sentence has gotten too long and needs a period. Such fragments can be corrected by removing the period between the independent clause and the fragment.

   Fragment: Ever since fifth grade I have participated in one or more team sports. *Beginning with the typical grammar school sports of basketball and volleyball.*
   (The second word group is a detached phrase that belongs to the sentence preceding it.)

   Revised: Ever since fifth grade I have participated in one or more team sports, beginning with the typical grammar school sports of basketball and volleyball.

   Fragment: Travelers going to Europe should consider going in the spring or fall. *Because airfares and hotels are often cheaper then.*
   (The second word group is a dependent clause that was detached from the sentence before it.)

   Revised: Travelers going to Europe should consider going in the spring or fall because airfares and hotels are often cheaper then.

HINT 1: To proofread for fragments caused by misplaced periods, read your paper backward, from the last sentence to the first. (For example, to proofread the paragraph in this hint, start with the last sentence that begins "Most, but not all, fragments...." Then, read the next to last sentence that begins "You will be able....") You will be able to notice the fragment more easily when you don't read it together with the sentence to which it belongs. Most, but not all, fragments occur *after* the main clause.

HINT 2: To find phrases separated from the main clause, check all your sentences to see that they have subjects and verbs. Watch especially for *-ing* words that are not complete verbs.

HINT 3: To find dependent clauses separated from the main clause, look for the marker word typically found at the beginning of the dependent clause. (See Chapter 7b.2) If the dependent clause is standing alone with no independent clause, attach it to the independent clause that completes the meaning. Typical marker words that begin dependent clauses are the following:

after	even though	what
although	if	whatever
as	since	when
as if	though	whenever
because	unless	whether
before	until	while
even if		

Fragment: Denise had breakfast at the doughnut shop near Hafter Hall. *After she went to her 8 A.M. biology class.*

Revised: Denise had breakfast at the doughnut shop near Hafter Hall after she went to her 8 A.M. biology class.

HINT 4: Another way to identify a dependent clause is to compare it to an independent clause (which can be a sentence). To find an independent clause, make up a yes-no question about the clause. Independent clauses that are not already questions will yield yes-no answers.

They frequently spend Sunday afternoons watching football games on TV.

Do they frequently spend Sunday afternoons watching football games on TV?

> (This question yields a yes-no answer and is, therefore, an independent clause.)

Because they frequently spend Sunday afternoons watching football games on TV.

Do because they frequently spend Sunday afternoons watching football games on TV?

> (This is not a reasonable question and is not, therefore, an independent clause.)

3. The intended fragment

Writers occasionally write an intentional fragment for its effect on the reader. Intended fragments should be used only when the rest of the writing clearly indicates to the reader that the writer could have written a whole sentence but preferred a fragment. In the following three sentences note that the second word group is an intended fragment. Do you like the effect it produces?

Fragment: Jessica walked quietly into the room, unnoticed by the rest of the group. *Not that she wanted it that way.* She simply didn't know how to make an effective entrance.

Exercise 13.1: Proofreading Practice

In these clusters of sentences there are both complete sentences and fragments. After you read each sentence, circle either F (fragment) or C (complete sentence).

A. (1) Pollution is a problem we have not really worked on (F or C). (2) Surely there is something that can be installed in factory smokestacks so that all the chemicals can be filtered out first (F or C). (3) Instead of just pouring right out in the open (F or C). (4) But factories are only part of the problem (F or C). (5) Every time you watch one of those big 747s take off, a big stream of smoke comes barreling out (F or C). (6) Or a big stream of pollution (F or C). (7) When a bus takes off, a cloud of black smoke comes pouring out (F or C). (8) Right through your car's vent into where you are sitting (F or C).

B. (1) Americans used to believe that the future would bring better jobs, better homes, and a better life for their children (F or C). (2) This confidence no longer exists (F or C). (3) Polls that have been reported in the news recently indicating that fewer Americans feel they are better off today than they were five years ago (F or C). (4) Many see themselves as lower on the ladder (F or C). (5) Maybe even with worse living conditions or further decline in the future (F or C).

Exercise 13.2: Pattern Practice

Read the following paragraph and note the pattern of dependent and independent clauses in each sentence. Practice using those patterns to write your own sentences, and check to see that you have not written any fragments. As a guide to help you, the first sentence has been done. For your own sentences, you may wish to write about some modern convenience you particularly like (or dislike) or some modern convenience you wish someone would invent.

(1) In France the National Electronic Directory has made the phone book obsolete because computer terminals are replacing the books. (2) Instead of a phone book, customers can choose a small computer hooked to their phones. (3) Using this computer they can call the directory along with a thousand other services such as banks, theater ticket offices, stock reports, and data bases. (4) The National Electronic Directory holds all twenty-five million French phone listings, and it handles about four million inquiries a month. (5) The directory finds the name of people anywhere in France, has a simple command structure, and is updated daily. (6) The equipment is given to customers free, although there is a charge for each minute a call is made to the directory or any of the other services.

Sample answer:

Sentence 1:

Pattern: independent clause—dependent clause

Sample sentence in this pattern: Those hot-air dryers in public restrooms are a Grade A nuisance because it's impossible to dry your face without messing up your hair.

14 *Dangling Modifiers* (dm)

A **dangling modifier** is a word or word group that refers to (or modifies) a word or phrase that has not been clearly stated in the sentence.

When an introductory phrase does not name the doer of the action, the phrase then refers to (or modifies) the subject of the independent clause that follows.

Having finished the assignment, Jill turned on the TV.

(Jill, the subject of the independent clause, is the doer of the action in the introductory phrase.)

However, when the intended subject (or doer of the action) of the introductory phrase is not stated, the result is a dangling modifier.

Dangling Modifer: Having finished the assignment, the TV set was turned on.

This sentence says that the TV set finished the homework. Since it is unlikely that TV sets can get our work done, the introductory phrase has no logical or appropriate word to refer to. Sentences with dangling modifiers say one thing while the writer means another.

Characteristics of dangling modifiers:

- They most frequently occur at the beginning of sentences but can also appear at the end.

- They often have an *-ing* word or a *to* + verb phrase near the start of the phrase.

Dangling Modifier: After getting a degree in education, more experience in the classroom is needed to be a good teacher.

Dangling Modifier: To work as a lifeguard, practice in CPR is required.

Dangling Modifier: As a teenager, moving tends to separate people.

Dangling Modifier: Relieved of your responsibilities at your place of work, your home should be a place to relax.

Dangling Modifer: The experiment was a failure, having not studied the lab manual carefully.

HINT: Two strategies for revising dangling modifiers are as follows:

1. Name the doer of the action in the dangling phrase.

   Dangling Modifier: Without knowing the guest's name, it was difficult for Maria to introduce him to her husband.

   Revised: Because Maria did not know the guest's name, it was difficult to introduce him to her husband.

2. Name the appropriate or logical doer of the action as the subject of the independent clause.

   Dangling Modifier: Having arrived late for practice, a written excuse was needed.

   Revised: Having arrived late for practice, the team member needed a written excuse.

14
dm

Exercise 14.1: Proofreading Practice

In the following paragraph there are several dangling modifiers. Identify them by underlining them.

According to some anthropologists, the fastball may be millions of years older than the beginning of baseball. To prove this point, prehistoric toolmaking sites, such as the Olduvai Gorge in Tanzania, are offered as evidence. These sites are littered with smooth, roundish stones not suitable for flaking into tools. Suspecting that they might have been used as weapons, anthropologists have speculated that these stones were thrown at enemies and animals being hunted. Searching for other evidence, historical accounts of primitive peoples have been combed for stories of rock throwing. Here early adventurers are described as being caught by rocks thrown hard and fast. Used in combat, museums have collections of these "handstones." So stone throwing may have been a major form of defense and a tool for hunting. Being an impulse that still has to be curbed, parents still find themselves teaching their children not to throw stones.

Exercise 14.2: Pattern Practice

Using the patterns of the sample sentences given here, sentences in which the modifiers do not dangle, write your own sentences. The first sentence is done as an example.

1. After seeing that there were no good movies on television that night, Brooke rented a home video movie for his VCR.

   Sentence in the same pattern:

   While walking home with her friends, Pam remembered the book she needed from the library.

2. To do well in biology, students have to be able to memorize many unfamiliar terms.

3. Unlike opera, rock videos usually don't have main characters or plots.

4. Undecided about his major, Mark registered for courses in several fields.

5. The movie was a thriller, having lots of blood and gore.

15 *Misplaced Modifiers* (mm)

> A **misplaced modifier** is a word or word group placed so far away from what it refers to (or modifies) that the reader may be confused.

Modifiers should be placed as closely as possible to the words they modify in order to keep the meaning clear.

Misplaced Modifier: The assembly line workers were told that they had been fired by the personnel director.

> (Were the workers told by the personnel director that they had been fired or were they told by someone else that the personnel director had fired them?)

Revised: The assembly line workers were told by the personnel director that they had been fired.

Misplaced modifiers are often the source of comedians' humor, as in the classic often used by Groucho Marx and others:

The other day I shot an elephant in my pajamas. How he got in my pajamas I'll never know.

Single-word modifiers should be placed immediately before the words they modify. Note the difference in meaning in these two sentences:

I earned nearly $30.
  (The amount was almost $30, but not quite.)
I nearly earned $30.
  (I almost had the opportunity to earn $30, but it didn't work out.)

HINT: Some one-word modifiers that may get misplaced:

almost	just	nearly
even	merely	only
hardly		

Exercise 15.1: Proofreading Practice

In these sentences there are some misplaced or unclear modifiers. Underline them and indicate a more appropriate place in the sentence by drawing an arrow to that place.

After finishing a huge dinner, he <u>merely</u> ate a few cherries for dessert.

(1) The man who was carrying the sack of groceries with an umbrella walked carefully to his car. (2) He had only bought food for his lunch because he was going to leave town that afternoon. (3) He whistled to his huge black dog opening the car door and set the groceries in the trunk. (4) The dog jumped into the trunk happily with the groceries.

Exercise 15.2: Pattern Practice

Choose one of the one-word modifiers listed in the Hint box and use it in several places in a series of sentences to create different meanings. Write out the meaning of each sentence.

Example (using the word *almost*):

Almost everyone in the office earned a $500 bonus last year.
  (Most of the people earned a $500 bonus, but a few people did not.)

Everyone in the office **almost** earned a $500 bonus last year.
  (There was almost a chance to earn a bonus, but it didn't work out.
  Therefore, no one earned a bonus.)

Everyone in the office earned **almost** a $500 bonus last year.
  (Everyone earned a bonus, but it was less than $500.)

16a
//

16 Parallel Constructions (//)

16a Parallel Structure

> **Parallel structure** is the use of the same grammatical form or structure for equal ideas in a list or comparison.

The balance of equal elements in a sentence helps to show the relationship between ideas. Often the equal elements repeat words or sounds.

Parallel: The instructor carefully explained <u>how to start the engine</u> and <u>how to shift gears</u>.
                                                                    1   2

  1 and 2 are parallel phrases in that both start with *how to*:
  • how to start the engine
  • how to shift gears

Parallel: <u>Getting the model airplane off the ground</u> was even harder than
                                                        1
<u>building it from a kit</u>.
        2

  1 and 2 are parallel phrases that begin with *-ing* verb forms:
  • getting the model airplane off the ground
  • building it from a kit

Parallel: She often went to the aquarium <u>to watch the fish</u>, <u>to enjoy the</u>
                                                      1   2
<u>solitude</u>, and <u>to escape from her roommate</u>.
                                3
    1, 2, and 3 are parallel phrases that begin with *to* + verb.

16b Faulty Parallelism

16b
//

    Non-parallel structure (or **faulty parallelism**) occurs when
like items are not in the same grammatical form or structure.

Nonparallel: Many companies are <u>reducing</u> their labor force as well as <u>eliminate</u>
                                          1   2
some employee benefits.

Revised: Many companies are <u>reducing</u> their labor force as well as <u>eliminating</u>
                                     1   2
some employee benefits.

Nonparallel: When the new investigator took over, he started his inquiry by <u>call-</u>
                                                                                    1
<u>ing</u> all the witnesses back and <u>requested</u> that they repeat their stories.
                                          2

Revised: When the new investigator took over, he started his inquiry by <u>calling</u>
                                                                                1
all the witnesses back and <u>requesting</u> that they repeat their stories.
                               2

Nonparallel: A visit home can help a student <u>stay informed of family activities</u>
                                                        1
and <u>to catch up with recent happenings in town</u>.
        2

Revised: A visit home can help a student <u>stay informed of family activities</u> and
                                                    1
<u>catch up with recent happenings in town</u>.
        2

      -or-

A visit home can help a student <u>to stay informed of family activities</u> and <u>to</u>
                                        1
<u>catch up with recent happenings in town</u>.
        2

Nonparallel: The article looked at <u>future uses of computers</u> and <u>what their role</u>

¹   ²

<u>will be in the next century</u>.

Revised: The article looked at <u>future uses of computers</u> and <u>their role in the</u>

¹   ²

<u>next century</u>.

16b
//

The following structures call for parallelism:

both . . . and . . .

Both by the way he dressed **and** by his attempts at humor, it was clear that he wanted to make a good impression.

either . . . or . . .   not only . . . but also . . .
neither . . . nor . . .   whether . . . or . . .

....

HINT 1: As you proofread, **listen** to the sound when you are linking or comparing similar elements. Do they balance by sounding alike? Parallelism often adds emphasis by the repetition of similar sounds.

HINT 2: As you proofread, **visualize** similar elements in a list. Check to see that the elements begin in the same way.

Isaiah wondered whether it was better to tell his girlfriend that he forgot or if he should make up some excuse.

Isaiah wondered whether it was better
• to tell his girlfriend that he forgot (or)
• if he should make up some excuse

Revised: Isaiah wondered whether it was better to tell his girlfriend that he forgot or to make up some excuse.

....

Exercise 16.1: Proofreading Practice
In this paragraph, underline the parallel elements in each sentence.

One of the great American cars was the J-series Duesenberg. The cars were created by Fred and August Duesenberg, two brothers from Iowa who began by making bicycles and who then gained fame by building racing cars. Determined to build an American car that would earn respect by its excellent quality and its high performance, the Duesenbergs completed the first Model J in 1928.

The car was an awesome machine described as having a 265-horse-power engine and a top speed of 120 mph. Special features of the car were its four-wheel hydraulic brakes and extensive quantities of light-weight aluminum castings. The masterpiece was the Duesenberg SJ, reputed to have a 320-horsepower engine and to accelerate from zero to 100 mph in 17 seconds.

Exercise 16.2: Pattern Practice

Using these sentences as patterns for parallel structures, write your own sentences using the same patterns. You may want to write about some favorite vehicle of your own, such as a car or bike.

1. A common practice among early Duesenberg owners was to buy a bare chassis and to ship it to a coachbuilder, who would turn the chassis into a dazzling roadster, cabriolet, or dual-cowl phaeton.
2. Duesenbergs that were originally purchased for six thousand dollars or so and that are now being auctioned off for more than a million dollars are still considered to be superb pieces of engineering brilliance.
3. After the Duesenberg first appeared on the market and people realized its excellence, the phrase "it's a doozy" became part of American slang.

17 Consistency (Avoiding Shifts) (shft)

Consistency in writing involves using the same (1) pronoun person and number, (2) verb tense, (3) tone, (4) voice, and (5) indirect or direct form of discourse and not shifting randomly or without good reason.

17a Shifts in Person or Number

Avoid shifts between first, second, and third person pronouns, and between singular and plural.

There are three "persons" in English pronouns:

	Singular	*Plural*

First person:
  (the person or
  persons speaking)
	I, me	we, us

Second person:
  (the person or
  persons spoken to)
	you	you

Third person:
  (the person or persons
  spoken about)
	he, she, it	they, them

  Those who view first or second person writing as too personal or informal suggest that writers use third person for formal or academic writing. Second person, however, is appropriate for giving instructions or helping readers follow a process:

First, (you) open the hood of the car and check the water level in the battery. (The pronoun *you* can be used or omitted.)

First person is appropriate for a narrative about your own actions and for essays that explore your personal feelings and emotions. Some teachers encourage writers to use first person to develop a sense of their own voice in writing.

(1) Unnecessary Shift in Person
Once you have chosen to use first, second, or third person, shift only with a good reason.

Unnecessary Shift: In a <u>person's</u> life, the most important thing <u>you</u> do is to
                              3rd   2nd
decide on a type of job.

  (This is an unnecessary shift from third to second person.)

Revised: In a **person's** life, the most important thing **he or she** does is to decide on a type of job.
  (This sentence stays in third person.)
          -or-

In **your** life, the most important thing **you** do is to decide on a type of job.
  (This sentence stays in second person.)

(2) Unnecessary Shift in Number

Another form of pronoun consistency is the avoidance of unnecessary shifts in number from singular to plural (or from plural to singular).

Unnecessary Shift: The working <u>woman</u> faces many challenges to advancement in a career. When <u>they</u> marry and have children, <u>they</u> may need to take
singular — plural — plural
a leave of absence and stay home for several months.

17b
shft

> (In the first sentence the writer uses the singular noun *woman* but then shifts unnecessarily to the plural pronoun, *they*, in the second sentence.)

Revised: The working **woman** faces many challenges to advancement in a career. When **she** marries and has children, **she** may need to take a leave of absence and stay home for several months.
(These sentences stay in the singular.)

-or-

Working **women** face many challenges to advancement in a career. When **they** marry and have children, **they** may need to take a leave of absence and stay home for several months.
(These sentences stay in the plural.)

17b *Shifts in Verb Tense*

> Because verb tenses indicate time, keep writing in the same time (past, present, or future) unless the logic of what you are writing about requires a switch.

Narrative writing can be in the past or present with time-switching if needed. Explanatory writing (exposition) that expresses general truth is usually kept in present time, though history is written in past time.

Necessary Verb Tense Shifting: Many people today generally **remember** very little about the Vietnam War except the filmed scenes of fighting they **watched** on television news at the time.
(The verb *remember* reports a general truth in the present, and the verb *watched* reports past events.)

Unnecessary Verb Tense Shifting: While we **were watching** the last game of the World Series, the picture suddenly **gets** fuzzy.

(The verb phrase *were watching* reports a past event, and there is no reason to shift to the present tense verb *gets*.)

Revised: While we **were watching** the last game of the World Series, the picture suddenly **got** fuzzy.

**17d
shft**

17c Shifts in Tone

Once you choose a formal or informal tone for a paper, keep that tone consistent in your word choices.

A sudden intrusion of a very formal word or phrase in an informal narrative or the use of slang or informal words in a formal report or essay indicates the writer's loss of control over tone.

Inconsistent Tone: The job of the welfare worker is to assist in a family's struggle to obtain funds for the **kids'** food and clothing.

(The use of the informal word *kids'* is a shift in tone in this formal sentence.)

Revised: The job of the welfare worker is to assist in a family's struggle to obtain funds for the **children's** food and clothing.

17d Shifts in Voice

Don't shift unnecessarily between active and passive voice in a sentence. (See Section 1d for a review of active and passive verbs.)

Active: He insisted that he was able to perform the magic trick.

Passive: The magic trick was not considered to be difficult by him.

Inconsistent Voice: He insisted that he was able to perform the magic trick, which was not considered to be difficult by him.

Revised: He insisted that he was able to perform the magic trick, which he did not consider to be difficult.

When choosing between passive and active, remember that many readers prefer active voice verbs because they are clearer, more direct, and more concise. The active voice also forces us to think about who the doer of the action is. For example, in the following sentence the writer uses passive rather than considering who the doer is:

Many arguments are offered against abortion.

(By whom?)

But there are occasions to use passive:

- When the doer of the action is not important or is not known.

    The pep rally was held before the game.

    For the tournament game, more than five thousand tickets were sold.

- When you want to focus on the action, not the doer.

    The records were destroyed.

- When you want to avoid blaming, giving credit, or taking responsibility.

    The candidate conceded that the election was lost.

- When you want a tone of objectivity or wish to exclude yourself.

    The experiment was performed successfully.

    It was noted that...

17e
shft

17e Shifts in Discourse

When you repeat the exact words that someone says, you are using **direct discourse**, and when you change a few of the words in order to report them indirectly, you are using **indirect discourse**. Mixing direct and indirect discourse results in unnecessary shifting, a problem that causes lack of parallel structure as well.

Direct Discourse: The instructor said, "Your reports are due at the beginning of next week. Be sure to include your bibliography."

Indirect Discourse: The instructor said that our reports are due at the beginning of next week and that we should be sure to include our bibliographies.

Unnecessary Shifting: The instructor said that our reports are due at the beginning of next week and be sure to include your bibliography.

(This sentence also mixes together a statement and a command, two different moods. For more on mood, see Section 1e.)

17e
shft

Exercise 17.1: Proofreading Practice

As you read the following paragraph, proofread for consistency and correct any unnecessary shifts. Underline the inconsistent word and write a more consistent form above it. You may also want to omit some words or phrases.

Many people think that recycling material is a recent trend. However, during World War II more than 43 percent of America's newsprint was recycled, and the average person saved bacon grease and other meat fat, which they returned to local collection centers. What you would do is to pour leftover fat and other greasy gunk from frying pans and pots into tin cans. Today, despite the fact that many trendy people are into recycling, only about 10 percent of America's waste is actually recycled. The problem is not to get us to save bottles and cans but to convince industry to use recycled materials. There is a concern expressed by manufacturers that they would be using materials of uneven quality and will face undependable delivery. If the manufacturer would wake up and smell the coffee, they would see the advantages for the country and bigger profits could be made by them.

18 Faulty Predication (pred)

Faulty predication occurs when the subject and the rest of the clause (the *predicate*) don't make sense together.

Faulty Predicate: The **reason** for her sudden success **proved** that she was very talented.

> (In this sentence the subject *reason* cannot logically *prove* "that she was talented.")

Revised: Her sudden success proved that she was very talented.

Faulty predication often occurs with forms of the verb *to be* because this verb sets up an equation in which the terms on either side of the verb should be equivalent:

Subject		Predicate
2 X 2	=	4
2 X 2	is	4
Dr. Streeter	is	our family doctor.

Faulty Predication: Success is when you have your own swimming pool.

> (The concept of success involves much more than having a swimming pool. Having a pool can be one example or a result of success, but it is not the equivalent of success.)

Revised: One sign of success is having your own swimming pool.

....

HINT: Faulty predication often occurs in sentences with the following constructions:

is when...
is where...
is why...
is because...

It is best to avoid these constructions in academic writing.

Faulty Predication: The reason I didn't show up is because I overslept.
Revised: The reason I didn't show up is that I overslept.

....

Exercise 18.1: Proofreading Practice

Rewrite the following examples of faulty predication so that they are correct sentences.

1. Relaxation is when you grab a bowl of popcorn, put your feet up, and watch football on television for two hours.
2. Computer science is where you learn how to program computers.
3. One of the most common methods of improving your math is a tutor.
4. The next agenda item we want to look at is to find out the cost of purchasing decorations.
5. His job consisted mainly of repetitious assembly line tasks.

Exercise 18.2: Pattern Practice

The patterns of the following five sentences avoid faulty predication. Practice these patterns by completing the second sentence in each set. Be sure to use the same pattern even though your subject matter will be different.

1. A good science fiction movie is one that has an exciting plot and realistic special effects.
   A good _____ is _____ .
2. His job as a receptionist is to direct people to the right office.
   His job as a _____ is _____ .
3. One sign of her excellent memory is her ability to remember the punch lines of all the jokes she hears.
   One sign of her _____ is _____ .
4. The reason I didn't buy those boots is that they are overpriced.
   The reason _____ is that _____ .
5. Stage fright is a kind of apprehension accompanied by a dry mouth, sweaty hands, and a fluttery stomach.
   _____ is _____ .

19 *Coordination and Subordination*

19a *Appropriate Coordination* (coord)

> When an independent clause is added to another independent clause to form a sentence, both clauses are described as **coordinate** because they are equally important and have the same emphasis.

Independent clauses are joined together by coordinators and appropriate punctuation (see Chapters 8a, 10b, and 23a). The two types of words that join coordinate clauses are:

- *Coordinating conjunctions* (the seven coordinating words used after a comma) are:

and	or	so
but	nor	yet
for		

- Coordinating words used after a semicolon. Some of the more commonly used ones are:

consequently	otherwise
furthermore	therefore
however	thus
moreover	

The following sentences illustrate appropriate coordination because they join two clauses of equal importance and emphasis.

Kathy is doing well as a real estate broker, and she hopes to become wealthy before she is thirty-five.

Some people take vitamin C tablets for colds; however, other people prefer aspirin.

19b *Inappropriate Coordination* (coord)

> **Inappropriate coordination** occurs when two clauses that are either unequal in importance or have little or no connection with each other are joined together as independent clauses.

Inappropriate coordination can be corrected by making one clause dependent on the other. However, if there is little connection between the clauses, they may not belong in the same sentence or paragraph.

Inappropriate Coordination: Winter in Texas can be very mild, and snow often falls in New England during the autumn.

(Because the connection between these two clauses is very weak, they don't belong together unless the writer can show more connection.)

Inappropriate Coordination: Jim was ill, and he went to the doctor.

Revised: Because Jim was ill, he went to the doctor.

(In this case the first clause can be shown to depend on the second clause.)

19c *Excessive Coordination* (coord)

> **Excessive coordination** occurs when too many equal clauses are strung together with coordinators. As a result, a sentence can ramble on and become tiresome or monotonous.

Excessive coordination can be corrected by breaking the sentence into smaller ones or by making the appropriate clauses into dependent ones.

Excessive Coordination: Kirsten is an excellent student from Holland, and she is visiting the United States for the first time, so she decided to drive through the Southwest during vacation.

Revised: Kirsten, an exchange student from Holland visiting the United States for the first time, decided to drive through the Southwest during vacation.

19∂ *Appropriate Subordination* (sub)

> When one clause has less emphasis or is less important in a sentence, it is **subordinate** to or dependent on the other clause.

The relationship of a dependent or subordinate clause to a main clause is shown by the marker word that begins the subordinate clause (See Chapters 8b and 10c). Some common marker words are:

after	before	unless
although	if	until
as	once	when
as though	since	whether
because	though	while

Although I like snow, I enjoy Florida vacations in winter.

Mr. Stratman, **who never missed a football game**, was one of the team's greatest supporters.

The house **that she grew up in** was torn down.

19e *Inappropriate Subordination* (sub)

> **Inappropriate subordination** occurs when the more important clause is placed in the subordinate or dependent position and has less emphasis.

Inappropriate Subordination: A career **that combines a lot of interaction with people and opportunities to use my creative talents** is my goal.

Revised: My career goal is to combine a lot of interaction with people and opportunities to use my creative talents.

19f *Excessive Subordination* (sub)

Excessive subordination occurs when a sentence has a string of clauses subordinate to each other. As a result, readers have difficulty following the confusing chain of ideas dependent on each other.

To revise excessive subordination, separate the string of dependent clauses into separate sentences with independent clauses.

Excessive Subordination: These computer software companies should inform their employees about advancements and promotions with the company because they will lose them if they don't compete for their services because the employees can easily find jobs elsewhere.

Revised: These computer software companies should inform their employees about advancements and promotions with the company. If these companies don't compete for the services of their employees, the companies will lose them because the employees can easily find jobs elsewhere.

Exercise 19.1: Proofreading Practice

In the following paragraph there are some sentences with inappropriate coordination and subordination. Rewrite these sentences so that the paragraph has appropriate coordination and subordination.

(1) Most people think of pigs as providers of ham, bacon, and pork chops, and they think of pigs as dirty, smelly, lazy, stupid, mean, and stubborn, but there's more to pigs than this bad press they've had, so we should stop and reevaluate what we think of pigs. (2) President Harry Truman once said that no man should be allowed to be president who does not understand hogs because this indicates a lack of appreciation for a useful farm animal. (3) Some people are discovering that pigs make excellent pets. (4) In fact, pigs have been favorite characters in children's fiction, and many people fondly remember Porky Pig and Miss Piggy, the Muppet creation, as well as the heroic pig named Wilbur in E.B. White's *Charlotte's Web*. (5) Now there are clubs for those who keep pigs as pets, and they are not just on farms where they have long been favorites as pets for farm children who are likely to be fond of animals. (6) People with pigs as pets report

that their pigs are curious, friendly little animals who are quite clean despite the "dirty as a pig" saying, though they are also not very athletic and have a sweet tooth. (7) Pigs can be interesting pets and are useful farm animals to raise.

Exercise 19.2: Pattern Practice

To practice using subordination and coordination appropriately use these suggested patterns in your own sentences. You can build your sentences from the short sentences offered here.

19f sub

1. Coordination: Join independent clauses with any of the following words (or others listed on previous pages).

, and	, but	, or
; moreover,	; however,	; therefore,

2. Subordination: Subordinate dependent clauses to independent clauses by using any of the following words (or others listed on previous pages) at the beginning of the dependent clause.

after	although	as
because	before	if
once	since	though
unless	until	when
whether	while	whose
that	which	who

You can use these clauses to build your paragraph:

Plastic used to be considered a cheap, shoddy material.
Now plastic is taking the place of traditional materials.
Cars are made of plastic.
Boats, airplanes, cameras, fishing rods, watches, suitcases, toothpaste tubes, and plates are made of plastic.
Plastic has replaced the glass in eyeglasses.
Plastic has replaced the wood in tennis rackets.
Plastic has replaced cotton and wool in our clothing.
Plastic seems new.
Plastic has been with us for a long time.
Amber is a natural form of plastic.
Celluloid is a nearly natural plastic.

Celluloid was developed in 1868 as a substitute for ivory in billiard balls.
Celluloid proved to be too flammable.
New types of plastic have mushroomed.
The use of plastics has steadily increased.
By the mid-1970s plastics had become the nation's most widely used material.

20 *Sentence Clarity* (clar)

The suggestions offered in this section will improve the clarity of your sentences. These suggestions are based on what is known about how to help readers follow along more easily and understand sentence content more fully.

20a *Moving from Known (Old) to Unknown (New) Information*

To help readers understand your writing, begin your sentences with something that is generally known or familiar before you introduce new or unfamiliar material later in the sentence. Then, when that new material is known, it becomes familiar, or "old," and you can go on to introduce more new material.

Note how these sentences move from familiar (or old) information to new:

Familiar ⟶ Unfamiliar: Every semester, after final exams are over, I'm always faced with the problem of what to do with old notebooks. **These lecture notes** might be useful some day, but they just keep piling up on my bookcase. Someday, **it** will collapse under the weight of information I might never need.

On the other hand, this example is not as clear:

Familiar ⟶ **Unfamiliar:** Second-rate entertainment is my categorization of most movies I've seen lately, but occasionally, there are some with worthwhile themes. In the Southwest, the mysterious and rapid disappearance of an Indian culture is the topic of a recent movie I saw that I would say has a worthwhile theme.

You probably found these sentences hard to read because the familiar information comes after the new information.

20c
clar

20b Using Positive Instead of Negative

Use the positive (or affirmative) instead of the negative because negative statements are harder for people to understand.

Unclear Negative: Less attention is paid to commercials that lack human interest stories.

Revised: People pay more attention to commercials with human interest stories.

20c Avoiding Double Negatives

Use only one negative at a time in your sentences.

Using more than one negative word creates a double negative, which is grammatically incorrect and leaves the reader with the impression that the writer isn't very literate. Some double negatives are also hard to understand.

Double Negative: He did not have no money.

Revised: He had no money.

-or-

He did not have any money.

Double Negative: I don't think he didn't have no money left after he paid for his dinner.

> (This sentence is particularly hard to understand because it uses both a double negative and negatives instead of positives.)

Revised: I think he had some money left after he paid for his dinner.

....

20d clar

HINT 1: Watch out for contractions with negatives in them. If you use contractions such as those in the following list, do not use any other negatives in your sentence.

aren't	hadn't	wasn't
couldn't	hasn't	weren't
didn't	haven't	won't
doesn't	isn't	wouldn't
don't		

Double Negative: She doesn't want no more riders in the car.

Revised: She doesn't want any more riders in the car.

         -or-

She wants no more riders in the car.

HINT 2: Watch out for other negative words such as the following:

hardly	no place	nothing
neither	nobody	nowhere
no one	none	scarcely

Double Negative: They hardly had no popcorn left.

Revised: They hardly had any popcorn left.

....

20∂ Using Verbs Instead of Nouns

Try to use verbs if possible rather than noun forms.

Actions expressed as verbs are more easily understood than actions named as nouns.

Unnecessary Noun Form: The decision was made to…

Revised: They decided to…

Some noun forms	*Verbs to use instead*
The determination of…	They determine…
The approval of…	They approve…
The preparation of…	They prepare…
The discovery of…	They discover…
The analysis of…	They analyze…

20f
clar

20e *Making the Intended Subject the Sentence Subject*

Be sure that the real subject or the real doer of the action in the verb is the grammatical subject of the sentence.

Sometimes the real subject of a sentence can get buried in prepositional phrases or other less noticeable places.

Subject buried in a propositional phrase: For real music lovers, it is preferable to hear a live concert instead of listening to the tape.

(The grammatical subject here is *it*, which is not the real subject of this sentence.)

Revised: Music lovers prefer hearing a live concert rather than listening to a tape.

Real subject buried inthe sentence: It seems like ordering from catalogs is something that Chris does too much.

Revised: Chris seems to order too much from catalogs.

20f *Using Active Instead of Passive*

The active verb (see Section 1d) is often easier to understand than the passive because the active voice explains who is "doing" the action.

Active: The committee <u>decided</u> to postpone the vote.
active

Not as clear: The decision that <u>was reached</u> by the committee was to postpone the vote.
passive

Exercise 20.1: Proofreading Practice

The following paragraph has numerous problems with clarity. Each of the sentences in the paragraph could be revised by using one or more of the suggestions in Chapter 20. List the section numbers of all the suggestions that could be followed to improve each of these sentences.

21
trans

(1) Beyond boomerangs and koala bears, knowledge about Australia was not common among Americans until a few years ago. (2) All that was changed by the appearance in the United States of Australian movies such as *My Brilliant Career* and *Mad Max*. (3) In addition, there was the appearance on American television of commercials of Paul Hogan, the Australian entertainer, reminding us that the America's Cup in yachting had been lost by the Americans to the Australians. (4) Now, American tourists are pouring into Australia, and hardly any big travel agency doesn't offer package tours "down under." (5) They are obviously happy to have discovered this new continent for sightseeing. (6) Not to be missed are sights to dazzle Americans, such as the Great Barrier Reef, a 1250-mile reef teeming with tropical fish, and the outback. (7) A vast collection of deserts and bush country where the aborigines live is also to be visited, with lovely cities such as Sydney and Melbourne for the traveler.

Exercise 20.2: Pattern Practice

Look back through Chapter 20 at the patterns for the changes you suggested in Exercise 20.1. Use those patterns to revise the paragraph above so that it is clearer.

21 *Transitions* (trans)

> **Transitions** are words and phrases that build bridges between sentences, parts of sentences, and paragraphs. These bridges show relationships and help to blend sentences together smoothly.

Several types of transitions are illustrated here.

21a Repetition of a Key Term or Phrase

Among the recent food fads sweeping America is the interest in **exotic foods**. While not everyone can agree on what **exotic foods** are, most of us like the idea of trying something new and different.

21b Synonyms

Since the repetition of a key word or phrase can become boring, the strategy of using a synonym (a word or phrase having essentially the same meaning) offers a way to add variety while not repeating.

One food Americans are not inclined to try is **brains**. A Gallup Poll taken one year found that 41 percent of the people who responded said they would never try **brains**. Three years later, the percentage of those who wouldn't touch **gray matter** had risen to 49 percent.

21c Pronouns

Pronouns such as *he, she, it, we,* and *they* are useful devices when you want to refer back to something mentioned previously. Similarly, *this, that, these,* and *those* can be used as links.

In addition to brains, there are many other foods that <u>Americans</u> now find more distasteful than <u>they</u> did several years ago. For example, more people now say they would never eat <u>liver, rabbit, pig's feet, or beef kidneys</u> than said so three years ago. Even restaurant workers who are exposed to <u>these</u> delicacies aren't always wild about <u>them.</u>

21∂ *Transitional Words and Phrases*

English has a huge storehouse of words and phrases that cue the reader to relationships between sentences. Without these cues the reader may be momentarily puzzled or unsure of how sentences relate to each other. For example, read these two sentences:

John is very tall. He does not play basketball.

If it took you a moment to see the connection, try reading the same two sentences with a transitional word added:

John is very tall. However, he does not play basketball.

The word *however* signals that the second sentence contradicts or contrasts with the first sentence. Read the following:

The state government was determined not to raise taxes. Therefore,…

As soon as you reached the word *therefore*, you knew that some consequence or result would follow.

The transitions listed here are grouped according to the categories of relationships they show.

Adding	*Comparing*	*Contrasting*
and	similarly	but
besides	likewise	yet
in addition	in like manner	however
also	at the same time	still
too	in the same way	nevertheless
moreover		on the other hand
further		on the contrary
furthermore		in contrast
next		nonetheless
first		conversely
second		in another sense
third		instead
finally		notwithstanding
last		rather
again		though
and then		whereas
likewise		after all

Adding
similarly
equally important
what's more

Contrasting
although

Emphasizing
indeed
in fact
above all
add to this
and also
even more
in any event
to repeat
in other words
that is
obviously
in any case

Ending
after all
finally
in sum
for these reasons

Giving Examples
for example
for instance
to illustrate
that is
namely
specifically

21d
trans

Pointing to cause and effect, proof, results or conclusions
thus
therefore
consequently
because of this
hence
as a result
then
so
accordingly

Showing place or direction
over
above
inside
next to
underneath
to the left
to the right
just behind
beyond
in the distance

Showing time
meanwhile
soon
later
afterward
now
in the past
then
next
before
during
while
finally
after this
at last
since then
whereupon
presently
temporarily
after a short time

Showing time

at the same time
in the meantime

Summarizing

to sum up	in conclusion	in general
in brief	that is	to recapitulate
on the whole	finally	to conclude
as has been noted	as has been said	
in other words	for these reasons	

HINT: In this list you'll notice words such as *and* and *but*, which some people prefer not to use to begin sentences. Others think of them as useful words to achieve variety and smooth transitions between sentences.

Although jet lag is a nuisance for travelers, it can be a disaster for flight crews. **But** flight crews can reduce the effects of jet lag by modifying their sleep patterns. **And** some airlines are even beginning to recognize the need for in-flight naps.

21e Transitions in and between Paragraphs

(1) Transitions between Sentences in a Paragraph

Readers can more easily understand your paragraphs when they see how every sentence in the paragraph is connected to the whole. You can signal these connections between sentences through the use of repetition, synonyms, pronouns, and transitional words and phrases, as explained in Chapters 21a through 21d. In the following example, these connections are highlighted.

◯ = repetition   ⌒ = pronouns

▢ = synonyms   ⌐┐ = transitional words and phrases

When drilling into Greenland's layers of ice, scientists have recently pulled up evidence from the last ice age showing that the island's climate underwent extreme shifts within a year or two. (This) unexpected [finding] is based on evidence from ice cores that the climate often shifted from glacial to warmer weather in less than a few years. In addition, other evidence indicates that the annual amount of snow accumulations also changed abruptly at the same time. As the climate went from cold to warm, the amount of snowfall jumped by as much as 100 percent in just a few years. This happens because more snow falls during warmer periods when the atmosphere holds more water. From this evidence, scientists therefore conclude that warming and cooling of the earth may be able to occur much faster than had been previously thought.

**21e
trans**

(2) Transitions between Paragraphs

As you start a new paragraph, you should also show the link to previous paragraphs, and an effective place to do this is in the first sentence of the new paragraph. Some strategies for making transitions between paragraphs are the following:

- *Use repetition as a hook*
  One way to make a connection or bridge is to reach back to the previous paragraph and refer to some element there in the beginning of your next paragraph. Some writers think of this strategy as using a hook. They "hook" an element from above and bring it down—through the use of repetition—to the next paragraph, providing a connecting thread of ideas.

  Suppose your whole paper discusses the changing role of women in combat. In a paragraph on the history of women's roles in warfare, you conclude with the example of Harriet Tubman, an African American who led scouting raids into enemy territory during the Civil War. In the next paragraph you want to move to new roles for women in modern combat. Your opening sentence can "hook" the older use of women as scouts and tie that to their new role as pilots in the Gulf War:

  While a few women served in more limited roles as <u>scouts</u> in previous
  ("hook" to previous paragraph)
  wars, in the recent Gulf War women took on more extensive roles as pilots

  flying supplies, troops, and ammunition into combat zones.

- *Use transitional words to show direction*

  Because every paragraph advances your paper forward, the first sentence of a paragraph can be used to point your readers in the general direction of your whole essay. Think of the first sentence of every paragraph as being like a road map, indicating to your readers where they are headed.

  For example, suppose your next paragraph in a paper on campaign reform presents a second reason in your argument against allowing large personal contributions to political candidates. If so, then use a transitional word which shows that you are building a list of arguments:

  <u>Another reason</u> why political candidates should not receive large personal
  (this shows the direction of adding another element)
  contributions is…

  Or suppose that your next paragraph is going to acknowledge that there are also arguments for the opposing side in this topic. You would then be going in the opposite direction or contrasting one side against the other:

  <u>Not everyone,</u> <u>however,</u> is in favor of making personal contributions to can-
  (this signals a turn in the opposite direction)
  didates illegal. Those who want to continue the practice argue that…

Exercise 21.1: Proofreading Practice

To practice recognizing different types of transitions, read the following paragraph and underline the transitions. Categorize them by putting the appropriate numbers under the words you mark, using these numbers:

1. *Repetition of key term or phrase*
2. *Synonyms*
3. *Pronouns*
4. *Transitional words or phrases*

International airports may soon have a high-tech machine that is really an unusually reliable nose. This sophisticated machine sniffs for drugs and will provide a more accurate means of trapping narcotics smugglers than has been possible so far. The walk-through narcotics vapor detector pulls in air samples from a passenger's clothes as he or she passes through. Several feet past the first sampling, the passenger is again sampled by having air blown across his or her body. Then, these vapor samples are funneled into a device called a thermionic sensor. If the sensor sets off an alarm, the passenger is then searched. However, it is not always certain that drugs will be found because there can be an occasional false alarm. But officials hope that the electronic nose will strike fear in the hearts of would-be smugglers. If so, this high-tech nose will act as a deterrent as well as a detector.

21e
trans

Exercise 21.2: Pattern Practice

In the following paragraph, the connections or transitional links are missing in paragraph 1, but they are added in paragraph 2. Paragraph 3, like 1, needs transitions. Use the types of transitional links described in Chapter 21 and illustrated in paragraph 2 to revise paragraph 3. Your revision will be paragraph 4.

Paragraph 1:
   I like autumn. Autumn is a sad time of year. The leaves turn to brilliant yellow and red. The weather is mild. I can't help thinking ahead to the coming of winter. Winter will bring snowstorms, slippery roads, and icy fingers. In winter the wind chill factor can make it dangerous to be outside. I find winter unpleasant. In the autumn I can't help thinking ahead to winter's arrival. I am sad when I think that winter is coming.

Paragraph 2:
   Although I like autumn, it is also a sad time of year. Of course, the leaves turn to brilliant yellow and red, and the weather is mild. Still, I can't help thinking ahead to the coming of winter with its snowstorms, slippery roads, and icy fingers. Moreover, in winter the wind chill factor can make it dangerous to be outside. Because I find these things unpleasant, in the autumn I can't help thinking ahead to winter's arrival. Truly, I am sad when I think that winter is coming.

Paragraph 3:

Caring for houseplants requires some basic knowledge about plants. The plant should be watered. The plant's leaves should be cleaned. The spring and summer bring a special time of growth. The plant can be fertilized then. The plant may also be repotted. The new pot should be only two inches (in diameter) larger than the pot the plant is presently in. Some plants can be put outside in summer. Some plants cannot be put outside. Being familiar with basic requirements for houseplants will result in having healthy plants.

22 *Sentence Variety* (var)

Sentences with the same word order and length produce the kind of monotony that is boring to readers. To make your sentences more interesting, add variety by making some longer than others and by finding alternatives to starting every sentence with the subject and verb. Following are strategies to help achieve that variety.

22a Sentence Combining

- You can combine two sentences (or independent clauses) into one longer sentence.

    Original: Doonesbury cartoons laugh at contemporary politicians. The victims of the satire probably don't read the cartoon strip.

    Revised: Doonesbury cartoons laugh at contemporary politicians, but the victims of the satire probably don't read the cartoon strip.

PUNCTUATION HINT: Remember that if you join an independent clause to another with *and, but, for, or, nor, so,* or *yet,* use a comma. Use a semicolon if you do not use connecting words or if you use other connecting words such as *therefore, however,* and so on.

- You can join the subject of two independent clauses into one sentence when the verb and the rest of the clause (called the *predicate*) are the same.

  Original: During the flood, the Wabash River overflowed its banks. At the same time, Wildcat Creek also did the same.

  Revised: During the flood, both the Wabash River and Wildcat Creek overflowed their banks.

- You can join two predicates when they have the same subject.

  Original: Ken often spends Sunday afternoons watching football on TV. He spends Monday evenings the same way.

  Revised: Ken often spends both Sunday afternoons and Monday evenings watching football on TV.

22b var

22b *Adding Words*

- You can add a description, a definition, or other information about a noun after the noun.

  Original: Dr. Lewis recently moved to Florida.

  Revised: Dr. Lewis, our family dentist, recently moved to Florida.

  Original: I plan to visit **New York**.

  Revised: I plan to visit **New York**, a city with a wide variety of ethnic restaurants.

  Original: Professor Smith is a political science teacher. She gives lectures in the community on current events.

  Revised: Professor Smith, a political science teacher, gives lectures in the community on current events.

- You can add a *who, which,* or *what* clause after a noun or turn another sentence into a *who, which,* or *what* clause.

  Original: Ed always arrives at his desk at 7:55 A.M.

  Revised: Ed, **who** takes his job very seriously, always arrives at his desk at 7:55 A.M.

  Original: The experiment failed because of Murphy's law. This law states that buttered bread always falls buttered side down.

Revised: The experiment failed because of Murphy's law, **which** states that buttered bread always falls buttered side down.

- Sometimes, you can delete the *who, which, what* words, as in the following example:

Original: The National Football League is very popular with TV fans. It is older than the American Football League.

Revised: The National Football League, **which** is popular with TV fans, is older than the American Football League.

Revised: The National Football League, popular with TV fans, is older than the American Football League.

- You can add phrases and clauses at the beginning of the sentence. For example, you can begin with the prepositional phrases. Some of the prepositions you might use include the following:

In...	Because of...
To...	In addition to...
For...	Under...
At...	Through...
From...	Between...
On...	

In addition to soup and salad, she ordered bread sticks and coffee.

From an advertiser's point of view, commercials are more important than the TV programs.

- You can begin with infinitives (*to* + verb) or with phrases beginning with *-ing* and *-ed* verbs.

To attract attention, the hijackers ordered the plane to fly to Africa.

Having finished his workout, the weightlifter headed for the shower.

Tired of hearing her dog whining, she finally opened the door and let the cold, wet pooch in the house.

- You can add transitional words (see Chapter 21) at the beginning of sentences.

However, I don't want to make a decision too quickly.

In addition, the new model for that sports car will have a turbo boost.

For example, whenever he tries to tell a joke, the whole group just stares at him.

22b
var

- You can begin with dependent clauses by starting these clauses with dependent markers such as the following:

After…	Since…
Although…	Until…
Because…	When…
If…	While…

After the parade was over, the floats were quickly taken apart.

When spring comes, I'll have to start searching for a summer job.

22c *Changing Words, Phrases, and Clauses*

- You can move adjectives after the *is* verb to the front of the sentence so that they describe the subject noun.

    Original: The Homecoming Queen was surprised and teary-eyed. She waved enthusiastically to the crowd.

    Revised: The surprised and teary-eyed Homecoming Queen waved enthusiastically to the crowd.

    -or-

    Surprised and teary-eyed, the Homecoming Queen waved enthusiastically to the crowd.

- You can expand your subject to a phrase or clause.

    Hunting is his favorite sport.

    Hunting grouse is his favorite sport.

    To hunt grouse in the early morning mists is to really enjoy the sport.

    Whoever has hunted grouse in the early morning mists knows the real joys of the sport.

    That grouse hunting is enjoyable is evident from the number of people addicted to the sport.

- You can change a sentence to a dependent clause (see Chapter 8b) or put it before or after the independent clause.

    Original: He overslept yesterday morning and missed class. He did not hear the announcement of the exam.

    Revised: Because he overslept yesterday morning and missed class, he did not hear the announcement of the exam.

Original: America is overly dependent on foreign oil. Scientists have not yet found enough alternate sources of energy.

Revised: Although America is overly dependent on foreign oil, scientists have not yet found enough alternate sources of energy.

Exercise 22.1: Pattern Practice

In the paragraphs included here, paragraph 1 (which you will probably find very choppy and boring) is composed of sentences in a very similar pattern. Paragraph 2 is a revision of that first paragraph and is composed of sentences that use the strategies for achieving variety that are described in Chapter 22. As you read through paragraph 2, identify the various strategies used to achieve sentence variety. Use those and other strategies described in Chapter 22 to revise paragraph 3, which (like paragraph 1) is composed of sentences in a very similar pattern.

Paragraph 1:

(1) Whistling is a very complex art. (2) It involves your lips, teeth, tongue, jaw, rib cage, abdomen, and lungs. (3) It occasionally also involves your hands and fingers. (4) Whistling sounds are produced by the vibration of air through a resonating chamber. (5) This resonating chamber is created by your mouth or hands. (6) One factor is particularly crucial. (7) This factor is the type of space produced in your mouth by your tongue. (8) Whistling is usually thought of as a means of entertainment. (9) It can also be a means of communication. (10) Some people include whistling as part of their language. (11) Others use whistling to carry messages over long distances.

Paragraph 2 (Revision of paragraph 1):

(1) Whistling is a very complex art that involves your lips, teeth, tongue, jaw, rib cage, abdomen, and lungs, and occasionally your hands and fingers. (2) Whistling sounds are produced by the vibration of air through the resonating chamber created by your mouth or hands. (3) One particularly crucial factor is the type of space produced in your mouth by your tongue. (4) Although whistling is usually thought of as a means of entertainment, it can also be a means of communication. (5) Some people include whistling as part of their language, and others use whistling to carry messages over long distances.

Paragraph 3:

Scientists neglect whistling. Amateurs and hobbyists do not neglect it. There are whistling contests all over the United States.

Accomplished whistlers whistle classical music, opera, jazz, Broadway show tunes, polkas, and even rock and roll at these contests. People whistle very differently. Some people pucker their lips. Other people use their throat, hands, or fingers to produce whistling sounds. These whistling sounds resemble the flute. Whistling has several advantages. One advantage is that it is a happy sound. Whistlers never lose their instrument. Their instrument doesn't need to be cleaned or repaired. Their instrument costs nothing. It is easily transported. Learning how to whistle is hard to explain. Whistling is something you either pick up at a young age or not at all.

two
ans

Answer Key for Exercises in Part 2

Exercise 11.1

(1) Chocolate has been grown in the Americas for several thousand years. (2) It was considered a treasure and was cultivated by the Aztecs for centuries before the Spanish discovered it in Mexico. (3) Cocoa reached Europe even before coffee or tea, and its use gradually spread from Spain and Portugal to Italy, France, and north to England. (4) In 1753 the botanist Linnaeus gave the cocoa plant its scientific name, *Theobroma cacao*, the food of the gods. (5) The tree is cacao, the bean is cocoa, and the food is chocolate, but it bears no relation to coca, the source of cocaine. (6) Most cacao is grown within ten degrees of the equator. (7) In the late nineteenth century the Portuguese took the plant to some islands off Africa, and it soon became an established crop in the Gold Coast, Cameroon, and Nigeria, where the temperature and humidity are ideal for it.

Exercise 11.2

Some possible answers are as follows:

1. There are many varieties of chocolate, but all varieties come from the same bean.
2. All varieties are the product of fermentation, and once fermented, beans must be dried before being packed for shipping.
3. Chocolate pods cannot be gathered when they are underripe or overripe, so chocolate pods are usually harvested very carefully by hand.
4. Dutch chocolate has the cocoa butter pressed out and alkali added, and Swiss chocolate has milk added.

5. Chocolate is loved by millions of people all over the world, yet some people are allergic to chocolate.

Exercise 12.1

1. is	**7.** study
2. do not	**8.** conclude
3. seem	**9.** are
4. become	**10.** insist
5. attempts	**11.** aren't
6. are	**12.** sets

two ans

Exercise 13.1

A.		**B.**	
1. C		**1.** C	
2. C		**2.** C	
3. F		**3.** F	
4. C		**4.** C	
5. C		**5.** F	
6. F			
7. C			
8. F			

Exercise 14.1

According to some anthropologists, the fastball may be millions of years older than the beginning of baseball. <u>To prove this point</u>, prehistoric toolmaking sites, such as the Olduvai Gorge in Tanzania, are offered as evidence. These sites are littered with smooth, roundish stones not suitable for flaking into tools. Suspecting that they might have been used as weapons, anthropologists have speculated that these stones were thrown at enemies and animals being hunted. <u>Searching for other evidence</u>, historical accounts of primitive peoples have been combed for stories of rock throwing. Here early adventurers are described as being caught by rocks thrown hard and fast. <u>Used in combat</u>, museums have collections of these "handstones." So stone throwing may have been a major form of defense and a tool for hunting. <u>Being an impulse that still has to be curbed</u>, parents still find themselves teaching their children not to throw stones.

Exercise 15.1

(1) The man who was carrying the sack of groceries with an umbrella walked carefully to his car. (2) He had only bought food for his lunch because he was going to leave town that afternoon. (3) He whistled to his huge black dog opening the car door and set the groceries in the trunk. (4) The dog jumped into the trunk happily with the groceries.

Exercise 16.1

One of the great American cars was the J-series Duesenberg. The cars were created by Fred and August Duesenberg, two brothers from Iowa who began by making bicycles and who then gained fame by building racing cars. Determined to build an American car that would earn respect by its excellent quality and its high performance, the Duesenbergs completed the first Model J in 1928. The car was an awesome machine described as having a 265-horsepower engine and a top speed of 120 mph. Special features of the car were its four-wheel hydraulic brakes and extensive quantities of light-weight aluminum castings. The masterpiece was the Duesenberg SJ, reputed to have a 320-horsepower engine and to accelerate from zero to 100 mph in 17 seconds.

Exercise 17.1

Many people think that recycling material is a recent trend. However, during World War II more than 43 percent of America's newsprint was recycled, and the average person saved bacon grease and other meat fat, which they [he (or she)] returned to local collection centers. What you would do is [a person did was] to pour leftover fat and other greasy gunk [grease] from frying pans and pots into tin cans. Today, despite the fact that many trendy people are <u>into</u> ^(involved in) recycling, only

about 10 percent of America's waste is actually recycled. The

problem is not to get <u>us</u> ^(people) to save bottles and cans but to convince

industry to use recycled materials. <u>There is a concern expressed</u> ^(Manufacturers have expressed a concern)

<u>by manufacturers</u> that they would be using materials of uneven

quality and <u>will</u> ^(would) face undependable delivery. If <u>the manufacturer</u> ^(manufacturers)

would wake up <u>and smell the coffee</u>, ^((this phrase can be omitted)) they would see the advan-

tages for the country and <u>bigger profits could be made by them</u>. ^(the bigger profits they could make.)

Exercise 18.1

1. One type of relaxation is to grab a bowl of popcorn, put your feet up, and watch football on television for two hours.
2. Computer science is a field of study in which you learn how to program computers.
3. One of the most common methods of improving your math is to hire a tutor.
4. The next agenda item we want to look at is the question of finding out the cost of purchasing decorations.
5. His job consisted mainly of handling repetitious assembly line tasks.

Exercise 19.1

Some suggested possibilities for rewriting this paragraph are as follows:

(1) While most people think of pigs as providers of ham, bacon, and pork chops, they also think of pigs as dirty, smelly, lazy, stupid, mean, and stubborn. Because there's more to pigs than this bad press they've had, we should stop and reevaluate what we think of pigs. (2) President Harry Truman once said that no man should be allowed to be president who does not understand hogs. This lack of understanding indicates a lack of appreciation for a useful farm animal. (3) Some people are discovering that pigs make excellent pets. (4) In fact, because pigs have been favorite characters in children's

fiction, many people fondly remember Porky Pig and Miss Piggy, the Muppet creation, as well as the heroic pig named Wilbur in E.B. White's *Charlotte's Web*. (5) Clubs for those who keep pigs as pets are now not just on farms, although pigs have long been favorite pets of farm children, who are likely to be fond of animals. (6) People with pigs as pets report that their pigs are curious, friendly little animals who are quite clean despite the "dirty as a pig" saying. However, pigs, who are also not very athletic, also have a sweet tooth. (7) Pigs can be interesting pets and useful farm animals to raise.

two
ans

Exercise 19.2

One possible paragraph is given here:

    Although plastic used to be considered a cheap, shoddy material, it is taking the place of traditional materials. In addition to cars made of plastic, there are also boats, airplanes, cameras, fishing rods, watches, suitcases, toothpaste tubes, and plates made of plastic. Plastic, which has replaced the glass in eyeglasses, the wood in tennis rackets, and cotton and wool in our clothing, seems new but has been with us for a long time. For example, amber is a natural form of plastic. Celluloid, which is a nearly natural plastic, was developed in 1868 as a substitute for ivory in billiard balls. However, celluloid proved to be too flammable. Now, because new types of plastic have mushroomed, the use of plastics has steadily increased. By the mid-1970s, in fact, plastics had become the nation's most widely used material.

Exercise 20.1
1. 20a; 20b
2. 20e; 20f
3. 20d; 20e; 20f
4. 20b; 20c
5. 20a
6. 20b; 20e; 20f
7. 20e; 20f

Exercise 20.2

One suggested revision is as follows:

    (1) Until a few years ago Americans knew little about Australia beyond boomerangs and koala bears. (2) However, Australian

movies such as *My Brilliant Career* and *Mad Max* have changed all that. (3) In addition, Paul Hogan, the Australian entertainer, has appeared on American TV commercials, reminding us that we lost the America's Cup to the Australians. (4) Now, tourists from America are pouring into Australia, and most tourist agencies are offering package tours "down under." (5) Tourists are obviously happy to have discovered this new continent for sightseeing. (6 and 7) Sights to dazzle Americans are the Great Barrier Reef, which is a 1250-mile reef teeming with tropical fish, the outback, a vast collection of deserts and bush country where the aborigines live, and lovely cities such as Sydney and Melbourne.

Exercise 21.1

International airports may soon have a high-tech machine that is really an unusually reliable nose. <u>This</u> sophisticated machine sniffs for drugs and will provide a more accurate means of trapping narcotics smugglers than has been possible so far. <u>The walk-through narcotics vapor detector</u> pulls in air samples from a passenger's clothes as <u>he or she</u> passes through. Several feet past the first sampling, the <u>passenger</u> is again sampled by having <u>air</u> blown across <u>his or her</u> body. <u>Then, these</u> vapor <u>samples</u> are funneled into a device called a thermionic sensor. <u>If</u> the <u>sensor</u> sets off an alarm, the <u>passenger</u> is then searched. <u>However,</u> it is not always certain that <u>drugs</u> will be found because there can be an occasional false alarm. <u>But</u> officials hope that the <u>electronic nose</u> will strike fear in the hearts of would-be smugglers. <u>If so, this high-tech nose</u> will act as a deterrent as well as a detector.

Exercise 21.2

One suggested version of paragraph 4 is as follows:

Caring for houseplants requires some basic knowledge about plants. For example, the plant should be watered and its leaves should be cleaned. Moreover, since spring and summer bring a special time of growth, the plant can be fertilized then. In addition, the plant may also be repotted, but the new pot should be only two inches (in diameter) larger than the pot the plant is presently in. Some plants can be put outside in summer; however, some plants cannot. In sum, being familiar with basic requirements for houseplants will result in having healthy plants.

Exercise 22.1

Paragraph 2 uses the following strategies to achieve sentence variety:

Sentence 1 of paragraph 2 is the result of adding the second sentence of paragraph 1 to the first one after turning the second sentence into a *which* clause. Sentence 3 of paragraph 1 is combined with this new sentence.

Sentence 2 of paragraph 2 is the result of combining sentences 4 and 5 of paragraph 1. This is achieved by adding the information in sentence 5 of paragraph 1 after the noun *chamber* in sentence 4 of paragraph 1.

Sentence 3 of paragraph 2 is the result of combining sentences 6 and 7 of paragraph 1. This is achieved by moving the adjective after the verb *is* in sentence 6 to the front of the new sentence so that it describes the subject. The predicates of sentences 6 and 7 can be joined because they have the same subject.

Sentence 4 of paragraph 2 is the result of changing sentence 8 of paragraph 1 into a dependent clause and joining it to sentence 9 of paragraph 1.

Sentence 5 of paragraph 2 is the result of combining sentences 10 and 11 of paragraph 1 into one longer sentence.

One suggested version of paragraph 4 is as follows:

While scientists neglect whistling, amateurs and hobbyists do not. There are whistling contests all over the United States, where accomplished whistlers whistle classical music, opera, jazz, Broadway show tunes, polkas, and even rock and roll. People whistle very differently. Some people pucker their lips while others use their throat, hands, or fingers to produce whistling sounds which resemble the flute. Some advantages of whistling are that it is a happy sound, that whistlers never lose their instrument, that their instrument doesn't need to be cleaned or repaired, that it costs nothing, and that it is easily transported. Because whistling is hard to explain, it is something you either pick up at a young age or not at all.

two
ans

3

Punctuation and Mechanics

This part reviews the rules for punctuation, those marks we add to the page to guide readers through our sentences, and the mechanics of noting capitals, abbreviations, and numbers in writing. The topics covered are as follows:

23 *Commas* (,)

Like other punctuation marks, commas are signals to help readers understand the meaning of written sentences. Just as the voice pauses or changes in pitch, commas help listeners understand what you are saying. Thus, the sound of your sentences may help to indicate where commas are needed. But sound isn't always a dependable guide because not every voice pause occurs where a comma is needed and not every comma needs a voice pause.

The rules in this section, along with some clues you get from pauses in your voice, will indicate where you'll need commas. For a summary of comma use in punctuating sentences, see the chart "Commas and Semicolons in Sentences."

23
,

Commas and Semicolons in Sentences

For simple sentences, use Pattern 1.
For compound sentences, use Patterns 2, 3, and 4.
For complex sentences, use Patterns 5, 6, and 7.

1. | Independent clause | .

2. | Independent clause | ,**coordinating** | independent clause | .
   conjunction:
   and   for
   but   or
   so   nor
   yet

3. | Independent clause | ; | independent clause | .

4. | Independent clause | ; **independent** | independent clause | .
   clause
   marker:
   however,
   nevertheless,
   therefore,
   consequently,
   (etc.)

5. Dependent marker: | dependent clause |, | independent | .
  Because   When   clause
  Since   While
  If   After
            (etc.)

6. | Independent clause | **dependent** | dependent clause | .
                               marker:
                               because   when
                               since   while
                               if   after
                               (etc.)

7. Subject | dependent clause | verb/predicate.

(Use commas before and after the dependent clause if it is
nonessential.)

23a *Commas in Compound Sentences*

There are three ways to join independent clauses together
into a compound sentence.

Use the comma only for the first pattern:
(1) Use one of the seven coordinating conjunctions:

    for   and   nor
    but   or   yet   so
    _____ (clause) _____ , and _____ (clause) _____ .

The television program was dull, but the commercials were entertaining.

After the storm, they collected seashells along the beach, and everyone found
some interesting specimens, but the conservationists asked them not to take the
shells home.

......

HINT: To remember the seven coordinating conjunctions,
think of the phrase "fan boys":

For
And
Nor

But
Or
Yet
So

(2) Join the independent clauses with a semicolon and a con-
    necting word such as the following:

however,	therefore,
thus,	moreover,
consequently,	then,

_____ (clause) _____; thus, _____ (clause) _____ .

23a
,

The camping sites were all filled; however, the park ranger allowed latecomers
to use empty spaces in the parking lot.

David's new sports car was designed for high speed driving; moreover, it was
also designed to be fuel efficient.

HINT: Use a comma after the connecting word.

(3) Join the independent clauses with a semicolon and no join-
    ing words.

_____ (clause) _____ ; _____ (clause) _____ .

Everyone in the room heard the glass shattering; no one moved until it was
clear that there was no danger.

For the errors caused by not following one of these three patterns, see Chapter 11.

Exercise 23.1: Proofreading Practice

*In the following paragraph there are compound sentences that need com-
mas or semicolons. Add the appropriate punctuation.*

   An inventor working on a "flying car" says that traveling several hundred miles by commercial airplane is a fairly inefficient
way to get around. First, you have to drive through traffic to the
airport and then you have to park your car somewhere in order

to board a plane. You fly to another crowded airport outside of a city but then you have to take another automobile to your final destination in town. A more practical solution would be a personal commuter flying vehicle. The inventor, working in a company supported by several government agencies, has developed a vertical takeoff and landing vehicle that has the potential to allow everyone to take to the air. The vehicle can take off and land vertically and it travels five times faster than an automobile. The most recently developed model looks more like a car than a plane however, it operates more like a cross between a plane and a helicopter. Above 125 mph in flight, it flies like a conventional plane or below 125 mph, it maneuvers like a helicopter. It has a number of safety features, such as six engines therefore it can recover if it loses an engine while hovering close to the ground.

23a
,

Exercise 23.2: Sentence Combining

Using the punctuation pattern for commas in compound sentences, combine the following short sentences into longer, compound sentences.
Remember, commas in compound sentences follow this pattern:

```
_____ (clause) _____ , and _____ (clause) _____.
                      but
                      for
                      or
                      nor
                      so
                      yet
```

1. The personal commuter flying vehicle now being designed has room for four passengers.
2. It can fly roughly 850 miles per tankful at a cruising speed of 225 mph.
3. The vehicle can rise above 30,000 feet.
4. It can also hover near the ground.
5. According to the inventor, it has taken two decades of theoretical studies to design the vehicle's shape.
6. It has also taken ten years of wind-tunnel tests to achieve the aerodynamic shape.
7. Government officials foresee an entire transportation network in the future based on the personal flying vehicle.

8. There will have to be automated air-control systems for these vehicles.
9. The technology for controlling these vehicles already exists.
10. The technology will create electronic highways in the sky.

23b *Commas after Introductory Words, Phrases, and Clauses*

A comma is needed after introductory words, phrases, and clauses that come before the main clause.

Introductory words include connecting words and comments such as the following:

Yes,
No,
However,
Well,

> Well, perhaps he meant no harm.

In fact,

> In fact, he wanted to help out.

Consequently,
First,

Introductory phrases include long prepositional phrases and phrases with *-ing* verbals, *-ed* verbals, and *to* + verb. Use a comma with the following:

Long prepositional phrases (usually four words or more):

> In the middle of a long dull movie, I decided to get some popcorn.
> Due to his determination not to get a C, he even did the homework problems that were not collected in class.

-ing verbals:

> Having finished the test before the bell rang, he left the room.

-ed verbals:

> Tired of never having enough money, she took a second job on weekends.

to + verb:

> To get a seat close to the stage, you'd better come early.

Introductory clauses include dependent clauses that begin with adverbs such as the following:

After…
Although…
As…
Because…
If…
Since…   While I was eating, the cat scratched at the door.
When…
While…

23b
,

HINTS: When dependent clauses come *after* the main clause, there is no comma.

When the telephone rang, the dog started to bark.
The dog started to bark *when the telephone rang*.

Use commas after introductory clauses, phrases, and words in the following cases:

If the introduction is long. Are there five or more words before the main clause?

If there is a distinct voice pause. When you read the sentence aloud, do you find your voice pausing a moment after the introductory part?

If it is necessary to avoid confusion. Is there a possibility that your reader might have to read the sentence more than once to have it make sense?

Possibly Confusing: As I stated the rules can be broken occasionally.

Revised: As I stated, the rules can be broken occasionally.

When your sentence starts with an *-ing* verbal, *-ed* verbal, or *to* + verb, be sure you don't have a dangling modifier (see Section 14).

Exercise 23.3: Proofreading Practice

In the following paragraph there are introductory words, phrases, and clauses that require commas. Add commas where needed.

(1) A recent study showed that small cars are tailgated more than big ones. (2) Moreover the drivers of subcompact and compact cars also do more tailgating themselves. (3) In the study traffic flow at five different locations was observed, and a variety of driving conditions was included, such as two-lane state roads, four-lane divided highways, and so on. (4) In all more than 10,000 vehicles were videotaped. (5) Although subcompact and compact cars accounted for only 38 percent of the vehicles on the tape their drivers were tailgating in 48 percent of the incidents observed. (6) In addition to having done all this tailgating these drivers were also the victims of tailgating 47 percent of the time. (7) Midsized cars made up 31 percent of the cars on the tapes but accounted for only 20 percent of the tailgaters and 24 percent of the drivers being tailgated. (8) Having considered various reasons for this the researchers suggest that drivers of other cars may avoid getting close to midsized cars because of the cars' contours. (9) Because midsized cars have more curves in the sloping backs and trunks people may have more trouble seeing around them.

23b
,

Exercise 23.4: Pattern Practice

The following sentences illustrate some of the rules for using introductory commas. Identify the rule by selecting the appropriate letter from the list given here, and then write your own sentence in this pattern.

A. Comma after an introductory word
B. Comma after an introductory phrase
C. Comma after an introductory clause

1. Because tailgating is a road hazard that is known to cause many accidents, other studies have searched for causes of tailgating.
2. For example, one study examined how people judge distances on the road.
3. Puzzled by the question of why small cars are tailgated so often, researchers studied other drivers' perceptions of how far away small cars appear to be.

4. Despite the fact that many of the people studied were generally able to guess distances accurately, they sometimes perceived small cars to be more than forty feet farther away than they actually were.

5. If drivers tend to think that small cars are really farther away than they actually are, this may explain why small cars are tailgated so often.

6. However, researchers continue to study this problem.

23c Commas with Essential and Nonessential Words, Phrases, and Clauses

**23c
,**

Nonessential word groups (see Chapter 9) require a pair of commas, one before the nonessential element and the other afterward (unless there is a period). Essential word groups do not have commas to set them off from the rest of the sentence.

....

HINTS:

- Take out the word or word group in your sentence. If the meaning is too general, you have an essential element, and you should not add commas.

  Students **who cheat** harm only themselves. (With the word group *who cheat* removed, the sentence would say that students harm themselves. That's too general and does not convey the meaning of the sentence.)

- Does the word group interrupt the flow of words in the original sentence? If so, it's a nonessential element and needs commas. Some people can hear a slight pause in their voice or a change in pitch as they begin and end a nonessential element.

- Can you move the word group around in the sentence or put it in a different sentence? If so, it is a nonessential element.

No one, **however**, wanted to tell her she was wrong.

No one wanted, **however**, to tell her she was wrong.

However, no one wanted to tell her she was wrong.

- Does the clause begin with *that*? *That* clauses after nouns are almost always essential.

  I'll return the sweater **that I borrowed** after I wear it again tonight.

  That clauses following verbs that express mental action are always essential:

  I think that…
  She believes that…
  He dreams that…
  They wish that…
  We concluded that…

- Word groups (called *appositives*) that follow nouns and identify or explain the nouns are nonessential and need commas:

  Uncle Ike, **a doctor**, smoked too much even though he continued to warn his patients not to smoke. (Uncle Ike = a doctor)

  The movie critic's review of *Heartland*, **a story about growing up in Indiana**, focused on the beauty of the scenery. (*Heartland* = a story about growing up in Indiana.)

  When this word group is the last element in the sentence, keep it attached to the sentence and set it off with a comma. Some fragments are appositives that became detached from the sentence.

  Fragment: She is a good friend. **A person whom I trust and admire.**

  Revised: She is a good friend, **a person whom I trust and admire.**

23c
,

Exercise 23.5: Proofreading Practice

Some of the sentences in the following paragraph have essential and nonessential words, phrases, and clauses. Underline these elements, write N (for nonessential) or E (for essential), and add commas where they are needed.

The use of technical advisers for TV programs is not new. For medical, legal, and police dramas that attempt to be realistic, producers have long called on experts to check the scripts. These experts who read the scripts before production make sure that TV surgeons, lawyers, and police officers use the right terminology and follow standard procedures. Now network shows are also calling on social scientists as consultants to add realism in sitcoms and to help networks conform to criteria that are required by Federal Communications Commission (FCC) standards. The FCC, a federal regulatory agency, says that shows with a potential audience of children even if they are not aired until after the early evening family viewing time must offer some content of educational value. But of course TV still wants to entertain, and sometimes there is some conflict with the writers. On the whole though television scriptwriters have come to recognize and value advice from social scientists and psychologists particularly on important topics such as how children react to divorce, how parents might handle children's drug abuse, or how families deal with emotional crises.

23c
,

Exercise 23.6: Pattern Practice

In the previous exercise (23.5) there are sentences illustrating the following patterns for punctuating essential and nonessential elements in sentences. Using these patterns and the examples from the paragraph above, write your own sentences in the same pattern with correct punctuation.

Pattern A: Subject,   nonessential clause,   verb   object.

Pattern B: Subject   essential clause   verb   object.

Pattern C: Introductory phrase,   nonessential word,   subject verb   object.

Pattern D: Subject   verb   object,   nonessential phrase.

23∂ Commas in Series and Lists

Use commas when three or more items are listed in a series.

A series of words:

> Would you prefer the poster printed in yellow, blue, green, or purple?

A series of phrases:

> First he spoke to Dan, then called his roommate, and finally phoned me.

A series of clauses:

> She never dreamed she'd be in the movies, she hadn't even tried out for a part, and she was sure she didn't have enough talent to act.

23d

,

There are some variations in using commas in lists. The comma after the last item before *and* or *or* is preferred, but it may be omitted if there is no possibility of misreading.

Americans' favorite spectator sports are football, baseball, and basketball. (optional)

However, the comma before *and* cannot be omitted in sentences where terms belong together, such as *bread and butter*, or where some misreading is possible.

He talked about his college studies, art, and history.
(This sentence means that he talked about three things: his college studies, art, and history.)

He talked about his college studies, art and history.
(This sentence means that his college studies were in art and history.)

If one or more of the items in a series have commas, semicolons should be used between items.

The group included Bill Packo, the guitarist; Jim Hinders, drums; and Art Clutz, electronic keyboard.

Exercise 23.7: Proofreading Practice

In the following paragraph there are some series of three or more items that need punctuation. Add commas where they are needed.

Imagine not being able to recognize the face of your sister your boss or your best friend from high school. Imagine looking into a mirror seeing a face and realizing that the face you see is totally unfamiliar. Though this may sound impossible, a small number of people do suffer from a neurological condition that leaves them unable to recognize familiar faces. The condition is called *prosopagnosia* and results from brain damage caused by infection or stroke. Many people with this problem who have been studied have normal vision reading ability and language skills. They know that a face is a face they can name its parts and they can distinguish differences between faces. But only through other clues, such as hearing a familiar voice remembering a specific feature like a mustache hearing a name or recalling a particular identifying mark such as an unusual scar, can the people who were studied call up memories of people they should know. Researchers studying this phenomenon have found evidence suggesting that the step leading to conscious recognition of the face by the brain is somehow being blocked.

Exercise 23.8: Pattern Practice

The following sentences all have examples of items in a series. Using these sentences as patterns, write your own sentences with correctly punctuated items in series.

A. His favorite pastimes are sleeping late on weekends, drinking too much beer, and watching game shows on television.

B. She's convinced that it's better to work hard when you're young, to save your money, and then to spend it all when you retire.

C. Do you prefer jogging shoes with leather, canvas, or mesh tops?

D. Some people try to forget their birthdays, some like to have big celebrations, and others don't have any strong preference.

23e Commas with Adjectives

Use commas to separate two or more adjectives that describe the same noun equally.

cold, dark water
happy, healthy baby

However, not all adjectives in front of a noun describe the noun equally. When they are not equal (or coordinate) adjectives, do not use commas to separate them.

six big dogs
bright green sweater (the color of the sweater is bright green)

HINT: Can you add an *and* between the adjectives? Can the adjectives be written in reverse order? If so, separate the adjectives with commas.

a greedy, stubborn child
> You can say the following:
> a greedy and stubborn child
> > -and-
> a stubborn, greedy child

an easy, happy smile
> You can say the following:
> an easy and happy smile
> > -and-
> a happy, easy smile

But notice the following examples, which do not describe the noun equally.

a white frame house
> You wouldn't normally say the following:
> a white and frame house
> > -or-
> a frame white house

two young men
> You wouldn't normally say the following:
> two and young men
> > -or-
> young two men

23e
,

Exercise 23.9: Proofreading Practice

In the following paragraph there are adjectives in front of nouns that need punctuation. Add commas where they are needed.

All those dazed exhausted football players who return to the sidelines to suck on oxygen could just as well be saving their breath. In a recent controlled test subjects who breathed 100 percent oxygen did not revive any better or more quickly than subjects who were given plain ordinary air. The biggest surprise was that the athletes being tested couldn't even tell the difference. But they did like the idea of having all those bright orange oxygen tanks nearby in case of emergency, even if the tanks didn't do any good.

23f
,

Exercise 23.10: Pattern Practice

Using the patterns given here as guides, write your own phrases correctly punctuated with commas. Write two different phrases for each pattern given.

A. Four little kittens (use a number and another describing word).
B. A shiny red door (use a color and another describing word).
C. Balding, skinny man (use at least two body features).
D. Happy, carefree smile (use at least two emotions).
E. Heavy wooden door (use a material and another describing word).

23f *Commas with Dates, Addresses, Geographical Names, and Numbers*

(1) Commas with Dates

June 12, 1960,   -or-   12 June 1960
(no commas are needed if the day comes before the month)

May, 1972,   -or-   May 1972
(commas may be omitted if only the month and year are given)

The order was shipped out on September 2, 1987, and not received until May 12, 1988.

The application deadline was 15 August 1988 with no exceptions.

(2) Commas with Addresses

In a letter heading or on an envelope:

> Jim Johnson, Jr.
> 1436 Westwood Drive
> Birlingham, ID 98900

In a sentence:

You can write to Jim Johnson, Jr., 1436 Westwood Drive, Birlingham, Idaho 98900 for more information.

(3) Commas with Geographical Names

Put commas after each item in a place name.

The planning committee has decided that Chicago, Illinois, will be the site of this year's conference and Washington, D.C., for next year's meeting.

(4) Commas with Numbers

Separate long numbers into groups of three going from right to left. Commas with four-digit numbers are optional.

> 4,300,150
> 27,000
> 4,401   -or-   4401

Exercise 23.11: Proofreading Practice

Add commas in the following paragraph where they are needed.

The United States Government Printing Office has a catalog of thousands of popular books that it prints. If you'd like a copy of this catalog, write to the Superintendent of Documents United States Government Printing Office Washington D.C. 20402. There are books on agriculture, business and industry, careers, computers, diet and nutrition, health, history, hobbies, space exploration, and other topics. To pay for the books, you can send a check or money order, but more than 30000 customers every year set up deposit accounts with an initial deposit of at least $50. Future purchases can then be charged against this account. There are also Government Printing Office bookstores all around the country where you can browse before buying. They do not stock all 16000 titles in their inventory, but they do carry the more popular ones. For example, if you live in Birmingham, you can find the Government Printing Office bookstore in Roebuck Shopping City 9220-B Parkway East Birmingham Alabama 35206. There is also a bookstore in Cleveland Ohio and Jacksonville Florida.

Exercise 23.12: Pattern Practice

Using the patterns and examples given here, write your own sentences correctly punctuated with commas. Write two different sentences for each pattern given.

Pattern A: sentence with a date

> Everyone knows that July 4, 1776, was a memorable day in American history.

Pattern B: sentence with an address

> His business address is Fontran Investments, 3902 Carroll Boulevard, Indianapolis, IN 46229.

Pattern C: sentence with a geographical name

> She enjoyed her car trip to Sante Fe, New Mexico, and plans to go again next spring.

Pattern D: sentence with two numbers of four digits or more

> The police estimated that more than 50,000 people took part in the demonstration, but the organizers of the event said they were sure that at least 100,000 had shown up.

23g *Other Uses for Commas*

Commas have other uses in sentences, including the following:

To prevent misreading:

> **Confusing:** To John Harrison had been a sort of idol.
> **Revised:** To John, Harrison had been a sort of idol.

Confusing: On Thursday morning orders will be handled by Jim.
Revised: On Thursday, morning orders will be handled by Jim.

-or-

Revised: On Thursday morning, orders will be handled by Jim.

To set off sharply contrasted elements at the end of a sentence:

He was merely ignorant, not stupid.

To set off a question:

You're one of the senator's right-hand people, aren't you?

To set off phrases at the end of the sentence that refer to the beginning or middle of the sentence:

Nancy waved enthusiastically at the departing boat, laughing happily in the process.

To set off direct quotations and after the first part of a quotation in a sentence:

Becky said, "I'll see you tomorrow."

"I was able," she explained, "to complete the job on time."

To set off the opening greeting and closing of a letter:

Dear David,

Sincerely yours,

Exercise 23.13: Proofreading Practice
The following paragraph needs some punctuation. Add commas where they are needed.

Have you ever thought about where all those oranges in your orange juice come from? You'd probably say that they come from Florida wouldn't you? Some oranges may, but the world's largest producer of orange juice is now Brazil. Says one of Florida's biggest orange growers "We're going to regain the market sooner than those rookie Brazilians think." Florida growers predict that overplanting and plunging prices have set the stage for a damaging glut in Brazil not in Florida. "We have never had excess juice" claims a major Brazilian grower "and I don't think we ever will." Know-how from American juice companies, along with subsidies from the Brazilian government, is helping

Brazilian growers stay on top of the market. Brazilian growers are confident knowing that Florida is more prone to drought and hard freezes. So it looks as if our orange juice will remain partly Brazilian for the foreseeable future.

Exercise 23.14: Pattern Practice

Using the patterns and examples given here, write your own sentences correctly punctuated with commas. Write two different sentences for each pattern given.

Pattern A: to prevent misreading

> After eating, the cat stretched out near the fire and fell asleep.
> (If the comma is left out, is there a possible misreading?)

Pattern B: to set off sharply contrasted elements at the end of the sentence

> Everyone thought the car had stopped, not broken down.

Pattern C: to set off a question

> They were at the game, weren't they?

Pattern D: to set off a phrase at the end of the sentence that refers to the beginning or middle of the sentence

> Jennie decided not to go out in the evening, preferring to enjoy the quiet in her apartment.

Pattern E: to set off direct quotations

> Professor Bender said, "Don't call me tonight to ask about your grade."

23h *Unnecessary Commas*

Putting in commas where they are not needed can mislead readers because unnecessary commas suggest pauses or interruptions not intended as part of the meaning. (Remember, though, that not every pause needs a comma.)

Don't separate a subject from its verb:

Unnecessary Comma: The eighteen-year-old in most states ⁽⁾ is now considered an adult.

Revised: The eighteen-year-old in most states is now considered an adult.

Don't put a comma between two verbs:

Unnecessary Comma: We laid out our music and snacks ⁽⁾ and began to study.

Revised: We laid out our music and snacks and began to study.

Don't put a comma in front of every *and* or *but.*

Unnecessary Comma: We decided that we should not lend her the money ⁽⁾ and that we should explain our decision.

(The *and* in this sentence joins two *that* clauses.)

Revised: We decided that we should not lend her the money and that we should explain our decision.

Don't put a comma in front of a direct object. (Remember, clauses beginning with *that* can be direct objects.)

Unnecessary Comma: He explained to me ⁽⁾ that he is afraid to fly on airplanes because of terrorists.

Revised: He explained to me that he is afraid to fly on airplanes because of terrorists.

Don't put commas before a dependent clause when it comes *after* the main clause, except for extreme or strong contrast.

Unnecessary Comma: She was late for class ⁽⁾ because her alarm clock was broken.

Revised: She was late for class because her alarm clock was broken.

Extreme Contrast: She was still quite upset, although she did win an Oscar Award.

Don't put a comma after *such as* or *especially.*

Unnecessary Comma: There are several kinds of dark bread from which to choose, such as ⁽⁾ whole wheat, rye, oatmeal, and bran bread.

Revised: There are several kinds of dark bread from which to choose, such as whole wheat, rye, oatmeal, and bran bread.

Exercise 23.15: Proofreading Practice

In the following paragraph there are some unnecessary commas. Put an X under the commas that should be removed.

23h
,

Although the dangers of alcohol are well known, and have been widely publicized, there may be another danger that we haven't yet realized. Several controlled studies of drunken animals have indicated to researchers, that in an accident there is more swelling and hemorrhaging in the spinal cord, and in the brain, if alcohol is present in the body. To find out if this is true with humans, researchers studied the data on more than one million drivers in automobile crashes. One thing already known is, that drunks are more likely to be driving fast, and to have seat belts unfastened. Of course, their coordination is also poorer than sober people, so they are more likely to get into serious accidents. To compensate for this, researchers grouped accidents into type, speed, and degree of vehicle deformation, and found that alcohol still appears to make people more vulnerable to injury. The conclusion of the study was, that the higher the level of alcohol in the person's body, the greater the chance of being injured or killed. In minor crashes, drunk drivers were more than four times as likely to be killed as sober ones. In average crashes, drunk drivers were more than three times as likely to be killed, and in the worst ones, drunks were almost twice as likely. Overall, drunks were more than twice as likely to die in an accident, because of the alcohol they drank.

Exercise 23.16: Pattern Practice

Using the sentence patterns and examples given here, write your own sentences correctly punctuated with commas. Write two different sentences for each pattern given.

Pattern A: subject   verb   *object*   *and*   verb   object

Before the test <u>Gerry</u> <u>studied</u> the botany <u>notes</u> from the lectures and <u>reread</u>
             subject verb   object   verb
the <u>textbook</u> several times.
    object

Pattern B: independent clause   dependent clause

<u>He decided not to live in the dorm</u> <u>because it was so expensive.</u>
     independent clause   dependent clause

Pattern C: a sentence with a *that* clause or phrase as direct object

My high school physical education teacher often told me **that** <u>eating a</u>
                                            that phrase
<u>good breakfast</u> was an important part of keeping in good shape.

Pattern D: a sentence with a subject that has many words modifying it

Almost <u>everyone</u> attending the recent meeting of the union <u>decided</u> not to
       subject   verb
vote for the strike.

24 Apostrophes (')

24a Apostrophes with Possessives

Use the apostrophe to show possession.

For singular nouns, use <u>'s</u>.

the book's author

a flower's smell

For a singular noun ending in <u>-s</u>, the *s* after the apostrophe is
optional if the *s* doesn't make the pronunciation difficult.

James's car   -or- James' car
the grass's color-or- the grass' color

But if adding the *s* after the apostrophe makes the pronunciation difficult, omit the *s*. This happens especially when the next word starts with *s* or *z*.

Euripides' story (Trying to say *Euripides's story* is a bit difficult.)

For plural nouns ending in -s, add only an apostrophe.

both teams' colors
six days' vacation

For plural nouns not ending in -s (such as *children, men, mice,* etc.), use 's.

the children's game
six men's coats

24a
'

For the indefinite pronoun (pronouns ending in *-body* and *-one,* such as *no one, someone, everybody,* etc.), use 's.

no one's fault
someone's hat

For compound words, add 's to the last word.

brother-in-law's job
everyone else's preference

For joint ownership by two or more nouns, add 's after the last noun in the group.

Mary and Tom's house
bar and restaurant's parking lot

For individual ownership when several nouns are used, add 's after each noun.

Mary's and Tom's houses (This indicates that there are two houses, one belonging to Mary and the other to Tom.)

....

HINTS: When you aren't sure if you need the apostrophe, turn the phrase around into an *of the* clause.

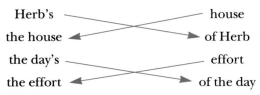

Sometimes, you'll have both the *of the* phrase and the apostrophe.

the painting of Cesar's (Without the 's this phrase would mean that Cesar was pictured in the painting as the subject.)

When you aren't sure if the word is plural or not, remember that you write the plural first and then add the possessive apostrophe marker. That is, everything to the left of the apostrophe is the word and its plural, if needed.

Word (and plural, if needed)	*Possessive marker*
cup	's handle
cups	' handles

24b Apostrophes with Contractions

Use the apostrophe to mark the omitted letter or letters in contractions.

it's = it is
don't = do not (informal usage)
o'clock = of the clock
'79 = 1979 (informal usage)
Jimmy's going = Jimmy is going (very informal usage)

24c Apostrophes with Plurals

Use apostrophes to form the plurals of lowercase letters and abbreviations with periods.

For capital letters, abbreviations without periods, numbers, symbols, and words used as words, the apostrophe before the *-s* is optional if the plural is clear. In all cases, the *'s* is not italicized or underlined.

Necessary apostrophes:

a's
B.A.'s

Optional apostrophes:

A's	-or-	As
9's	-or-	9s
1950's	-or-	1950s
UFO's	-or-	UFOs
and's	-or-	ands
&'s	-or-	&s

24d
,

HINT: Be consistent in choosing one or the other of these options.

24d Unnecessary Apostrophes

Do not use the apostrophe with possessive pronouns or with the regular plural forms of nouns.

Possessive pronouns not needing apostrophes include the following:

his	hers	its
ours	yours	theirs
whose		

Wrong Is that umbrella yours' or mine?
Revised: Is that umbrella yours or mine?

Wrong: I think it's leg is broken.
Revised I think its leg is broken.

Remember, *it's* and *who's* are contractions, not possessives:

it's = it is

It's a good time to clean out the closet.

who's = who is

Who's going to run for vice-president?

Do not use the apostrophe with regular plural forms of nouns that do not show possession.

Wrong: The Smiths' went to Disney World for vacation.

Revised: The Smiths went to Disney World for vacation.

Exercise 24.1: Proofreading Practice

The following paragraph has some words that should show possession. Add apostrophes where they are needed.

Although teachers commonly use tests to grade their students learning, taking a test can also help students learn. Peoples memory seems to be more accurate after reading some material and taking a test than after merely reading the material with no testing. In fact, studies have shown that students who take several tests learn even more than those who take only one test after reading material. Although everyones ability to memorize material generally depends on how well the material was studied, scientists research does indicate that test-taking aids memory. The type of test is also important because multiple-choice exams help us to put facts together better while fill-in-the-blank questions promote recall of specific facts. These questions ability to test different types of learning suggests that teachers ought to include different types of tests throughout the semester.

24d
'

Exercise 24.2: Pattern Practice

Using the patterns and examples given here, write your own sentences correctly punctuated with apostrophes. Write two different sentences for each pattern given.

Pattern A: two singular nouns with *'s*

If **Daniel's** car doesn't start, we can borrow **Alicia's** van.

Pattern B: a singular noun ending in *-s* with *'*

Does anyone know Mr. **Myconos'** zip code?

Pattern C: two plural nouns ending in *-s* with *'*

Although the **girls'** coats were on sale, all the **boys'** coats were still selling at regular prices.

Pattern D: a plural noun not ending in -*s* with '*s*

We helped collect money for the **Children's** Fund.

Pattern E: an indefinite pronoun with '*s*

I would really appreciate **someone's** help right now.

Pattern F: one compound word with '*s*

It was the **president-elect's** decision not to campaign on TV.

Pattern G: one example of joint ownership with '*s*

The next morning he felt the **pizza and beer's** effects.

Exercise 24.3: Proofreading Practice

In the following informal paragraph there are contractions that should be marked. Add apostrophes where they are needed.

Magazine racks used to be for magazines, but that was before mail-order catalogs began invading the market. In 1985, when some catalogs began taking paid ads for such products as liquor and cologne, the line between magazines and catalogs began to blur. In some cases its hard to distinguish the difference. And customers have good reasons to prefer buying catalogs when theres the advantage of having discount coupons tucked in. The catalogs that began appearing on magazine racks in 85 sold for $1 to $3 apiece, but customers would get a $5 discount on their first order. National distributors now estimate that more than five thousand stores and newsstands stock catalogs for such well-known companies as Sharper Image and Bloomingdale's. Waldenbooks was among the first to display these catalogs on its magazine racks. Its big business now, and magazines have a tough rival to beat.

Exercise 24.4: Pattern Practice

Using the patterns and examples given here, write your own sentences correctly punctuated with apostrophes. Write one sentence for each pattern given.

Pattern A: a sentence with *its* and *it's*

Whenever **it's** raining out, our cat races inside the house in order to keep **its** fur dry.

Pattern B: a sentence with two contractions

They're quite sure they **didn't** owe us any money.

Pattern C: a sentence with *who's* and *whose*

> I wonder **whose** skates those are and whether you know **who's** going to the skating rink with us.

Exercise 24.5: Proofreading Practice
The following paragraph needs apostrophes to mark plurals. Add the apostrophe even if it is optional.

In the late 1970s the M.B.A. became one of the most desirable degrees awarded by American universities. In large part this was due to the high salaries offered to new graduates. Students graduating with B.A.s or B.S.s in most fields could expect starting salaries thousands of dollars below new M.B.A.s, especially those graduating at the top of the class from the more prestigious universities. It was a case of having those hard-earned As translate into better salaries. When huge numbers of M.B.A.s began flooding the market in the mid-1980s, the value of the degree declined somewhat.

24d
,

Exercise 24.6: Pattern Practice
Using the patterns and examples given here, write your own sentences correctly punctuated with apostrophes. Write a sentence for each pattern given.

Pattern A: the plural of two lowercase letters

> On his new typewriter the **e's** and **c's** looked alike.

Pattern B: the plural of two abbreviations without periods

> The electronics stores sold their **TV's** at a better discount than their **CB's**.

Pattern C: the plural of a number and a capital letter

> There were several **3's** in her new license plate number and some **M's** too.

Pattern D: the plural of a date and a word

> He dressed like a **1960's** hippie and sprinkled lots of **far out's** and other outdated slang in his speech.

Exercise 24.7: Proofreading Practice
Add apostrophes if needed in the following paragraph.

Erica Johns, a recent contestant on one of the game shows, was embarrassed to see herself in the reruns. There she was on the screen, yelling out the answer and claiming the big prize was hers, even when someone else sounded the buzzer before she did. "Its difficult," she said, "not to act foolish when so much money is involved." But she did win some dance lessons and a cute puppy with its own diamond-studded leash. Still, she wished she had pushed the buzzer and answered the question worth $2000.

Exercise 24.8: Pattern Practice

Using the patterns and examples given here, write your own correctly punctuated sentences. Write your own sentence for each pattern given.

Pattern A: a sentence with two possessive pronouns

> I can never remember whether the car is **hers** or **his**.

Pattern B: a sentence with *it's* and *its*

> **It's** never clear whether that dumb dog wants **its** ears scratched or **its** water dish filled.

Pattern C: a sentence with a plural noun that does not show possession and a plural noun that does show possession

> There are six pages of **ads** in that issue of the magazine with all of the different **dealers'** prices.

25 *Semicolons* (;)

The semicolon is a stronger mark of punctuation than a comma. It is almost like a period, but it does not come at the end of a sentence. Semicolons are used only between closely related equal elements, that is, between independent clauses and between items in a series. See the chart of "Commas and Semicolons in Sentences" in Section 23.

25a *Semicolons in Compound Sentences*

Use the semicolon when joining independent clauses *not* joined by the seven connectors that require commas: *and, but, for, or, nor,* so, or *yet.*

25a
;

Two patterns for using semicolons are:

independent clause; independent clause

independent clause; (other joining word or transitional phrase), independent
clause

Some of the joining words or transitional phrases that require
a semicolon include the following:

Joining words:

also,	meanwhile,
besides,	nevertheless,
consequently,	otherwise,
finally,	still,
furthermore,	then,
hence,	therefore,
however,	thus,
instead,	

Transitional phrases:

after all,	in addition,
as a result,	in fact,
at any rate,	in other words,
by the way,	in the second place,
even so,	on the contrary,
for example,	on the other hand,

He often watched TV even when there were only reruns; she preferred to read
instead.

-or-

He often watched TV even when there were only reruns; however, she preferred to read instead.

(1) Variations in Compound Sentences

A semicolon can be used instead of a comma with two independent clauses joined by *and, but, for, or, nor, so,* or *yet* when one or
more of the clauses has its own comma. The semicolon thus
makes a clearer break between the two independent clauses.

independent clause (with commas);   and   independent clause.

Congressman Dow, who headed the investigation, leaked the story to the press;
independent clause with commas
but he would not answer questions during an interview.

25a
;

A colon can be used between two independent clauses when the second clause restates the first (see Chapter 26).

Her diet was strictly vegetarian: she ate no meat, fish, poultry, or eggs.

Exercise 25.1: Proofreading Practice

In the following paragraph there are compound sentences that need punctuation. Add semicolons and commas where they are needed.

Even before children begin school, many parents think they should take part in their children's education and help the children to develop mentally. Such parents usually consider reading to young toddlers important moreover they help the children memorize facts such as the days of the week and the numbers from one to ten. Now it is becoming clear that parents can begin helping when the children are babies. One particular type of parent communication, encouraging the baby to pay attention to new things, seems especially promising in helping babies' brains develop for example handing the baby a toy encourages the baby to notice something new. Some studies seem to indicate that this kind of activity resulted in children scoring higher on intelligence tests several years later. Parents interested in helping their babies' brain development have been encouraged by this study to point to new things in the baby's environment as part of their communication with their babies thus their children's education can begin in the crib.

Exercise 25.2: Pattern Practice

Using the patterns and examples given here, write your own sentences correctly punctuated with semicolons. Write two sentences for each pattern given.

Pattern A: independent clause;   independent clause

I didn't know which job I wanted; I was too confused to decide.
      independent clause   independent clause

Pattern B: independent clause; (joining word or transitional phrase),   independent clause

That movie was recommended by three different friends; however, I was
             independent clause   joining

bored by it.   word
independent clause

25a
;

Pattern C: independent clause,   *and*   independent clause.

-or-

but

<u>The shirt is a little small,</u> but <u>he has nothing else to wear.</u>

independent clause   independent clause

25b Semicolons in a Series

For clarity, use semicolons to separate a series of items in which one or more of the items contain commas. Use semicolons also if items in the series are especially long.

Items with their own commas:

Among her favorite videotapes to rent were old Cary Grant movies, such as *Arsenic and Old Lace*; any of Woody Allen's movies; and children's classics, including *The Sound of Music*, *Willy Wonka and the Chocolate Factory*, and *The Wizard of Oz*.

Long items in a series:

When planning the bus schedule, they took into consideration the length of travel time between cities where stops would be made for additional passengers; the number of people likely to get on at each stop; and the times when the bus would arrive at major cities where connections would be made with other buses.

25c Semicolons with Quotation Marks

If a semicolon is needed, put it after the quotation marks.

Her answer to every question I asked was, "I'll have to think about that"; she clearly had no answers to offer.

25∂ Unnecessary Semicolons

Don't use a semicolon between unequal parts of a sentence such as between a clause and a phrase or between an independent clause and a dependent clause.

Unnecessary Semicolon: <u>They wanted to see some of the government build-</u>

<u>ings in the city</u>; <u>especially the courthouse and the post office</u>.

clause

phrase

Revised: They wanted to see some of the government buildings in the city, especially the courthouse and the post office.

Unnecessary Semicolon: <u>She always chooses some variety of chocolate ice</u>

<u>cream</u>; <u>such as mocha fudge, chocolate mint, or almond chocolate</u>.

clause

phrase

Revised: She always chooses some variety of chocolate ice cream, such as mocha fudge, chocolate mint, or almond chocolate.

Unnecessary Semicolon: <u>He kept trying to improve his tennis serve</u>; <u>because</u>

<u>that was the weakest part of his game</u>.

independent clause

dependent clause

Revised: He kept trying to improve his tennis serve because that was the weakest part of his game.

Don't use a semicolon in place of a dash, comma, or colon.

Unnecessary Semicolon: When Mike kept spinning his car wheels to get out of the sand, I realized he was really just persistent; not stupid.

Revised: When Mike kept spinning his car wheels to get out of the sand, I realized he was really just persistent—not stupid.

Unnecessary Semicolon: The office clearly needed several more pieces of equipment; a computer, a phone-answering machine, and a paper shredder.

Revised: The office clearly needed several more pieces of equipment: a computer, a phone-answering machine, and a paper shredder.

Exercise 25.3: Proofreading Practice

In the following paragraph there are some unnecessary semicolons to delete and some necessary semicolons to add. Put an X under semicolons that are incorrect, and write in the appropriate punctuation above. Add semicolons and other punctuation where needed, and replace any wrong punctuation with semicolons. Underline the added semicolons and other punctuation. Also, underline the semicolons you put in to replace wrong punctuation.

In the not-too-distant future, when airline passengers board their flights, they will be able to enjoy a number of new conveniences; such as choosing their snacks and drinks from on-board vending machines, selecting movies, TV programs, or video games for screens mounted on the seat in front of them, and making hotel and car-rental reservations from an on-board computer. Such features are what aircraft designers envision within the next five years for passenger jets. Their plans, though, may not be realized until much further in the future; if ever. But the ideas reflect the airline industry's hopes. If fare wars stop and ticket prices become similar, passengers may begin choosing different airlines on the basis of comfort, not cost; if that happens, airlines will have to be ready with new and better in-flight features. A Boeing Company executive says that "cabin environment will be a major factor;" that is, designers must make the cabin so attractive that it will offset lower fares on other airlines. The problem, however, is added weight caused by some of the suggested features; such as; computers, video screens, and more elaborate kitchens. Added weight will mean that the plane consumes more fuel; thus driving up the price of the ticket. Still, some carriers, determined to find answers, are studying ways to

25d
;

use the new services to generate income; particularly in the area of commercial-supported or pay-as-you-use video entertainment.

Exercise 25.4: Pattern Practice

Using the patterns and examples given here, write your own sentences correctly punctuated with semicolons. Write one sentence for each pattern given.

Pattern A: semicolons with a series of items that have their own commas

> The McDonnell Douglas Corporation's new wide-body jet, scheduled to begin service soon, is designed for greater passenger comfort and will have refrigerators to hold fresh food; aisles wide enough so that passengers, even heavyset people, can walk past a serving cart; and high-resolution video monitors for every ten rows.

Pattern B: a comma before the phrase *such as*

> Other planes are being built with changes sought by passengers, such as larger overhead storage bins, handrails above the seats, and fresher air in the cabins.

Pattern C: a semicolon after the quotation marks

> One airline executive says that, for now, it's "hard to justify the costs of some suggested innovations"; however, airlines must be ready to meet the challenge if more passengers start choosing their carrier on the basis of comfort.

26 *Colons* (:)

The colon is used in more formal writing to call attention to words that follow it.

26a *Colons to Announce Elements at the End of a Sentence and Quotations*

Use the colon at the end of a sentence to introduce a list, an explanation (or intensification) of the sentence, or an example.

The university offers five different majors in engineering: mechanical, electrical, civil, industrial, and chemical engineering.

After so many weeks of intensive study, there was only one thing she really wanted: a vacation. (A dash can also be used here, though it is more informal.)

HINT: Think of the colon as the equivalent of the phrase *that is*. For most elements at the end of the sentence, you could have said "that is" where the colon is needed.

When the company president decided to boost morale among the employees, the executive board announced the one improvement that would surely please everyone: pay raises. (: = that is)

26b *Colons to Separate Independent Clauses*

Use the colon as a substitute for a semicolon to separate two independent clauses when the second amplifies or restates the first clause.

Again, think of the colon as the equivalent of *that is*. An independent clause following a colon may begin with a capital or lowercase letter, although the lowercase letter is preferred.

Some say that lobbying groups exert too much influence on Congress: they can buy votes as a result of their large contributions to the right senators and representatives.

26c *Colons to Announce Long Quotations*

Use the colon to announce long quotations (more than one sentence) or a quotation not introduced by such words as *said, remarked,* or *stated.*

The head of the company's research department, Ms. Mann, said: "We recommended budgeting $1 million for the development of that type of software, but we were turned down. We regrouped and tried to think of a new approach to change their minds. We got nowhere."

He offered an apology to calm her down: "I'm truly sorry that we were not able to help you."

26d Colons in Salutations and Between Elements

Use the colon in the salutation of a formal or business letter, in scriptural and time references, between a title and subtitle, with proportions, between city and publisher in bibliographical format, and after an introductory label.

Dear Mayor O'Daly:
Genesis 1:8
6:15 A.M.
Jerusalem: A City United
built on a scale of 4:1
Philadelphia: Able Publishing Company
Correct:

26e Colons with Quotation Marks

If a colon is needed, put it after the closing quotation mark.

"To err is human; to repeat an error is stupid"_:_ that was my chemistry teacher's favorite saying in the lab.

26f Unnecessary Colons

Do not use the colon after a verb or after a phrase like *such as* or *consisted of.*

Remember, the colon can only be used after an independent clause.

Unnecessary: The people who applied for that were: Mr. Orland, Mr. Johnson, and Ms. Lassiter.

Revised: The people who applied for that were Mr. Orland, Mr. Johnson, and Ms. Lassiter.

-or-

Revised: The people who applied for that were the following: Mr. Orland, Mr. Johnson, and Ms. Lassiter.

Unnecessary: She wanted to try out for a non-contact sport, such as: tennis, swimming, or golf.

Revised: She wanted to try out for a non-contact sport, such as tennis, swimming, or golf.

26f
:

> **HINT:** When you revise for unnecessary colons, you can either omit any punctuation or add a word or phrase such as *the following* after the verb.

Exercise 26.1: Proofreading Practice

The following paragraph needs some colons and has some correct and incorrect colons. Add colons where they should be, and put an X under colons or other punctuation that is incorrect. If other punctuation is needed instead, put it above the incorrect punctuation. Underline colons that are added.

When the Apollo astronauts brought back bags of moon rocks, it was expected that the rocks would provide some answers to a perennial question; the origin of the moon. Instead, the Apollo's moon rocks suggested a number of new theories. One that is gaining more supporters is called: the giant impact theory. Alan Smith, lunar scientist, offers an explanation of the giant impact theory "Recently acquired evidence suggests that the moon was born of a monstrous collision between a primordial, just-formed Earth and a protoplanet the size of Mars." This evidence comes from modeling such a collision on powerful super-computers. The theory proposes the following sequence of events (1) as Earth was forming, it was struck a glancing blow by a projectile the size of Mars; (2) a jet of vapor then spurted out, moving so fast that some of it escaped from Earth and the rest condensed into pebble-sized rock fragments; and (3) gravitational attraction fused this cloud of pebbles into the moon. There are several reasons that make some scientists favor this theory, such as: it dovetails with what is known about the moon's chemistry and it explains why the moon's average composition resembles Earth. Another lunar scientist says, "We may be close to tracking down the real answer."

Exercise 26.2: Pattern Practice

Using the patterns and examples given here, write your own sentences correctly punctuated with colons. Write one sentence for each pattern given.

Pattern A: sentence with a list following a colon

> The coffee shop offered samples of five new coffee flavors: mocha java, chocolate fudge, Swiss almond, cinnamon, and French roast.

Pattern B: independent clause, colon, second independent clause that restates or explains the first clause

> <u>That cat has only one problem</u>: <u>she thinks she is a human</u>.
>   independent clause   independent clause

Pattern C: sentence with a quotation not introduced by words such as *said, remarked,* or *stated.*

> Jim clarified his views on marriage: "It should be a commitment for a lifetime, not a trial run for a relationship."

27 *End* Punctuation

At the end of a sentence, use a period, question mark, or exclamation point.

27a *Periods* (.)

(1) Periods at the End of the Sentence

Use the period to end sentences that are statements, mild commands, indirect questions, or polite questions where an answer is not really expected.

He's one of those people who don't like pets.
    statement
Hand in your homework by noon tomorrow.
    mild comment
She asked how she could improve her backstroke in swimming.
    indirect question
Would you please let me know when the bus arrives.
    polite question

(2) Periods with Abbreviations

Use the period after most abbreviations.

Mr.	etc.
Mrs.	9 P.M.
Ms.	Ave.
A.D.	Ph.D.
R.S.V.P.	Inc.

Don't use a second period if the abbreviation is at the end of the sentence.

She studied for her R.N.

Periods are not needed after certain common abbreviations or names of well-known companies, agencies, organizations, and the state abbreviations used by the U.S. Postal Service.

27a

NAACP	NATO
NBA	CIA
IBM	CA
VW	MA
TV	VT (and other state postal abbreviations)
NFL	

(3) Periods with Quotation Marks

Put periods that follow quotations inside the quotation marks.

As she said, "No one is too old to try something new."

However, if there is a reference to a source, put the period after the reference.

Hemmings states, "This is, by far, the best existing example of Renaissance art" (144).

If words are omitted in a quotation, use three periods (called an ellipsis) to signal the omission.

The newspaper's editorial that day warned of the need for snow fences: "If we don't begin now to investigate ways to prevent drifting snow on our highways, we will have more winters...with stranded motorists." (The original quotation was as follows: "If we don't begin now to investigate ways to prevent drifting snow on our highways, we will have more winters like this one we just weathered and blizzards like the last few years with stranded motorists.")

Exercise 27.1: Proofreading Practice

Add periods where they are needed in the following paragraph. Take out any periods used incorrectly.

Several years ago the nation's print and broadcast media joined with advertising agencies to launch a massive media campaign against drugs. Some, like ABC-TV, announced that they would donate prime time T.V. spots, but CBS Inc, while agreeing to cooperate, announced its intention to continue to commit funds for campaigns for other public issues such as AIDS prevention. James R Daly, a spokesman for the anti-drug campaign said, "We were glad to see other companies joining in to help the campaign". For example, the Kodak Co donated the film needed for TV spots, and in Washington, D C, a group of concerned parents volunteered to do additional fund raising. In the first two years of this media campaign, more than $500 million was raised Says Dr Harrison Rublin, a leading spokesperson for one of the fund-raising groups, "One effective thirty-second ad aired at 8 PM is ten times more effective than a hundred brochures on the subject".

Exercise 27.2: Pattern Practice

Using the patterns and examples given here, write your own correctly punctuated sentences. Write two sentences for each pattern given.

Pattern A: statement (with a period at the end)

> Louise started guitar lessons at the age of six.

Pattern B: mild command (with a period at the end)

> Return that pencil to me when you are done.

Pattern C: indirect quotation (with a period at the end)

> Jennifer asked the gas station attendant if he had a wrench.

Pattern D: polite question (with a period at the end)

> Would you please send the material I am requesting as soon as possible.

Pattern E: an abbreviation with periods

> He couldn't decide whether to enroll for a B.S. or a B.A. degree.

Pattern F: an abbreviation without periods

> The computer shop featured IBM PC and Apple computers.

Pattern G: with a quotation

> His father announced, "If you use the car tonight, then you pay for the gas."

Pattern H: with a quotation and a reference

> According to the article, "Smokers can no longer demand rights that violate the air space of others" (Heskett 27).

27b
?

27b *Question Marks* (?)

(1) Question Marks at the End of the Sentence
Use a question mark after direct quotations but not after indirect quotations.

Direct Quotation: "Do you have another copy of this book in stock?"

Indirect Quotation: She asked the salesperson if he had another copy of the book in stock.

Use the question mark in statements that contain direct quotations.

"Did Henry ever pay back that loan?" she wondered.

Enclose the question mark inside the quotation marks only if the question mark belongs to the quotation.

Alice said, "Who's that standing by the door?"
Did Alice really say, "Get lost"?

(2) Question Marks in a Series

Question marks may be used between parts of a series.

Would you prefer to eat at a restaurant? go on a picnic? cook at home?

(3) Question Marks to Indicate Doubt

Question marks can be used to indicate doubt about the correctness of the preceding word, figure, date, or other piece of information.

The city was founded in 1837 (?) but did not grow significantly until about fifty years later.

(4) Unnecessary Question Marks

Don't use a question mark within parentheses to indicate sarcasm. Instead, rewrite the sentence so that the meaning is clear from the use of appropriate words.

Unnecessary Question Mark She was sure that it was her intelligence (?) that charmed him.

Revised: Although she was sure that it was her intelligence that charmed him, she was greatly mistaken.

Exercise 27.3: Proofreading Practice

In the following paragraph add question marks where they are needed and delete any incorrect, unnecessary, or inappropriate ones.

Oxford University has a chancellor, but members of the Oxford faculty wonder if anyone in the general public knows who the chancellor is? As the principal of one of the colleges said, "Does anyone care"? The post of chancellor at Oxford is mostly ceremonial, carrying very few responsibilities. One previous chancellor, Lord Curzon, did try to get involved with running the university but was soon discouraged from continuing such unseemly action. When Prime Minister Harold Macmillan was installed as chancellor, he delivered a speech in Latin saying that he was quite clear on the point that it was not one of his duties to run the university. He underscored his recognition of the heavy duties (?) of his new job by wearing his cap backward throughout the whole proceedings. Many old Oxonians fear that they'll never see his lackadaisical like again. Is there anyone who can be trusted to keep a campaign promise when he or she says, "If elected, I won't stir things up?"

27b
?

Exercise 27.4: Pattern Practice

Using the patterns and examples given here, write your own correctly punctuated sentences. Write two sentences for each pattern given.

Pattern A: sentence with a question mark

> Which way should I turn this knob?

Pattern B: statement with a direct question

> "Can you speak French?" he asked.

Pattern C: quotation with question mark inside the quotation marks

> Jeff kept on asking, "Did she really ask my name?"

Pattern D: quotation with the question mark outside the quotation marks

> Why did the coach say, "No more practice this week"?

Pattern E: question mark to indicate doubt about a piece of information

> The cavalry unit had 1000 (?) horses before the battle.

27c Exclamation Points (!)

(1) Exclamation Points at the End of the Sentence

Use an exclamation mark after strong commands, statements said with great emphasis, interjections, and sentences intended to express surprise, disbelief, or strong feeling.

What a magnificent surprise!

I am not guilty!

Definitely!

Don't overuse the exclamation mark, don't use more than one, and don't combine it with other end punctuation.

Overuse of the exclamation mark:

> Wow! What a party! There was even a live band!
>
> I won $500!
>
> Is he for real?!

(2) Exclamation Points with Quotation Marks

Enclose the exclamation mark inside quotation marks only if it belongs to the quotation.

He burst into the room and yelled, "We are surrounded!"

In the middle of the meeting Maude quietly explained, "My committee has already vetoed this motion"!

Exercise 27.5: Proofreading Practice

Add exclamation marks where they are needed in the following paragraph, and delete any that are incorrect, unnecessary, or inappropriate.

At the end of winter when gardeners are depressed from the long months indoors, plant catalogs start flooding the mail! With their large type the catalogs blare out their news to hungry gardeners. "AMAZING!!" "FANTASTIC!!!" "INCREDIBLE!!!!" The covers always belong to some enormous new strain of tomatoes. "Bigger than Beefsteaks" or "Too Big to Fit on This Page"! they yell. Even the blueberries are monsters. "Blueberries as big as quarters!" they promise. All you do, according to these enticing catalogs is "plant 'em and stand back!?!" On a gloomy February afternoon, many would-be gardeners are probably ready to believe that this year they too can have "ASPARAGUS THICKER THAN A PERSON'S THUMB"!!!

Exercise 27.6: Pattern Practice
Using the patterns and examples given here, write your own correctly punctuated sentences. Write one sentence for each pattern given.

Pattern A: sentence with an exclamation mark

This is the happiest day of my life!

Pattern B: quotation with an exclamation mark enclosed

After the ballots were counted, Dan yelled, "I won!"

Pattern C: quotation with an exclamation mark outside

Every time we try to study, Bob always says, "Let's go out instead"!

28a
" "

28 *Quotation Marks* (" ")

28a *Quotation Marks with Direct and Indirect Quotations*

Use quotation marks with direct quotations of prose, poetry, and dialogue.

(1) Quotation Marks with Prose Quotations

Direct quotations are the exact words said by someone or the exact words you saw in print and are recopying. Use a set of quotation marks (" at the beginning of the quotation and " at the end) to enclose direct quotations included in your writing.

Indirect quotations are not the exact words, but the rephrasing or summarizing of someone else's words. Do not use quotation marks for indirect quotations. (For more information on quoting from prose sources, see Chapter 51c.)

• Direct quotation (whole sentence):

Mr. & Mrs. Allen, owners of a 300-acre farm, said, "We refuse to use that pesticide because it might pollute the nearby wells."

HINT: Use a capital letter to start the first word of a direct quotation of a whole sentence.

- Direct quotation (part of a sentence):

  Mr. & Mrs. Allen stated that they "refuse to use that pesticide" because of possible water pollution.

HINT: Do *not* use a capital letter to start the first word of a direct quotation of part of a sentence.

28a
" "

- Indirect quotation:

  According to their statement to the local papers, the Allens refuse to use the pesticide because of potential water pollution.

Use single quotations (' at the beginning and ' at the end) for a quotation enclosed inside another quotation.

- Quotation within a quotation:

  The agricultural reporter for the newspaper explained, "When I talked to the Allens last week, they said, 'We refuse to use that pesticide.'"

If you leave some words out of a quotation, use an ellipsis mark to indicate omitted words. If you need to insert something within a quotation, use a pair of brackets ([]) to enclose the addition.

- Full direct quotation:

  The welfare agency representative said, "We are unable to help this family whom we would like to help because we don't have the funds to do so."

- Omitted material with ellipsis:

  The welfare agency representative said, "We are unable to help this family...because we don't have the funds to do so."

- Added material with brackets:

  The welfare agency representative explained that they are "unable to help this family whom [they] would like to help."

For long quotations (questions that extend more than four typed or handwritten lines on a page), set the quotation off by indenting ten spaces from the left margin and double-space the quotation. Do not use quotation marks for this indented material.

(2) Quotation Marks in Poetry

When you quote a single line of poetry, write it like other short quotations. Two lines can be run into your text with a slash mark to indicate the end of the first line. If the quotation is three lines or longer, set it off like a longer quotation. (Some people prefer to set off two-line quotations also for emphasis.) Quote the poem line by line as it appears on the original page, and do not use quotation marks. Indent ten spaces from the left margin. (For more information on quoting poetry, see Chapter 51c.)

28a
" "

- Poetry quoted in your writing:

  In his poem "Mending Wall," Robert Frost says: "Something there is that doesn't love a wall,/That sends the frozen-ground-swell under it."

- Longer quotation from a poem:

  In his poem "Mending Wall," Robert Frost questions the building of barriers and walls:

  > Before I built a wall I'd ask to know
  > What I was walling in or walling out,
  > And to whom I was like to give offense.

(3) Quotation Marks in Dialogue

Write each person's speech, however short, as separate paragraphs. Use commas to set off *he* or *she said.* Closely related bits of narrative can be included in the paragraph. If one person's speech goes on for several paragraphs, use quotation marks at the beginning of each paragraph but not at the end of the paragraphs before the last one. To signal the end of the person's speech, use quotation marks at the end of the last paragraph. (For more information on quoting dialogue, see Chapter 51c.)

"May I help you?" the clerk asked as she walked over to the customer.

"No, thanks," responded the woman in a quiet voice.

"We have a special sale today on sweaters," persisted the salesperson. She continued to stand next to the customer, waiting for the woman to indicate why she was there.

"How nice for you," the customer replied as she walked out, leaving a puzzled clerk wondering what she meant.

28b Quotation Marks for Minor Titles and Parts of Wholes

Use quotation marks for titles of parts of larger works (titles of book chapters, magazine articles, and episodes of television and radio series) and for short or minor works (songs, short stories, essays, short poems, one-act plays, and other short literary works that are less than three-act plays or book length.)

For larger, complete works, see Chapter 29, on italics. Neither quotation marks nor italics are used for referring to the Bible or legal documents.

Whenever he got involved with hard work in his garden, he'd hum his favorite song, "Old Man River."

Mark Twain's short story "The Celebrated Jumping Frog of Calaveras County" helped frog-jumping contests gain their great popularity.

28c Quotation Marks for Words

Use quotation marks for words used as words, not for their meaning, and for words used in special ways, such as for irony (when the writer means the opposite of what is being said). Italics (underlining) can also be used.

Be consistent throughout your papers in choosing either quotation marks or italics.

Quotation marks can also be used to introduce unfamiliar or technical terms when they are used for the first time (and defined). No quotation marks are needed in later uses of the word after it has been introduced the first time.

"Neat" is a word I wish she'd omit from her vocabulary.

The three-year-old held up his "work of art" for the teacher to admire.

28d Use of Other Punctuation with Quotation Marks

Put commas and periods before the second set of quotation marks, except when a reference follows the quotation. (For more information on punctuating quotations, see Chapter 51c.)

"The Politics of Hunger," a recent article in *Political Quarterly*, discussed the United Nations' use of military force to help victims of hunger.

He said, "I may forget your name, but I never remember a face."

Jenkins said, "Moshenberg's style of writing derives from his particular form of wit" (252).

Put the colon and semicolon after the quotation marks.

The critic called the movie "a potential Academy Award winner"; I thought it was a flop.

Put the dash, question mark, and exclamation point *before* the second set of quotation marks when the dash, question mark, or exclamation point apply to the quotation and *after* the second set of quotation marks when one of these punctuation marks applies to the whole sentence.

He asked, "Do you need this book?"
(The quotation here is a question.)

Does Dr. Lim always say to her students, "You must work harder"?
(The quotation here is a statement, but it is included in a sentence that is a question.)

28e Unnecessary Quotation Marks

Don't put quotation marks around the titles of your essays (though someone else will use quotation marks if referring to your essay), and don't use quotation marks for common nicknames, bits of humor, technical terms, and trite or well-known expressions.

Unnecessary Quotation Marks: The crew rowed together like "a well-oiled machine."

Revised: The crew rowed together like a well-oiled machine.

Unnecessary Quotation Marks: He decided to save his money until he could buy a "digital audio tape deck."

Revised: He decided to save his money until he could buy a digital audio tape deck.

Exercise 28.1: Proofreading Practice

Add quotation marks where they are needed in the following paragraph, and delete any quotation marks that are incorrect, unnecessary, or inappropriately placed.

28e
" "

Remember Silverton wine coolers? Silverton, like hundreds of other products that appeared in the same year, was pulled from the shelf after it failed to gain a market. Silverton didn't seem to have any connotation as a cooler, explains G. F. Strousel, the company's vice-president in charge of sales. Every year new products appear briefly on the shelf and disappear, and established products that no longer have "customer appeal" are canceled as well. "Either way," experts say, "the signs that point to failure are the same." Companies looking to cut their losses pay attention to such signs. In a recent newspaper article entitled *Over 75% of Business Ideas Are Flops*, T. M. Weir, a professor of marketing, explains that products that don't grow but maintain their percentage of the market are known as cash cows, and those that are declining in growth and in market share are called dipping dogs. Says Weir, "Marketers plot the growth and decline of products, especially of the dipping dogs, very closely." According to several sources at a New York research firm that studies new product development, "the final decision to stop making a product is a financial one." When the "red ink" flows, the product is pulled.

Exercise 28.2: Pattern Practice

Using the patterns and examples given here, write your own correctly punctuated sentences. Write two sentences for each pattern given.

Pattern A: direct quotation with a whole sentence being quoted

> The president of the university stated, "It is my fervent hope that next year there will be no tuition increase."

Pattern B: direct quotation with a part of a sentence being quoted

The president of the university vowed that next year "there will be no tuition increase."

Pattern C: a quotation within a quotation

The announcer said, "You heard it live on this station, Coach Williams predicting that his team 'will run away with the game tomorrow.'"

Pattern D: dialogue between two speakers

"Can you help me with the chem lab report?" his roommate asked.
"I'll try, but my notes aren't very complete," he said as he ambled off to turn up the stereo.
"That's OK. They have to be better than mine."

Pattern E: quotation marks with a minor title or a title of a part of a whole

In his autobiography Evans entitled his first chapter "In the Beginning."

Pattern F: quotation marks with a word used as a word

I can't believe that any grown person really says "Golly, gee whiz."

29 *Underlining/Italics* (under)

When you are typing or writing by hand, use underlines as described in this section. When you have italic lettering on a computer, you can use the italics instead.

29a *Underlines for Titles*

Use underlines (or italics) for titles and names of books, magazines, newspapers, pamphlets, works of art, and long works such as plays with three or more acts, movies, long musical works (operas, concertos, etc.), radio and television programs, and long poems.

For the use of quotation marks for titles of minor works and parts of whole works, see Chapter 8b.

29a
under

Do not use underlines, italics, or quotation marks for references to the Bible or legal documents.

Underlines	*-or-*	*Italics*
<u>Catcher in the Rye</u>		*Catcher in the Rye*
<u>U.S. News and World Report</u>		*U.S. News and World Report*
<u>New York Times</u>		*New York Times*
Shakespeare's <u>King Lear</u>		Shakespeare's *King Lear*
<u>Family Ties</u>		*Family Ties*
<u>Star Wars</u>		*Star Wars*

29b *Other Uses of Underlines*

Names of ships, airplanes, and trains are underlined or italicized. (With spacecraft, practice varies: Apollo 7 or *Apollo 7*.)

Queen Mary

Concorde

Orient Express

Foreign words and phrases, scientific names of plants, animals, diseases, and so on are underlined or italicized.

in vino veritas

Hedera helix

But many words that were once foreign are now part of English and no longer italicized:

alumni	cliché	karate
rouge	genre	hacienda

Words used as words, or letters, numbers, and symbols used as examples or terms are underlined or italicized. (Remember, quotation marks can also mark words being used in special ways. [See Chapter 28c.] Choose either quotation marks or italics and use them consistently throughout a paper.)

Some words, such as *Kleenex* and *Scotch tape*, are brand names for products.

In English the letters *ph* and *f* often have the same sound.

The keys for *9* and *&* on that typewriter are broken.

Underlines and italics are used sparingly for emphasis.

It *never* snows here at this time of year.

Do not use underlines or italics with titles of your own papers.

Exercise 29.1: Proofreading Practice

Add italics (underlines) where they are needed in the following paragraph and delete any other punctuation that is incorrect.

Because of her interest in the influence of the media on people's attitudes, Sarah chose as the topic for her research project the media's image of the Japanese during the last ten years. For source material Sarah began by reading news magazines such as Time and Newsweek, but she soon found that news articles were less likely to portray attitudes than features in magazines such as "People" and "Fortune", which have articles on sushi bars, Japanese electronics, and *karate.* The index to the New York Times also led her to articles such as *The Japanese Influence on American Business* and *Japanese Technology in America.* Sarah also read reviews of old television programs, including the short-lived series Ohara, which featured a Japanese-American detective, and old movies, such as The Karate Kid. Sarah rapidly found herself buried under mounds of notes and decided to limit her topic to one of the media, though she couldn't decide which one.

29b under

Exercise 29.2: Pattern Practice

Using the patterns and examples given here, write your own correctly italicized sentences. Write two sentences for each pattern given.

Pattern A: italics with titles of books, magazines, newspapers, and long works of art

> After surveying its recently checked out materials, the library concluded that the most popular items on the shelves were murder mysteries, such as Blodgen's *The Dead Hero;* current big city newspapers, such as the *New York Times;* and videotapes of old movies, such as *North by Northwest* and *Gone With the Wind.*

Pattern B: italics with names of ships, airplanes, and trains

> When the old *Queen Mary* was no longer fit for sailing, it became a floating hotel.

Pattern C: italics with foreign words or phrases and scientific names

> Dr. Galland diagnosed the cause of his illness as a combination of *candidiasis* and *giardiasis.*

Pattern D: italics with words used as words or figures used as examples

> If she would stop overusing empty words such as *great* or *nice* in her composition class papers, she would probably be able to get an A.

Pattern E: italics for emphasis

> When Mike woke up, he couldn't believe that he felt so refreshed even though he had been asleep for *only* ten minutes.

30 Hyphens (hyph)

30a Hyphens to Divide Words

Use the hyphen to indicate that the last part of a word appears on the next line.

Be sure to divide words between syllables. Check your dictionary to see how words are split into syllables. Most dictionaries use dots to show the syllable separation. When you split words, do so in a way that is most helpful to your reader. Follow these guidelines:

- Don't divide one-syllable words.
- Don't leave one or two letters at the end of the line.
- Don't put fewer than three letters on the next line.
- Don't divide the last word in a paragraph or the last word on a page.

Wrong: She took the big package a-

part very carefully.

(If there is no room for the whole word *apart* on the first line, move the word to the next line.)

Revised: She took the big package

apart very carefully.

Wrong: Twila was so hungry she ordered **panc-akes**, eggs, and sausage.

Revised: Twila was so hungry she ordered *pan-cakes*, eggs, and sausage.

30b Hyphens to Form Compound Words

Use the hyphen to form compound words.

This includes fractions and numbers that are spelled out, from twenty-one to ninety-nine. Because accepted usage and dictionaries vary, words forming compounds may be written separately, as one word, or connected by hyphens.

mother-in-law	thirty-six
clear-cut	two-thirds

For words in a series, use hyphens as follows:

mother-, father-, and sister-in-law

four-, five-, and six-page essays

30c Hyphens to Join Two-Word Units

Use the hyphen to join two or more words that work together and serve as a single descriptive word before a noun.

When the words come after the noun, they are usually not hyphenated. Don't use hyphens with *-ly* modifiers.

The office needed up-to-date scores.

-or-

The office needed scores that were up to date.

The repair involved a six-inch pipe.

30c hyph

-or-

The repair involved a pipe that was six inches long.

They brought along their nine-year-old son.

-or-

They brought along their son, who was nine years old.

30d Hyphens to Join Prefixes, Suffixes, and Letters to a Word

Use the hyphen between words and the prefixes *self-*, *all-*, and *ex-*.

For other prefixes, such as *anti-*, *non-*, *pro-*, and *co-*, use the dictionary as a guide. Use the hyphen when you add a prefix to a capitalized word (for example, *mid-August*) and when you add the suffix *-elect* to a word. In addition, use the hyphen to join single letters to words.

co-author	self-supporting
anti-abortion	president-elect
pro-American	T-shirt
D-day	all-encompassing

The hyphen is also used to avoid doubling vowels and tripling consonants:

anti-intellectual (not: antiintellectual)
bell-like (not: belllike)

30e Hyphens to Avoid Ambiguity

Use the hyphen to avoid confusion between those words that are spelled alike but have different meanings.

re-creation (to make again)   vs.   recreation (fun)

re-cover (cover again)   vs.   recover (regain health)
co-op (something jointly owned) vs.   coop (cage for fowls)

Exercise 30.1: Proofreading Exercise
Add hyphens where they are needed in the following paragraph and delete any that are incorrect.

For health conscious people who cringe at the thought of using a toothpaste with preservatives and dyes, there are now alternative toothpastes made entirely from plants. One brand of these new, all natural toothpastes advertises that its paste includes twenty nine different herbs, root and flower-extracts, and seaweed. Some of these toothpastes have a pleasant taste and appearance, but the owner of a San Francisco health food store decided not to carry one brand because it is a reddish-brown paste. "When squeezed from a tube, it resembles a fat earthworm," she explained. She prefers a brand made of propolis, the sticky stuff bees use to line their hives, and myrrh. Another brand, a black paste made of charred eggplant powder, clay, and seaweed, is favored by the hard core macrobiotic crowd. This interest in natural toothpastes may be cyclical, explains the director of an oral health institute. He recalls a gray striped, mint flavored paste from the Philippines that sought to capitalize on a spurt of interest several years ago. It was a big-seller for awhile and then disappeared.

30e
hyph

Exercise 30.2: Pattern Practice
Using the patterns and examples given here, write your own correctly hyphenated sentences. Write one sentence for each pattern given.

Pattern A: hyphen that splits a word at the end of a line

It was clear that they would have to sell off a quarter of the herd that summer.

Pattern B: hyphen with at least two compound words

Japanese-Americans in the area helped to elect more than twenty-seven delegates of Japanese descent to the convention.

Pattern C: hyphen with two words serving as a single descriptive word in front of a noun (and, if possible, the same two words after the noun)

The plastic-trimmed suitcase was promptly returned by unhappy customers who said the plastic trim fell off within several weeks.

Pattern D: hyphen with prefixes or suffixes

The slogan on her T-shirt announced her pro-feminist views.

31 Dashes (dash)

Dashes, which are considered somewhat informal, can add emphasis and clarity. But they shouldn't be overused, especially as substitutes for commas or colons.

> **HINT:** When you are typing, use two hyphens to indicate the dash. Do not leave a space before or after the hyphens. For handwritten papers, draw a dash as an unbroken line, at least twice as long as a hyphen.

31a Dashes at the Beginning or the End of a Sentence

Use the dash at the beginning or the end of the sentence to set off added explanation or illustration and to add emphasis or clarity.

If the added explanation is of less importance than the rest of the sentence, use parentheses.

Fame, fortune, and a Ferrari—these were his goals in life. (When dashes are used this way at the beginning of a sentence, they tend to come after a series of items that are explained in the main part of the sentence, which usually then begins with *these, all,* or *none.*

Her acting added an extra touch of humor to the play—an added sparkle.

31b Dashes to Mark an Interruption

Use the dash as an interrupter to mark a sudden break in thought, an abrupt change or surprise, or a deliberate pause and to show in a dialog that the speaker has been interrupted.

According to her way of looking at things—but not mine—this was a worth-while cause.

The small child stood there happily sniffing a handful of flowers—all the roses from my garden.

Of course Everett was willing to work hard to get good grades—but not too hard.

Sherri announced, "I'm going to clean up this room so that—"
"Oh no, you don't," yelled her little brother.

31c Dashes to Set Off a Phrase or Clause with a Comma

31c
dash

When a phrase or clause already has commas within it, you can use dashes to set off the whole word group.

Hildy always finds interesting little restaurants—such as Lettuce Eat, that health-food place, and Ho Ming's Pizza Parlor—to take us to after a concert.

Exercise 31.1: Proofreading Practice
Add dashes where they are needed in the following paragraph.

Businesspeople, laborers, children, private clubs, and senior citizens these are some of the groups who have parade floats in New Orleans' Mardi Gras. Every year more than fifty different parading organizations trundle their floats through the streets. All kinds of difficulties have to be anticipated, including rain, tipsy float riders who will fall off, and mechanical failures in the tractor engines pulling the floats, and have to be overcome. Rain can slow the parade but not stop it. Too much money, time, and dedication go into parade preparation to let anything prevent it or so the parade organizers say.

Exercise 31.2: Pattern Practice
Using the patterns and examples given here, write your own sentences with dashes. Write two sentences for each pattern given.

Pattern A: at the beginning or end of the sentence for added explanation or illustration

> Those leather boots cost about $100—almost half a week's salary.

Pattern B: to mark an interruption or break in thought

> Rick is always borrowing—but not returning—everyone else's ballpoint pens.

Pattern C: to set off phrases and clauses with their own commas

> There were several exercise programs—including aerobic dancing, gymnastics, and aquatic exercises in the pool—to choose from in the students' recreational program at the gymnasium.

32a

32 Slashes (/)

32a Slashes to Mark the End of a Line of Poetry

When you quote two or three lines of poetry within a paragraph, indicate the end of each line with a slash (with a space before and after the slash).

Don't use the slash mark when you indent and quote three or more lines of poetry.

Andrew Marvell's poem "To His Coy Mistress" begins by reminding the lady that life is indeed short: "Had we but world enough, and time / This coyness, lady, were no crime." And as the poem progresses, the imagery of death reinforces this reminder of our brief moment of life:

> But at my back I always hear
> Time's winged chariot hurrying near;
> And yonder all before us lie
> Deserts of vast eternity.

32b Slashes to Indicate Acceptable Terms

Use the slash mark, with no space before or afterward, to indicate that either of two terms can apply.

pass/fail   either/or

HINT: The slash mark on a typewriter or computer keyboard is the slanting line /.

Exercise 32.1: Pattern Practice

Using the patterns and examples given here, write your own sentences with slashes. Write one sentence for each pattern given.

Pattern A: with poetry quoted within a sentence

> Whenever she was asked to discuss her ability to cope with great difficulties, she quoted John Milton: "The mind is its own place, and in itself / Can make a Heaven of Hell, a Hell of Heaven."

Pattern B: with two terms when either is acceptable

> Because the reading list for History 227 was so long, he decided to register for it on a pass/fail option.

33 *Parentheses* ( )

A dash gives emphasis to an element in the sentence, whereas a pair of parentheses indicates that the element enclosed is less important. *Parentheses* is the plural form of the word and indicates both the parenthesis at the beginning and the parenthesis at the end of the enclosed element.

33a Parentheses to Set Off Supplementary Matter

Use parentheses to enclose supplementary or less important material that you include as further explanation or as added detail or examples.

That added material does not need to be part of the grammatical structure of the sentence. If the material is inside the sentence, any punctuation needed for the rest of the sentence is outside the closing parentheses. If a whole sentence is enclosed with parentheses, put the end punctuation for that sentence inside.

33b
( )

The officers of the fraternity (the ones elected last month) decided to call a chapter meeting just before the dance to remind everyone of the new alcohol regulations.

33b Parentheses to Enclose Figures or Letters

Use parentheses to enclose figures or letters that enumerate items in a series.

The three major items on the agenda were as follows: (1) the budget review, (2) the new parking permits, and (3) the evaluation procedures.

Exercise 33.1: Pattern Practice

Using the patterns and examples given here, write your own sentences with parentheses. Write a sentence for each pattern given.

Pattern A: to enclose less important material

The sixth-grade teacher decided to offer his art class an opportunity to try out different drawing materials (such as pastel chalks and charcoal) that they hadn't used before.

Pattern B: to enclose figures and letters

The job offer included some very important fringe benefits that similar positions in other companies did not include: (a) a day-care center in the building, (b) retirement benefits for the employee's spouse, and (c) an opportunity to buy company cars after they were used for a year or so.

34 *Brackets* [ ]

34a *Brackets to Add Your Comments within a Quotation*

When you are quoting material and have to add your own explanation, comment, or addition within the quotation, enclose your addition within brackets [ ].

The word *sic* in brackets means that you copied the original quotation exactly as it appeared, but you think that the word just before *sic* may be an error or a questionable form.

After the town meeting, the newspaper's lead story reported the discussion: "The Town Board and the Mayor met to discuss the mayor's proposal to raise parking meter rates. The discussion was long but not heated, and the exchange of views was fiendly [*sic*] despite some strong opposition."

Everyone agreed with Phil Brown's claim that "this great team [the Chicago Bears] is destined for next year's Superbowl."

34b *Brackets to Enclose Something Inside Parentheses*

When you find that you need to enclose something already within parentheses, use brackets instead of a second set of parentheses.

"Baby busters, the children born between 1965 and 1980, will have more choices in the job market and better prospects for advancement than the previous 'baby boom' generation," says John Sayers in his recent study of population trends (*The Changing Face of Our Population* [New York: Merian Co., 1978] 18).

Exercise 34.1: Pattern Practice

Using the patterns and examples given here, write your own sentences with brackets. Write one sentence for each pattern given.

Pattern A: brackets to add comments within a quotation

> The lab assistant explained that "everyone [who has finished the lab experiment] should hand in notebooks by Friday."

Pattern B: brackets to replace parentheses within parentheses

> The new library guide (distributed by the Freshman Council [a subcommittee of the Student Government Board] at no cost to students) is intended to help freshman composition students become acquainted with resources for researching term paper topics.

34b
[ ]

Exercise 34.2: Proofreading Practice

Add slashes, parentheses, and brackets where they are needed in the following paragraph. Correct any wrong punctuation.

The last two lines of Archibald MacLeish's poem "Ars Poetica" (written in 1924 are often quoted as his theory of poetry. "A poem should not mean But be," he wrote. In his notebooks, he expanded on this statement: "The purpose of the expression of emotion in a poem is not to recreate the poet's emotion in someone else…. The poem itself is a finality, an end, a creation." G. T. Hardison, in his analysis of MacLeish's theory of poetry ("The Non-Meaning of Poetry," *Modern Poetics* 27 (1981): 45, explains that "when MacLeish says the poem 'is a finality, an ending sic,' he means that a good poem is self-sufficient; it is, it does not mean something else. One might as well ask the meaning of a friend or brother."

35 *Omitted Words/Ellipsis* (...)

Use an **ellipsis** (a series of three dots) to indicate that you are omitting words or a part of a sentence from material you are quoting.

To indicate the omission, use three spaced periods with a space before and after each period.

Original: "In 1891, when President Benjamin Harrison proclaimed the first forest reserves as government land, there were so many people opposed to the idea that his action was called undemocratic and un-American."

Some Words Omitted: "In 1891, when President Benjamin Harrison proclaimed the first forest reserves . . . his action was called undemocratic and un-American."

If you are omitting a whole sentence or paragraph, add a fourth period with no space after the last word:

"federal lands. . . . were designated"

An ellipsis is not needed if the omission occurs at the beginning or end of the sentence you are quoting. But if your sentence ends with quoted words that are not the end of the original sentence, use an ellipsis mark. Add your period (the fourth one) with no space after the last word if there is no documentation included. But if there is documentation, such as a page number, add the last period after the parentheses.

"the National Forest System. . . ."

"the National Forest System . . ." (Smith 27).

If you omit words immediately after a punctuation mark in the original, include that mark in your sentence.

"because of this use of national forests for timbering, mining, and grazing, . . ."

In addition to indicating the omission of quoted words, three dots are also used to show hesitation or an unfinished statement.

The lawyer asked: "Did you see the defendant leave the room?"

"Ah, I'm not sure . . . ," replied the witness.

35
. . .

36 Capitals (caps)

Capitalize words that name one particular thing, most often a person or place rather than a general type or group of things.

Names that are capitalized can be thought of as legal titles that identify a specific thing. For example, you can take a course in history (a word not capitalized because it is a general field of study), but the course is offered by a particular department with a specific name, such as History Department or Department of Historical Studies. The name of that specific department is capitalized. However, if you take a course in French, the word *French* is capitalized because it is the name of a specific language.

Listed here are categories of words that should be capitalized. If you are not sure whether a particular word fits in these categories, check your dictionary.

- Persons: Vincent Baglia, Rifka Kaplan

- Places, including geographical regions: Indianapolis, Ontario, Midwest

- Peoples and their languages: Spanish, Dutch

- Religions and their followers: Buddhist, Judaism, Christianity, Lutheran

- Members of national, political, racial, social, civic, and athletic groups: Democrat, African-American, Chicago Bears, Danes

- Institutions and organizations: Supreme Court, Legal Aid Society, Lions Club

- Historical documents: The Declaration of Independence, Magna Carta

- Periods and events: Middle Ages, Boston Tea Party, World War II

  But not century numbers: eighteenth century

- Days, months, and holidays: Monday, August, Thanksgiving

  But not seasons: spring, winter

- Trademark names: Coca-Cola, Kodak, Ford
- Holy books and words denoting the Supreme Being: Bible, Talmud, Allah, Lord

  Some people also capitalize pronouns referring to the Supreme Being: the wonders of His creation

- Words and abbreviations from specific names: Stalinism, Freudian, NATO, CBS

  But some names have lost this specific association and now refer more generally to the type of thing: french fry, pasteurize, italics

- Place words, such as *street, park, city,* that are part of specific names: New York City, Wall Street, Madison Avenue, Zion National Park
- Titles that precede people's names: Aunt Sylvia, Governor Lionel Washington

  But not titles that follow names:

  > Sylvia, my aunt
  > Lionel Washington, governor

- Words that indicate family relationships when used as a substitute for a specific name:

  > Here is a gift for Mother.
  > Ling Chen sent a gift to his mother.

HINT: If you put an article (*a, an, the*) or possessive pronoun (*my, your, his, her, our, their*) in front, don't capitalize:

> my father
> their cousin

- Titles of books, magazines, essays, movies, plays, and other works:
  Capitalize the first and last words and all other words except articles (*a, an, the*), short prepositions (*to, by, on, in*), and short joining words (*and, but, or*). With hyphenated words, capitalize the first word and the word following the hyphen

if it is a noun, adjective, or another word equal in importance to the first word.

> *The Taming of the Shrew*
> *A Dialog Between Soul and Body*
> "The Sino-Soviet Conflict"
> "A Brother-in-Law's Lament"

(For APA style, which has different rules for capitalizing titles in documentation, see Chapter 51e.)

- The pronoun *I* and the interjection *O*:

> "Sail on, sail on, O ship of state,"
> I said as the canoe began to sink.

But do not capitalize the word *oh* unless it begins a sentence.

**36
caps**

- The first word of every sentence and the first word of a comment in parentheses if the comment is a full sentence:

The American Olympic Ski Team (which receives very little government support) spent six months in training before the elimination trials while the German team trained for over two years. (Like most European nations, the German government provides financial support for all team members.)

....

HINT: Full sentences in parentheses can also be placed within a sentence, but they are cumbersome to read and should be avoided unless absolutely necessary.

....

But for a series of questions in which the questions are not full sentences, no capitals are needed.

What did the settlers want from the natives? food? animal skins? to be left alone?

- The first word of directly quoted speech:

She answered, "No one will understand."

But capitals are not used for the second portion of interrupted direct quotations:

"No one," she answered, "will understand."

But quoted phrases or clauses integrated into your own sentence are not capitalized:

When Hemmings declined the nomination, he explained that he "would try again another year."

- The first word in a list after a colon if each item in the list is a complete sentence:

The rule books were very clear: (1) No player could continue to play after committing two fouls, (2) Substitute players would be permitted only with the consent of the other team, and (3) Every eligible player had to be designated before the game.

     -or-

The rule books were very clear:
1. No player could continue to play after committing two fouls,
2. Substitute players would be permitted only with the consent of the other team,
3. Every eligible player had to be designated before the game.

But do not capitalize items in a list that are not complete sentences:

The rise in popularity of walking as an alternative to jogging has already led to commercial successes of various kinds: (1) new designs for walking shoes, (2) an expanding market for walking sticks, and (3) a rapid growth in the number of manufacturers selling walking shoes.

     -or-

The rise in popularity of walking as an alternative to jogging has already led to commercial successes of various kinds:
1. new designs for walking shoes,
2. an expanding market for walking sticks, and
3. a rapid growth in the number of manufacturers selling walking shoes.

- Words that are normally capitalized when placed after a prefix: un-American, anti-Semitic

Exercise 36.1: Proofreading Practice

In the following sentences there are some errors in capitalization. Revise the sentences so that the capitals are used correctly.

1. Every Spring when the Madison avenue advertisers compete for Clio Awards for the best commercials, my Cousin Bert makes bets on who will win.
2. At the Dallas-fort Worth international airport, the Pan-am plane landed with a cargo of dutch cigars and african diamonds.

36
caps

3. When Marta signed up for an advanced course in Psychology, she was already familiar with Freudian Psychology and various Twentieth-Century views on dream interpretation.

4. Floyd Martin, a Washington, D.C., Physician, has recently completed his study of the effects of Asthma as his contribution to a Task Force convened by the National Institutes of Health.

5. When Aleen drove South from Minnesota to Tennessee, she wondered whether "Every restaurant, including McDonald's, would serve grits."

Exercise 36.2: Pattern Practice

For each of the capitalization patterns listed here, write a sentence of your own that uses capitals correctly.

**37
ab**

Pattern A: a sentence with the name of a national, political, racial, social, civic, or athletic group; the name of a season of the year; and a person's name and title.

> When Matthew Given, superintendent of the Monticello School Corporation, suggested a summer program for additional study, many parents vigorously supported his idea.

Pattern B: a sentence with a quotation interrupted by other words in the sentence

> "Thanks," said the customer to the salesclerk, "this is just what I was looking for."

Pattern C: two place names and a holiday

> On the Fourth of July, Chicago hosts an art and food fair in Grant Park.

37 Abbreviations (ab)

In the fields of social science, science, and engineering, abbreviations are used frequently, but in other fields and in academic writing in the humanities, only a limited number of abbreviations are generally used.

37a Abbreviating Numbers

Write out any numbers that can be expressed in one or two words: nine   twenty-seven   135

The dollar sign abbreviation is generally acceptable when the whole phrase will be more than three words:

$23 thousand   one million dollars

For temperatures, use words if only a few temperatures are cited in the whole paper, but use figures if temperatures are cited frequently:

ten degrees below zero, Fahrenheit   -10°F

37b
ab

37b Abbreviating Titles

Mr., *Mrs.* and *Ms.* are acceptable abbreviations when used as titles before the name.

Dr. and *St.* (*saint*) are acceptable only when these immediately precede a name. Write the words out when they appear after the name.

Dr. Marlen Chaf

Marlen Chaf, doctor of internal medicine

Prof., *Sen.*, *Gen.*, *Capt.*, and similar abbreviated titles can be used when they appear in front of a full name or before initials and a last name. But do not abbreviate when such a title appears before the last name only.

Gen. R. G. Fuller

General Fuller

Sr., *Jr.*, *J.D.*, *Ph.D.*, *M.F.A.*, *C.P.A.*, and other abbreviations of academic titles and professional degrees can be used after the name.

Leslie Millen, Ph.D.,

Charleen Phipps, C.P.A.,

Bros., *Co.*, , and similar abbreviations are retained only if they are part of the exact name.

Marshall Field & Co.

HINT: Don't indicate the same title before and after a name.
Redundant: Dr. Michael Wagnal, M.D.
Correct: Dr. Michael Wagnal   -or-   Michael Wagnal, M.D.

37c Abbreviating Places

In general, spell out names of states, countries, continents, streets, rivers, etc.

Use the abbreviation *D.C.* in Washington, D.C. Use *U.S.* only when it is used as an adjective, not a noun.

U.S. training bases

training bases in the United States

If you include a full address in a sentence, citing the street, city, and state, you can use the postal abbreviation for the state.

For further information, write to the company at 100 Peachtree Street, Atlanta, GA 30300 for a copy of their free catalog.

The company's headquarters in Atlanta, Georgia, will soon be moved.

37d Abbreviating Measurements

Spell out units of measurement such as an acre, a meter, foot, percent, kilobyte, etc., but use abbreviations in tables, graphs, and figures. In technical writing abbreviations are often used.

37e Abbreviating Dates

Spell out months and days of the week.

With dates and times, the following are acceptable:

57 B.C. or 57 B.C.E. (the abbreviation B.C. and B.C.E. [Before the Common Era] are placed after the year)
A.D. 329 (the abbreviation A.D. is placed before the date)
a.m., p.m., (or A.M., P.M.)
EST (or E.S.T., est)

37f Abbreviating Initials Used as Names

Use abbreviations for names of organizations, agencies, countries, and things usually referred to by their capitalized initials.

NASA	IBM
UNICEF	U.S.S.R.
NAACP	VCR

If you are using the initials for a term that may not be familiar to your readers, spell it out the first time and give the initials in parentheses. From then on, you can use the initials.

The study of children's long-term memory (LTM) has been a difficult one because of the lack of a universally accepted definition of LTM.

37g Abbreviating Latin Expressions

Some Latin expressions always appear as abbreviations.

cf.	(compare)
e.g.	(for example)
et al.	(and others)
etc.	(and so forth)
i.e.	(that is)
n.b.	(note carefully)
vs. -or- v.	(versus)

37h Abbreviating Documentation

For bibliographical information, use the abbreviations found in the style manual of the particular format for bibliographical information that you are using. (See Chapter 51d and 51e.)

abr.	(abridged)
anon.	(anonymous)
b.	(born)
c. -or- c	(copyright)
c. -or- ca.	(about—used with dates)
ch. -or- chap.	(chapter)
col., cols.	(column, columns)
d.	(died)
ed., eds.	(editor, editors)
esp.	(especially)
f., ff.	(and the following page, pages)
illus.	(illustrated by)
ms., mss.	(manuscript, manuscripts)
no.	(number)
n.d.	(no date of publication given)
n.p.	(no place of publication given)
n. pag.	(no page number given)
p., pp.	(page, pages)
trans. -or- tr.	(translated by)
vol., vols.	(volume, volumes)

Exercise 37.1: Proofreading Practice

Proofread the following paragraph and correct the errors in using abbreviations. Underline the words you correct.

Some forms of illegal fishing are hard to define. For example, "noodling," the practice of catching fish by snagging them in the gills or flesh, is illegal in most places in the U.S. However, in a recent case, a man who had caught two fish, weighing 25 and 31 lbs., in a Texas lake, argued that he wasn't noodling when he dived under water with a fishing pole & a very short line. This was not noodling, he claimed, because he poked his rod & baited hook into catfish nets instead of dragging his lines through the water to snag fish the way noodlers do. The local game warden charged the angler with noodling, a misdemeanor that carries a fine of up to $250. Residents of the area, near Cloud Creek Lake, TX, agreed that he was fishing illegally. But, after much debate, the man won his claim that while his unusual method was very close to noodling, he was innocent.

37h
ab

Exercise 37.2: Pattern Practice

Using the patterns listed here, write a sentence of your own that correctly uses abbreviations.

Pattern A: a sentence with a number that can be written as one or two words; a name with a degree after it, and a place name without a full address (street, city, and state)

> When Cleon Martin, C.P.A., looked for office space in Rochester, New York, he found a slightly expensive but convenient office on the thirty-sixth floor of a new high-rise office building near his home.

Pattern B: a sentence with the abbreviation for the United States used correctly and the name of a month and day of the week.

> Because of recent changes in the U.S. Post Office, many local post offices are now open on Saturday mornings, especially in December.

Pattern C: a sentence with a unit of measurement and a specific dollar amount.

> The luxurious boat, more than sixty feet long, was purchased for $555 thousand.

38 *Numbers* (num)

While style manuals for different fields and companies vary, the suggestions for writing numbers given here are generally useful as a guide for academic writing.

Spell out numbers that can be expressed in one word or two, and use figures for other numbers.

Words	*Figures*
two pounds	126 days
six million dollars	$31.50
thirty-one years	6381 bushels
eighty-three people	4.78 liters

38
num

Use a combination of figures and words for numbers when such a combination will keep your writing clear.

The club celebrated the birthdays of six 90-year-olds who were born in the city.

Use figures for the following:

* Days and years

December 12, 1963	-or-	12 December 1963
A.D. 1066		
in 1971–1972	-or-	in 1971–72
the 1980's	-or-	the 1980s

    But, for numbers that can be expressed in one or two words:

the eighties	the twentieth century

    Forms such as *1st* and *2nd,* as well as forms such as *fourth* and *fifth,* are sometimes used in dates but only when the year is omitted:

June 6th	June sixth

* Time of day

8:00 A.M. -or- a.m.	-or-	eight o'clock in the morning
4:30 P.M. -or- p.m.	-or-	half-past four in the afternoon

- Addresses

  15 Tenth Street
  350 West 114 Street   -or-   350 West 114th Street
  Prescott, AZ 86301

- Identification numbers

  Room 8
  Channel 18
  Interstate 65
  Henry VIII

- Page and division of books and plays

  page 30
  chapter 6
  act 3, scene 2   -or-   Act III, Scene ii

- Decimals and percentages

  2.7 average
  13 1/2 percent
  0.037 metric ton

- Numbers in series and statistics (Be consistent)

  two apples, six oranges, and three bananas
  115 feet by 90 feet
  scores of 25 to 6 (or) scores of 25–6
  The vote was 9 in favor, 5 opposed, and 3 undecided.

- Large round numbers

  four billion dollars   -or- $4 billion
  16,500,000   -or-   16.5 million

- Numbers beginning sentences
  Ten percent of the year's crop was harvested.

- Repeated numbers (in legal or commercial writing)
  The bill will not exceed one hundred (100) dollars.

Exercise 38.1: Pattern Practice

For each of the sentences given here, compose a sentence of your own using that suggestion for writing numbers. The first sentence is done as an example.

1. There was a 7.2 percent decrease in sales of cigarettes after the Surgeon General's speech.
   The study showed that 16.7 percent of the population in the country did not have running water.
2. The plane was due at 4:15 P.M. but arrived at 5:10 P.M.
3. That book was Volume 23 in the series.
4. The astronomer calculated that the star is 18 million light years from our planet.
5. In the sixties, during the height of the anti-war movement, the senator's political actions were not popular, but by the time of the 1972 election more people agreed with him.
6. The television commercial warned buyers that there were only 123 days until Christmas.

Answer Key for Exercises in Part 3

Exercise 23.1

An inventor working on a "flying car" says that traveling several hundred miles by commercial airplane is a fairly inefficient way to get around. First, you have to drive through traffic to the airport, and then you have to park your car somewhere in order to board a plane. You fly to another crowded airport outside of a city, but then you have to take another automobile to your final destination in town. A more practical solution would be a personal commuter flying vehicle. The inventor, working in a company supported by several government agencies, has developed a vertical takeoff and landing vehicle that has the potential to allow everyone to take to the air. The vehicle can take off and land vertically, and it travels five times faster than an automobile. The most recently developed model looks more like a car than a plane; however, it operates more like a cross between a plane and a helicopter. Above 125 mph in flight, it flies like a conventional plane, or below 125 mph, it maneuvers like a helicopter. It has a number of safety features, such as six engines; therefore it can recover if it loses an engine while hovering close to the ground.

Exercise 23.3

(1) A recent study showed that small cars are tailgated more than big ones. (2) Moreover, the drivers of subcompact and compact cars also do more tailgating themselves. (3) In the study traf-

fic flow at five different locations was observed, and a variety of driving conditions was included, such as two-lane state roads, four-lane divided highways, and so on. (4) In all, more than 100,000 vehicles were videotaped. (5) Although subcompact and compact cars accounted for only 38 percent of the vehicles on the tape, their drivers were tailgating in 48 percent of the incidents observed. (6) In addition to having done all this tailgating, these drivers were also the victims of tailgating 47 percent of the time. (7) Midsized cars made up 31 percent of the cars on the tapes but accounted for only 20 percent of the tailgaters and 24 percent of the drivers being tailgated. (8) Having considered various reasons for this, the researchers suggest that drivers of other cars may avoid getting close to midsized cars because of the cars' contours. (9) Because midsized cars have more curves in the sloping backs and trunks, people may have more trouble seeing around them.

three
ans

Exercise 23.4

1. C.	**4.** B.
2. B.	**5.** C.
3. B.	**6.** A.

Exercise 23.5

The use of technical advisers for TV programs is not new. For medical, legal, and police dramas <u>that attempt to be realistic</u>, $\qquad$ E producers have long called on experts to check the scripts. These experts, <u>who read the scripts before production</u>, make $\qquad$ N sure <u>that TV surgeons, lawyers and police officers use the right</u> $\qquad$ E <u>terminology and follow standard procedures</u>. Now network shows are also calling on social scientists as consultants to add realism in sitcoms and to help networks conform to criteria <u>that</u> <u>are required by (FCC) standards</u>. The FCC, <u>a federal regulatory</u> $\qquad$ E $\qquad$ N

agency, says <u>that TV shows with a potential audience of</u>
<u>E</u>
<u>children,</u> <u>even if they are not aired until after the early evening</u>
<u>N</u>
<u>family viewing time</u>, must offer some content of educational

value. But, <u>of course</u>, TV still wants to entertain, and sometimes
<u>N</u>
there is some conflict with the writers. On the whole, <u>though,</u>
<u>N</u>
television scriptwriters have come to recognize and value advice

from social scientists and psychologists, <u>particularly on impor-</u>

<u>tant topics such as how children react to divorce, how parents</u>
<u>N</u>
<u>might handle children's drug abuse, or how families deal with</u>

<u>emotional crises.</u>

three
ans

Exercise 23.7

Imagine not being able to recognize the face of your sister, your boss, or your best friend from high school. Imagine looking into a mirror, seeing a face, and realizing that the face you see is totally unfamiliar. Though this may sound impossible, a small number of people do suffer from a neurological condition that leaves them unable to recognize familiar faces. The condition is called *prosopagnosia* and results from brain damage caused by infection or stroke. Many people with this problem who have been studied have normal vision, reading ability, and language skills. They know that a face is a face, they can name its parts, and they can distinguish differences between faces. But only through other clues, such as hearing a familiar voice, remembering a specific feature like a mustache, hearing a name, or recalling a particular identifying mark such as an unusual scar, can the people who were studied call up memories of people they should know. Researchers studying this phenomenon have found evidence suggesting that the step leading to conscious recognition of the face by the brain is somehow being blocked.

Exercise 23.9

All those dazed, exhausted football players who return to the sidelines to suck on oxygen could just as well be saving their breath. In a recent controlled test subjects who breathed 100 percent oxygen did not revive any better or more quickly than subjects who were given plain, ordinary air. The biggest surprise was that the athletes being tested couldn't even tell the difference. But they did like the idea of having all those bright orange oxygen tanks nearby in case of emergency, even if the tanks didn't do any good.

Exercise 23.11

The United States Government Printing Office has a catalog of thousands of popular books that it prints. If you'd like a copy of this catalog, write to the Superintendent of Documents, United States Government Printing Office, Washington, DC 20402. There are books on agriculture, business and industry, careers, computers, diet and nutrition, health, history, hobbies, space exploration, and other topics. To pay for the books, you can send a check or money order, but more than 30,000 customers every year set up deposit accounts with an initial deposit of at least $50. Future purchases can then be charged against this account. There are also Government Printing Office bookstores all around the country where you can browse before buying. They do not stock all 16,000 titles in their inventory, but they do carry the more popular ones. For example, if you live in Birmingham, you can find the Government Printing Office bookstore in Roebuck Shopping City, 9220-B Parkway East, Birmingham, AL 35206. There is also a bookstore in Cleveland, Ohio, and Jacksonville, Florida.

Exercise 23.13

Have you ever thought about where all those oranges in your orange juice come from? You'd probably say that they come from Florida, wouldn't you? Some oranges may, but the world's largest producer of orange juice is now Brazil. Says one of Florida's biggest orange growers, "We're going to regain the market sooner than those rookie Brazilians think." Florida growers predict that overplanting and plunging prices have set the stage for a damaging glut in Brazil, not in Florida. "We have never had excess juice," claims a major Brazilian grower, "and I don't think we ever will." Know-how from American juice companies, along with subsidies from the Brazilian government, is helping Brazilian growers stay on top of the market. Brazilian growers are confident, knowing that Florida is more prone to drought and hard freezes. So it looks as if our orange juice will remain partly Brazilian for the foreseeable future.

Exercise 23.15

three
ans

Although the dangers of alcohol are well known, and have

been widely publicized, there may be another danger that we

haven't yet realized. Several controlled studies of drunken ani-

mals have indicated to researchers, that in an accident there is

more swelling and hemorrhaging in the spinal cord, and in the

brain, if alcohol is present in the body. To find out if this is true

with humans, researchers studied the data on more than one

million drivers in automobile crashes. One thing already known

is, that drunks are more likely to be driving fast, and to have seat

belts unfastened. Of course, their coordination is also poorer

than sober people, so they are more likely to get into serious

accidents. To compensate for this, researchers grouped acci-

dents into type, speed, and degree of vehicle deformation, and

found that alcohol still appears to make people more vulnerable

to injury. The conclusion of the study was, that the higher the

level of alcohol in the person's body, the greater the chance of

being injured or killed. In minor crashes, drunk drivers were more than four times as likely to be killed as sober ones. In average crashes, drunk drivers were more than three times as likely to be killed, and in the worst ones, drunks were almost twice as likely. Overall, drunks were more than twice as likely to die in an accident, because of the alcohol they drank.

x

Exercise 24.1

Although teachers commonly use tests to grade their students' learning, taking a test can also help students learn. People's memory seems to be more accurate after reading some material and taken a test than after merely reading the material with no testing. In fact, studies have shown that students who take several tests learn even more than those who take only one test after reading some material. Although everyone's ability to memorize material generally depends on how well the material was studied, scientists' research does indicate that test-taking aids memory. The type of test is also important because multiple-choice exams help us to put facts together better while fill-in-the-blank questions promote recall of specific facts. These questions' ability to test different types of learning suggests that teachers ought to include different types of tests throughout the semester.

three ans

Exercise 24.3

Magazine racks used to be for magazines, but that was before mail-order catalogs began invading the market. In 1985, when some catalogs began taking paid ads for such products as liquor and cologne, the line between magazines and catalogs began to blur. In some cases it's hard to distinguish the difference. And customers have good reasons to prefer buying catalogs when there's the advantage of having discount coupons tucked in. The catalogs that began appearing on magazine racks in '85 sold for $1 to $3 apiece, but customers would get a $5 discount on their first order. National distributors now estimate that more than 5000 stores and newsstands stock catalogs for such well-known companies as Sharper Image and Bloomingdale's. Waldenbooks was among the first to display these catalogs on its magazine racks. It's big business now, and magazines have a tough rival to beat.

Exercise 24.5

In the late 1970's the M.B.A. became one of the most desirable degrees awarded by American universities. In large part this was due to the high salaries offered to new graduates. Students graduating with B.A.'s or B.S.'s in most fields could expect starting salaries thousands of dollars below new M.B.A.'s, especially those graduating at the top of the class from the more prestigious universities. It was a case of having those hard-earned A's translate into better salaries. When huge numbers of M.B.A.'s began flooding the market in the mid-1980's, the value of the degree declined somewhat.

Exercise 24.7

three ans

Erica Johns, a recent contestant on one of the game shows, was embarrassed to see herself in the reruns. There she was on the screen, yelling out the answer and claiming the big prize was hers, even when someone else sounded the buzzer before she did. "It's difficult," she said, "not to act foolish when so much money is involved." But she did win some dance lessons and a cute puppy with its own diamond-studded leash. Still, she wished she had pushed the buzzer and answered the question worth $2000.

Exercise 25.1

Even before children begin school, many parents think they should take part in their children's education and help the children to develop mentally. Such parents usually consider reading to young toddlers important; moreover, they help the children memorize facts such as the days of the week and the numbers from one to ten. Now it is becoming clear that parents can begin helping when the children are babies. One particular type of parent communication, encouraging the baby to pay attention to new things, seems especially promising in helping babies' brains develop; for example, handing the baby a toy encourages the baby to notice something new. Some studies seem to indicate that this kind of activity resulted in children scoring higher on intelligence tests several years later. Parents interested in helping their babies' brain development have been encouraged by this study to point to new things in the baby's environment as part of their communication with their babies; thus, their children's education can begin in the crib.

Exercise 25.3

In the not-too-distant future, when airline passengers board their flights, they will be able to enjoy a number of new conveniences; such as choosing their snacks and drinks from on-board vending machines; selecting movies, TV programs, or video games from screens mounted on the seat in front of them; and making hotel and car-rental reservations from an on-board computer. Such features are what aircraft designers envision within the next five years for passenger jets. Their plans, though, may not be realized until much further in the future—if ever. But the ideas reflect the airline industry's hopes. If fare wars stop and ticket prices become similar, passengers may begin choosing different airlines on the basis of comfort, not cost; if that happens, airlines will have to be ready with new and better in-flight features. A Boeing Company executive says that "cabin environment will be a major factor;"; that is, designers must make the cabin so attractive that it will offset lower fares on other airlines. The problem, however, is added weight caused by some of the suggested features; such as; computers, video screens, and more elaborate kitchens. Added weight will mean that the plane consumes more fuel; thus driving up the price of the ticket. Still, some carriers, determined to find answers, are studying ways to

three
ans

use the new services to generate income'; particularly in the area

                          x

of commercial-supported or pay-as-you-use video entertainment.

Exercise 26.1

When the Apollo astronauts brought back bags of moon

rocks, it was expected that the rocks would provide some answers

to a perennial question; the origin of the moon. Instead, the

              x

Apollo's moon rocks suggested a number of new theories. One

that is gaining more supporters is called: the giant impact theory.

                                     x

Alan Smith, lunar scientist, offers an explanation of the giant

impact theory: "Recently acquired evidence suggests that the

moon was born of a monstrous collision between a primordial,

just-formed Earth and a protoplanet the size of Mars." This evi-

dence comes from modeling such a collision on powerful super-

computers. The theory proposes the following sequence of

events: (1) as Earth was forming, it was struck a glancing blow by

a projectile the size of Mars; (2) a jet of vapor then spurted out,

moving so fast that some of it escaped from Earth and the rest

condensed into pebble-sized rock fragments; and (3) gravita-

tional attraction fused this cloud of pebbles into the moon.

There are several reasons that make some scientists favor this

theory, such as it dovetails with what is known about the moon's

three
ans

chemistry and it explains why the moon's average composition resembles Earth. Another lunar scientist says, "We may be close to tracking down the real answer."

Exercise 27.1

Several years ago the nation's print and broadcast media joined with advertising agencies to launch a massive media campaign against drugs. Some, like ABC-TV, announced that they would donate prime time TV spots, but CBS Inc., while agreeing to cooperate, announced its intention to continue to commit funds for campaigns for other public issues such as AIDS prevention. James R. Daly, a spokesman for the antidrug campaign, said, "We were glad to see other companies joining in to help the campaign." For example, the Kodak Co. donated the film needed for TV spots, and in Washington, D.C., a group of concerned parents volunteered to do additional fund raising. In the first two years of this media campaign, more than $500 million was raised. Says Dr. Harrison Rublin, a leading spokesperson for one of the fund-raising groups, "One effective 30-second ad aired at 8 P.M. is ten times more effective than a hundred brochures on the subject."

Exercise 27.3

Oxford University has a chancellor, but members of the Oxford faculty wonder if anyone in the general public knows who the chancellor is. As the principal of one of the colleges said, "Does anyone care?" The post of chancellor at Oxford is mostly ceremonial, carrying very few responsibilities. One previous chancellor, Lord Curzon, did try to get involved with running the university but was soon discouraged from continuing such unseemly action. When Prime Minister Harold Macmillan was installed as chancellor, he delivered a speech in Latin saying that he was quite clear on the point that it was not one of his duties to run the university. He underscored his recognition of the heavy duties of his new job by wearing his cap backward throughout the whole proceedings. Many old Oxonians fear that they'll never see his lackadaisical like again. Is there anyone who can be trusted to keep a campaign promise when he or she says, "If elected, I won't stir things up"?

Exercise 27.5

At the end of winter when gardeners are depressed from the long months indoors, plant catalogs start flooding the mail. With their large type the catalogs blare out their news to hungry gardeners. "AMAZING!" "FANTASTIC!" "INCREDIBLE!" The covers always belong to some enormous new strain of tomatoes. "Bigger than Beefsteaks!" or "Too Big to Fit on This Page!" they yell. Even the blueberries are monsters. "Blueberries as big as quarters!" they promise. All you do, according to these enticing catalogs is "plant 'em and stand back!" On a gloomy February afternoon, many would-be gardeners are probably ready to believe that this year they too can have "ASPARAGUS THICKER THAN A PERSON'S THUMB!"

Exercise 28.1

Remember Silverton wine coolers? Silverton, like hundreds of other products that appeared in the same year, was pulled from the shelf after it failed to gain a market. "Silverton didn't seem to have any connotation as a cooler," explains G. F. Strousel, the company's vice-president in charge of sales. Every year new products appear briefly on the shelf and disappear, and established products that no longer have customer appeal are canceled as well. Either way, experts say, the signs that point to failure are the same. Companies looking to cut their losses pay attention to such signs. In a recent newspaper article entitled "Over 75% of Business Ideas Are Flops," T. M. Weir, a professor of marketing, explains that products that don't grow but maintain their percentage of the market are known as "cash cows," and those that are declining in growth and in market share are called "dipping dogs." Says Weir, "Marketers plot the growth and decline of products, especially of the dipping dogs, very closely." According to several sources at a New York research firm that studies new product development, the final decision to stop making a product is a financial one. When the red ink flows, the product is pulled.

Exercise 29.1

Because of her interest in the influence of the media on people's attitudes, Sarah chose as the topic for her research project the media's image of the Japanese during the last ten years. For source material Sarah began by reading news magazines such as

Time and *Newsweek,* but she soon found that news articles were less likely to portray attitudes than features in magazines such as *People* and *Fortune,* which have articles on sushi bars, Japanese electronics, and karate. The index to the *New York Times* also led her to articles such as "The Japanese Influence on American Business" and "Japanese Technology in America." Sarah also read reviews of old television programs, including the short-lived series *Ohara,* which featured a Japanese-American detective, and old movies, such as *The Karate Kid.* Sarah rapidly found herself buried under mounds of notes and decided to limit her topic to one of the media, though she couldn't decide which one.

Exercise 30.1

For health-conscious people who cringe at the thought of using a toothpaste with preservatives and dyes, there are now alternative toothpastes made entirely from plants. One brand of these new, all-natural toothpastes advertises that its paste includes twenty-nine different herbs, root and flower extracts, and seaweed. Some of these toothpastes have a pleasant taste and appearance, but the owner of a San Francisco health-food store decided not to carry one brand because it is a reddish-brown paste. "When squeezed from a tube, it resembles a fat earthworm," she explained. She prefers a brand made of propolis, the sticky stuff bees use to line their hives, and myrrh. Another brand, a black paste made of charred eggplant powder, clay, and seaweed, is favored by the hard-core macrobiotic crowd. This interest in natural toothpastes may be cyclical, explains the director of an oral health institute. He recalls a gray-striped, mint-flavored paste from the Philippines that sought to capitalize on a spurt of interest several years ago. It was a big seller for awhile and then disappeared.

Exercise 31.1

Businesspeople, laborers, children, private clubs, and senior citizens—these are some of the groups who have parade floats in New Orleans' Mardi Gras. Every year more than fifty different parading organizations trundle their floats through the streets. All kinds of difficulties have to be anticipated—including rain, tipsy float riders who will fall off, and mechanical failures in the tractor engines pulling the floats—and have to be overcome.

three
ans

Rain can slow the parade—but not stop it. Too much money, time, and dedication go into parade preparation to let anything prevent it—or so the parade organizers say.

Exercise 34.2

The last two lines of Archibald MacLeish's poem "Ars Poetica" (written in 1924) are often quoted as his theory of poetry. "A poem should not mean / But be," he wrote. In his notebooks, he expanded on this statement: "The purpose of the expression of emotion in a poem is not to recreate the poet's emotion in someone else…. The poem itself is a finality, an end, a creation." G. T. Hardison, in his analysis of MacLeish's theory of poetry ("The Non-Meaning of Poetry," *Modern Poetics* 27 [1981]: 45), explains that "when MacLeish says the poem 'is a finality, an ending [*sic*],' he means that a good poem is self-sufficient; it is, it does not mean something else. One might as well ask the meaning of a friend or brother."

Exercise 36.1

1. Every Spring when the Madison Avenue advertisers compete for Clio Awards for the best commercials, my cousin Bert makes bets on who will win.
2. At the Dallas-Fort Worth International Airport, the Pan-Am plane landed with a cargo of Dutch cigars and African diamonds.
3. When Marta signed up for an advanced course in psychology, she was already familiar with Freudian psychology and various twentieth-century views on dream interpretation.
4. Floyd Martin, a Washington, D.C., physician, has recently completed his study of the effects of asthma as his contribution to a task force convened by the National Institutes of Health.
5. When Aleen drove south from Minnesota to Tennessee, she wondered whether "every restaurant, including McDonald's, would serve grits."

Exercise 37.1

Some forms of illegal fishing are hard to define. For example, "noodling," the practice of catching fish by snagging them in the gills or flesh, is illegal in most places in the United States. However, in a recent case, a man who had caught two fish, weigh-

three ans

ing <u>twenty-five</u> and <u>thirty-one pounds</u>, in a Texas lake, argued that he wasn't noodling when he dived under water with a fishing pole <u>and</u> a very short line. This was not noodling, he claimed, because he poked his rod <u>and</u> baited hook into catfish nets instead of dragging his lines through the water to snag fish the way noodlers do. The local game warden charged the angler with noodling, a misdemeanor that carries a fine of up to $250. Residents of the area, near Cloud Creek Lake, <u>Texas</u>, agreed that he was fishing illegally. But, after much debate, the man won his claim that while his unusual method was very close to noodling, he was innocent.

three
ans

4

Spelling

English spelling can be difficult because many words in English have been imported from other languages that have different spelling conventions. But despite the difficulty, it is important to spell correctly. Some misspelled words can cause confusion in the reader's mind (for example, writing *preform* when the word *perform* is meant), but any misspelled word can send a signal to the reader that the writer is a person who is either careless or not very knowledgeable. Since no writer wants to lose credibility, correct spelling is important.

Some people shrug off work on spelling because they expect to rely on someone else—or the spell-checker on their computers—to correct misspellings. But these resources are not always available when we need them. So it is wise to spend some time on spelling, doing one or more of the following:

- **Learn some spelling rules.**
- **Make up your own rules.**
  - Think up some rules or letter associations that will help you remember particularly troublesome words.

- **Learn your own misspelling patterns.**
- **Learn how to proofread.**

This Part covers the following topics related to spelling:

39 *Proofreading* (sp)

Proofreading means carefully reading your final written work to ensure that it is free from misspellings and typographical errors.

Like editing (the rereading that is done with last drafts to catch grammatical errors), proofreading is best done after you are finished writing and are preparing to turn your paper over to your readers.

Here are some useful proofreading strategies:

Slow down. Proofreading requires slowing down your eye movement to see *all* the letters in each word. This is unlike normal reading when your eyes skip across the line and notice only groups of words.

Focus on each word. One very helpful way to slow yourself down is to point a pencil or pen at each word as you say it aloud or to yourself.

Read backward. Don't read left to right as you would normally do because you will soon slip back into a more rapid reading rate. Instead, move backward through each line from right to left. In this way, you won't be listening for meaning or checking for grammatical correctness.

Cover up any distractions. To focus on each word so that you can see it more completely, hold a sheet of paper or a note card under the line being read. This way you won't be distracted by other words on the page.

Watch for your patterns of misspellings. Remember to look for those groups or patterns of misspellings that occur most frequently in your writing.

Read forward. End-to-beginning proofreading will not catch problems with omitted words or sound-alike words. To check for those, you need to do a second proofreading moving forward, from left to right, so that you can watch the meaning of your sentences. Listen for each word as you read aloud or to yourself.

Exercise 39.1: Proofreading Practice

Practice the proofreading strategies described in Chapter 39 by proofreading the following paragraph, which has a number of typos and misspellings and some omitted words. First, read each line in the paragraph very slowly from the end of the line to the beginning. It should take you at least ten seconds to read each line this way. Underline each word that is spelled incorrectly, and correct the spelling. Then, when you are done, read each line from beginning to end (left to right) very slowly, again allowing at least ten seconds per line, to look for omitted words. Write in above the line any word or words that are missing.

**39
sp**

Turkish people do'nt think of St. Nicholas as having reindeer or elfs, living at North Pole, or climbing down chimneys with gifts on Christmass Eve. Accept for a twist of history, Santa Claus might well speak Turkish, ride a camel, dress for a warmmer climate, bring gifts of oranges and tomatoes, and appear on December 5 instead of Christmas Eve. According to the story of the Turkish church about his backround, Nicholas was the frist bishop of Myra, on the coast Turkey. Turkish scholars say he was known far and wide for his peity and charity. He was killed around A.D. 245, and after his martyrdom, on December 6, tails of his good deeds lived on. His faime was so great that in the eleventh centruy when the Italian branch of the Catholic church began a drive to bring to Italy the remains of the most famous saints, theives stole most of Nicholas's bones from the church tomb in Turkey and took them to a town in southren Italy. Nicholas was abbreviated to Claus, and St. Nick became Santa. Since there are no docuiments or records of the original Nicholas of Myra, some sholars doubt his existance. But others are convinced there really was a St. Nicholas, even if he didn't have reindeer or live at North Pole.

40 *IE/EI* (sp)

> Write *i* before *e*
> Except after *c*
> Or when sounded like *ay*
> As in *neighbor* and *weigh.*

This rhyme may help you remember the rules for using *ie* and *ei* correctly.

As the rule says, you should generally write *ie*, except under two conditions: (1) when the two letters follow a *c* and (2) when the two letters sound like *ay* (as in day).

Some *ie* words: believe, chief, field, grief, niece, relief, yield
Some *ei* words: ceiling, conceit, deceive, eight, receive, vein

> **HINT:** The major exceptions to this rule are the following words:
>
> | | | |
> |---|---|---|
> | conscience | forfeit | seize |
> | counterfeit | height | sheik |
> | either | leisure | species |
> | financier | neither | sufficient |
> | foreign | science | weird |

Exercise 40.1: Proofreading Practice

*Spell these words correctly by writing **ie** or **ei** in the blanks.*

1. There are _____ght candles on the cake.
2. I have not rec _____ved a letter from her.
3. Her n _____ce is coming to visit next week.
4. Drop that silver, you th _____f!
5. She is not a conc _____ted person, despite her beauty.
6. The ch _____f of the tribe led the dancing.
7. May I have a p _____ce of cheese?
8. The fr _____ght train woke the n _____ghbors.
9. He wanted n _____ther the pants nor the shirt the salesperson showed him.
10. I bel _____ve that I already returned that to you.
11. There was a spider web hanging from the c _____ling.
12. What did you w _____gh before your diet?
13. I'll need a rec _____pt for this purchase.
14. The f _____ld of wheat waved in the wind.
15. The dollar bill was obviously a counterf _____t.

41 Doubling Consonants (sp)

There are a few rules about doubling the last consonant of the base word that will help you spell several thousand words correctly.

41a Doubling Consonants in One-Syllable Words

If the word ends in a consonant, preceded by a single vowel, double that last consonant when you are adding a suffix beginning with a vowel.

drag	dragged	dragging	
flip	flipped	flipping	flipper
nap	napped	napping	
shop	shopped	shopping	shopper
slip	slipped	slipping	slipper
star	starred	starring	
tap	tapped	tapping	
wet	wetted	wetting	wettest

Note that in one-syllable words with two vowels, you do not double the last consonant:

beat		beating	beater
foot	footed	footing	
look	looked	looking	
lock	locked	locking	locker

Note also that when one-syllable words end in final -*e* instead of a consonant, you do not double the consonant:

hope	hoped	hoping
stare	stared	staring
tape	taped	taping

Note also that you don't double the last consonant when adding a suffix that starts with a consonant:

star   starless

41b Doubling Consonants in Two-Syllable Words

For words with two or more syllables that end with a consonant preceded by a single vowel, double the consonant when both of these conditions apply:

1. You are adding a suffix beginning with a vowel.
2. The last syllable of the word is accented.

begin		beginning	beginner
occur	occurred	occurring	occurrence
omit	omitted	omitting	
prefer	preferred	preferring	
refer	referred	referring	
regret	regretted	regretting	regrettable
submit	submitted	submitting	
unwrap	unwrapped	unwrapping	

Note that when the last syllable of a two-syllable word is not stressed, the final consonant is not doubled:

labor	labored	laboring

Exercise 41.1: Proofreading Practice

Underline the words that are misspelled in the following paragraph, and write the correct spelling above the word.

Last week Michael planed to have his bicycle repaired, though he admitted that he was hopping he had stopped the leak in the front tire with a patch. Even though he concealled the patch with some heavy tape, he found that he had to keep tapping the patch back on the tire. Yesterday, when Michael looked at the bicycle on the way to his first class, he could see that the front tire had become flatter than it should be because it was lossing air. With no time to spare, he jogged off to class, resolved that he would take the bicycle to a shop that afternoon.

42
sp

42 *Prefixes* (sp)

A **prefix** is a word part added at the beginning of a base word. Knowing prefixes helps to improve both your vocabulary and your spelling.

Some common prefixes are the following:

Prefix	Meaning	Examples
ante-	before	anteroom
anti-	against	antidote, antiliberal
auto-	self	automobile
bene-	good	benefit
bi-	two, twice	bicycle, biweekly
bio-	life	biography, biology
de-	away, down	depress
dis-	not, no longer, away	disappear
ex-	out, no longer	exclude, expel, ex-wife
im-	in, not	immense, immodest
in-	in, not	inflow, incorrect
inter-	between, among	interact, interstate
intra-	within, between members of the same group	intramural, intrastate
mis-	wrong, bad	misspell, misdeed
per-	entirely, through	perfect, pertain
post-	after	postgame, postdate
pre-	before	pregame, prefix
pro-	for, take place of	prohibit, proslavery, proclaim
re-	again, back	retell, redo, readmit
semi-	half, partially	semicircle, semiautomatic
un-	not, contrary to	unhappy, unable

42 sp

HINT: Don't double letters when prefixes are added to words. However, a double consonant is needed when a prefix ends with the same letter as the beginning of the word. Be sure to write the whole prefix before writing the base word. (For rules on doubling before suffixes, see Chapter 41.)

Incorrect	Correct
disatisfied	dissatisfied (dis/satisfied)
mispelling	misspelling (mis/spelling)
tommorrow	tomorrow (to/morrow)

Exercise 41.1. Pattern Practice

Using your dictionary, look up three examples of words that include the prefixes listed here:

1. ante-
2. anti-
3. auto-
4. bene-
5. bio-
6. de-
7. dis-
8. ex-
9. im-
10. in-
11. inter-
12. intra-
13. mis-
14. per-
15. post-
16. pre-
17. pro-
18. re-
19. semi-
20. un-

43 *Suffixes*

A **suffix** is a word-part added to the end of the word. Although the prefix does not change the spelling of the base word, some changes do occur when suffixes are added to base words.

43a sp

43a *Suffixes with Words Ending in -e*

If the word ends in *-e* and the suffix begins with a vowel (for example, *-able, -ary, -ing,* and *-ous*), drop the *-e.*

age	aging
desire	desirable
fame	famous
imagine	imaginary
use	usable

Exception: To keep the "ess" sound of *-ce* and the "je" sound of *-ge,* don't drop the final *-e* before *-able* or *-ous:*

change	changeable
courage	courageous

knowledge	knowledgeable
marriage	marriageable
notice	noticeable

There are also a few exceptions for other words in which the *-e* is kept in the word before a suffix starting with a vowel:

acre	acreage
mile	mileage

If the word ends in *-e* and the suffix begins with a consonant (for example, *-less, -ly, -ment, -ness, -some*), keep the *-e.*

care	careful
entire	entirely
name	nameless
safe	safety
same	sameness
state	statement
whole	wholesome

**43b
sp**

Exception: There are some words in which the *-e* is dropped before a suffix starting with a consonant:

argue	argument
awe	awful
nine	ninth
true	truly

43b The -ly Suffix

If a word ends in *-l,* don't drop that *-l* when adding the suffix *-ly:*

formal	formally
real	really
usual	usually

But if the word already ends with two *-l's,* merely add the *-y* of the *-ly* suffix:

chill	chilly
hill	hilly

43c *Suffixes with Words Ending in -ic*

When a word ends in *-ic*, add a *-k* before suffixes starting with *-i*, *-e*, or *-y:*

picnic	picnicking
politic	politicking
traffic	trafficking

Some words that end in *-ic* add the suffix *-ally*, not *-ly:*

logic	logically
tragic	tragically

Exercise 43.1: Pattern Practice

Using your dictionary to check the correct spelling, add the suffixes to the words listed here:

1. *-ing:*   rise, guide, come
2. *-ly:*   like, sure, true
3. *-ful:*   care, use, stress
4. *-ous:*   continue, courage, nerve
5. *-able:*   desire, notice, knowledge

**44
sp**

44 *Y to I* (sp)

When adding a suffix to words that end with *-y*, change the *-y* to an *-i*. But to avoid a double *i* in a word, keep the *-y* before the *-ing* suffix.

apply	applies, applied	(but) applying
carry	carries, carried	(but) carrying
study	studies, studied	(but) studying
apology	apologies	
beauty	beautiful	
ceremony	ceremonious	
busy	busied, business	
easy	easily, easiness	
happy	happily, happiness	

Exception: If there is a vowel before the final *-y*, keep the *-y* before adding *-s* or *-ed:*

stay	stays, stayed
enjoy	enjoys, enjoyed
day	days
attorney	attorneys
key	keys

Exercise 44.1: Pattern Practice

Using your dictionary to check the correct spelling, add the suffixes in parentheses to the words listed here:

1. tray + (-s)
2. apology + (-s)
3. ally + (-ed)
4. steady + (-ing)
5. accompany + (-ing)
6. study + (-ing)
7. lonely + (-ness)
8. vary + (-ed)
9. ninety + (-eth)
10. mercy + (-ful)
11. funny + (-er)
12. monkey + (-s)
13. bury + (-al)
14. likely + (-er)
15. story + (-s)
16. employ + (-er)
17. study + (-ous)
18. pretty + (-ness)

45 *Plurals* (sp)

There are seven major ways to form plurals of words.

45a Forming Plurals of Most Words

(See also Chapter 2a.) The plurals of most words are formed by adding *-s* to the singular form

one boy	two boys
one wall	three walls
a shoe	a pair of shoes
the page	two pages
one ribbon	six ribbons
Mr. Herron	all the Herrons
Mrs. Smith	the Smiths

For phrases and hyphenated words, pluralize the last word unless another word is more important:

one videocassette recorder	two videocassette recorders
one systems analyst	two systems analysts
one sister-in-law	two sisters-in-law

When words end in *-s, -sh, -ch, -x,* or *-z,* add *-es* for the plural form (because an extra syllable is needed):

one box	five boxes
a loss	some losses
the church	several churches
a buzz	two buzzes
a brush	a pair of brushes

45b Plurals of Words Ending in -f or -fe

For some words that end in *-f* or *-fe,* change the *-f* to *-ve* and add *-s*

one thief	six thieves
a leaf	some leaves
a wife	several wives
one life	their lives

For other words that end in *-f,* add *-s* without making any change in the base word:

a roof	two roofs
his belief	their beliefs
the chief	two chiefs
one sheriff	all of the sheriffs

45c
sp

45c Plurals of Words Ending in -y

For words ending in a consonant plus *-y,* change the *y* to *i* and add *-es:*

one company	four companies
one candy	some candies

For words ending in a vowel plus -*y*, add an *s:*

one boy	several boys
a monkey	two monkeys

45d Plurals of Words Ending in -o

For words ending in a vowel plus -*o*, add an -*s:*

one radio	several radios
one patio	two patios

For words ending in a consonant plus -*o*, add an -*s* for some plurals, an -*es* for other plurals, and either -*s* or -*es* for still other plurals:

-s only	-es only	either -s or -es
autos	echoes	zeros -or- zeroes
memos	heroes	cargos -or- cargoes
pianos	potatoes	

45e Words with Irregular Plurals

For some words, the plural is formed by changing the base word:

one child	several children
one woman	two women
one goose	nine geese
one mouse	some mice

45f Words with No Separate Plural Forms

Some words have the same form for both singular and plural:

deer   sheep
pliers   wheat
rice

45g Plurals of Foreign Words

Some words from other languages keep their original plural endings:

for men: one alumnus	some alumni
for women: one alumna	several alumnae
one antenna	two antennae
an appendix	three appendices
a basis	some bases
a criterion	some criteria
a crisis	two crises
one piece of datum	several pieces of data
a medium	all the media
one memorandum	two memoranda
a phenomenon	some phenomena
one psychosis	many psychoses
one radius	two radii
a thesis	several theses

45g
sp

Some of these words are beginning to acquire an English plural, such as *antennas* and *memorandums*.

Exercise 45.1: Proofreading Practice
Which of the following words has an incorrectly spelled plural? Use your dictionary if needed.

1. foxs
2. papers
3. companys
4. latchs
5. analyses
6. womans
7. passer-bys
8. attorneys
9. stereos
10. tariffs
11. brother-in-laws
12. bushes
13. windows
14. heroes
15. freshmans

46 *Sound-alike Words (Homonyms)* (sp)

English has a number of words that sound alike but are spelled differently and have different meanings. These are called **homonyms.**

Here are the most commonly misspelled sound-alike words:

accept (a verb meaning *to agree, to receive*): She accepted the gift.

except (a preposition meaning *all but, other than*): Everyone danced except Tom.

affect (a verb meaning *to influence*): Lack of sleep affects his performance.

effect (a noun meaning *result*): What effect does that medicine have?

> commonly used phrases:
> in effect   take effect   to that effect

effect (a verb meaning *to accomplish*): to effect a cure

hear (a verb): Did you hear that?

here (indicates a place): over here

its (shows possession): its leg

it's (is a contraction): it is

passed (verb): The time passed by.

past (adjective meaning *before the present*): this past week

than (word used in comparisons): She is richer than I.

then (a time word): Then he went home.

their (shows possession): their books

there (indicates a place): over there

they're (a contraction): they are

to (a preposition): to the store

too (adverb meaning *also, very*): too tired, too bad

were (verb): They were singing.

we're (contraction): we are

where (in what place): Where is he?

who's (contraction): Who's going to the game?

whose (shows possession or means *of which, of whom*): whose book, the family whose house I admired

your (shows possession): your hat
you're (a contraction): you are

Here are other commonly misspelled sound-alike words:

advice (noun meaning a *recommendation* or *piece of information*): That was good advice.
advise (verb meaning *to give advice* or *recommend*): I advise caution.
angel (noun meaning a *heavenly being* or *good person*): She drew a picture of angels wearing white robes.
angle (noun meaning *the space between two lines*): a sharp angle
bare (adjective meaning *nude, plain*): the bare tree
bear (verb meaning *to carry;* noun naming the animal): bear a burden, a big brown bear
buy (verb meaning *to purchase*): buy some tapes
by (preposition meaning *next to, through*): by the side of the road
cite (verb meaning *to point out*): She cited the traffic code rule
sight (noun meaning *vision*): The dawn was a lovely sight.
site (noun meaning *place*): The site of the construction was moved.
council (noun meaning an *organizing or governing group*): The town council voted on the bill.
counsel (noun meaning *advice, suggestions;* verb meaning *to give advice*): He offered wise counsel. He counseled her to quit her job.
desert (noun meaning *dry, arid place;* verb meaning *to abandon*): They explored the Mojave Desert. They deserted their friends when danger appeared.
dessert (noun meaning *sweet course at the end of a meal*): They ordered cherry pie for dessert.
forth (adverb meaning *forward*): from this day forth
fourth (adjective meaning *next after third*): the fourth inning
hole (noun meaning *opening*): a deep hole in the ground
whole (adjective meaning *complete*): the whole story
knew (past tense form of the verb *know*): He knew the name but couldn't spell it.
new (adjective meaning *not existing before*): That was a new melody.
know (verb meaning *to have in one's mind, to learn*): Do you know the answer?
no (adjective meaning *not any*): no more money

**46
sp**

peace (noun meaning *calm, free from war*): They all wished for peace.

piece (noun meaning *part of a whole*): piece of pie

quiet (adjective meaning *no sound or noise*): a quiet time

quit (verb meaning *to give up, abandon*): He quit working on it.

quite (adverb meaning *very, entirely*): quite nice

stationary (adjective meaning *not moving*): The bird remained stationary.

stationery (noun meaning *writing paper*): She always used gray stationery.

weather (noun meaning *the condition of the atmosphere or climate*): stormy weather

whether (conjunction meaning *if*): whether or not it rains

There are also many single and two-word phrases that sound alike but have different meanings.

all ready (adjective expressing complete readiness): Finally, the whole family was all ready to leave.

already (adverb expressing time): Everyone had already left.

all right (adverb meaning *satisfactorily*): They were all right on their own without a guide.

alright: common misspelling for *all right* (However, a few dictionaries accept this as an alternate spelling.)

all together (adverb meaning *in a group*): The students were all together in the cafeteria.

altogether (adverb meaning *thoroughly*): Her actions were altogether unnecessary.

any body (phrase referring to any person or thing): Any body of water in the park is safe to swim in.

anybody (pronoun referring to any person): Has anybody seen my glasses?

any more (phrase referring to one or more items): Are there any more potato chips?

anymore (adverb meaning *now, henceforth*): I don't want to see her anymore.

any one (phrase referring to a specific person or thing): Any one of those newspapers will have the story.

anyone (a pronoun meaning *any person at all*): Can anyone hear me?

any time (phrase referring to a time): I can make the appointment for any time that is convenient.

anytime (adverb meaning *at any time*): Anytime tomorrow is fine.

any way (adverb meaning *any course or direction*): Any way will lead back to town.

anyway (adverb meaning *in any case*): She objected, but he went anyway.

a while (an article and a noun meaning *a period of time*): It will take a while to finish this.

awhile (adverb meaning *for a short while*): I can only stay for awhile.

every body (a phrase referring to a specific person or thing): Every body he examined was listed on the chart.

everybody (pronoun meaning *every person*): Is everybody here?

every day (adjective and a noun referring to *each day*): Every day last week it rained.

everyday (adjective meaning *daily*): I take the bus everyday.

every one (phrase referring to a specific person or thing): Every one of the bottles was cracked.

everyone (pronoun meaning *everybody*): He bought everyone a drink.

in to (two prepositions): He came in to get his hat.

into (preposition meaning *to the inside of*): It fell into the river.

may be (a verb form): They may be late.

maybe (adverb meaning *perhaps*): Maybe we should wait.

some body (phrase referring to an unspecified person or thing): Some body of data was lost.

somebody (pronoun referring to an unspecified person): Has somebody moved this bookcase?

some one (phrase referring to an unspecified person or thing): Some one of these pearls should match the ones on your necklace.

someone (pronoun referring to an unspecified person): Someone can pick up the package for me.

> **46**
> **sp**

Some words have different spellings in the noun and verb forms:

Noun	*Verb*
advice	advise
breath	breathe
choice	choose
device	devise

envelope	envelop
past	passed

Nouns with *-nce* and *-nts* endings sound the same but are spelled differently.

assistance (help): I needed her assistance in completing the form.
assistants (helpers): The potter trained his assistants.
patience (perseverance): That hobby needed patience.
patients (people receiving treatment by doctors and dentists): The doctor kept her patients waiting for more than an hour.

Exercise 46.1: Proofreading Practice

Select the correctly spelled word for each of the following sentences.

1. The weather always (affects, effects) my moods.
2. She was (to, too) tired to join in.
3. It was a (quite, quiet) summer evening.
4. Would (anyone, any one) of these shirts be acceptable?
5. I need another (envelop, envelope) for these letters.
6. Her tardiness was an (every day, everyday) occurrence.
7. The coach offered some useful (advice, advise).
8. It seemed that (any way, anyway) he threw the hoop it landed on the rung.
9. It is always cooler in the woods (than, then) in the city.
10. I often drive (by, buy) the Smiths' house.
11. When (it's, its) snowing, the street sounds seem muffled.
12. The table remained (stationary, stationery) when the wind shook the room.
13. When the teacher asked a question, the students answered (all together, altogether).
14. The dictionary (maybe, may be) helpful in deciding which word you want.
15. Whenever the train (passed, past) the station, the conductor waved to the stationmaster.
16. The salesclerk asked his supervisor for some (assistants, assistance) with the computer.
17. The committee agreed that it was (alright, all right) to table the motion being discussed.
18. The football game was nearing the end of the (forth, fourth) quarter.

46
sp

19. The teacher asked everyone to (sight, cite, site) all the sources used in the term paper.

20. What does (there, their, they're) car horn sound like?

47 Using the Dictionary (dict)

Because your dictionary helps you learn both the meaning and spelling of words, spend some time reading the introduction and learning how to use this helpful tool.

The entries for each word will indicate some or all of the following:

- Syllables (to help you hyphenate)
- Pronunciation
- Part of speech
- Various forms of the word, such as irregular tenses for verbs and irregular plurals for nouns (regular forms are not included)
- Origins of the word
- Various meanings
- Phrases and idioms using the word
- List of related words (synonyms)
- Words with opposite meanings (antonyms)

47
dict

Note all the information given in the following example from the Second College Edition of the *Webster's New World Dictionary of the American Language* (1986):

for•get (f ə r get′, fôr-) *vt.* **-got′** or archaic **gat′**, **-got′ten** or **-got′**, **-get′ting** [ME. *forgeten* < OE. *forgitan* (akin to G. *vergessen*): see FOR- & GET] **1.** to lose (facts, knowledge, etc.) from the mind; fail to recall; be unable to remember **2.** to fail to do, bring, etc. as because of carelessness; overlook, omit, or neglect unintentionally [don't *forget* to write] **3.** to overlook, omit, or neglect intentionally [let's *forget* our differences] —*vi.* to forget things; be forgetful —*SYN.* see NEGLECT — ☆ **forget it** don't trouble to think about or mention it —**forget oneself 1.** to think only of others; be altruistic or unselfish **2.** to behave in an improper or unseemly manner —**for•get′ta•ble** *adj.* —**for•get′ter** *n.*

This entry for *forget* includes the following information.

Spelling: The entry begins with the correct spelling of the base word and indicates the syllables by separating them with dots. Words that are hyphenated have hyphens, not dots, in the appropriate places.

Pronunciation: The next entry, in parentheses, indicates the pronunciation. Two acceptable pronunciations are given for the first syllable, and as with any word of more than one syllable, the pronunciation guide also indicates which syllable to accent.

Part of speech: The *vt* indicates that the word is a verb (v) and is transitive (t), meaning that it takes a direct object. A definition near the end of the entry indicates that *forget* also has an intransitive (vi) meaning, "to forget things, be forgetful," which does not take a direct object.

Various forms: Other forms of the word are included because they are irregular. Dictionaries include entries for verbs with irregular forms in other tenses and also for nouns with irregular plurals.

Origins: The next entry, in brackets, gives information on the origins of the word in Middle English, as derived from Old English, and the related form in German.

Meanings: The next entries are different definitions for the word with accompanying phrases illustrating each definition.

Related words: The entry for SYN. (the abbreviation for *synonym,* meaning a word with similar meaning) has one possible synonym, *neglect.* Dictionaries also include entries for *antonyms,* words with opposite meanings. Following the synonym in this entry for *forget* are several phrases that include the word and their definitions. At the end of the entry are the correct spellings for the adjective and noun forms of the word.

In entries for other words you may note labels that indicate the difference in British and American spellings (for example, the British form *realise* and the American form *realize*); labels that indicate out-of-date, informal, and slang definitions; and variations in spelling. If two spellings appear separated by a slash mark (for example, *hijacker/highjacker*), either is acceptable, though the first one is usually the more common or preferred one. When words are broken into syllables, be careful to distinguish between dots used to indicate syllabification and hyphens used to indicate hyphenated words.

Exercise 47.1: Dictionary Practice

Spend a few minutes reading the introduction to your dictionary, and then use the dictionary to answer the following questions. Your diction-ary's answers may differ slightly from the suggested answers given in the answer key, which are based on entries in the Second College Edition of Webster's New World Dictionary of the American Language.

1. What are some synonyms and antonyms for the following words?
   a. begin
   b. big
   c. new
2. What are some short phrases using the word *walk* and what do these phrases mean?
3. Use your dictionary to find the syllables of the following words. Write the word so that you indicate the syllables.

   photographic   pho•to•graph•ic

   a. goggle
   b. honorable
   c. metallurgy
   d. humidity
   e. presentation
4. What are the past tense, participle, and *-ing* forms of the fol-lowing verbs?
   a. break
   b. lay
   c. swim
   d. take
   e. tread
5. Suppose you weren't sure whether you should write "The river has swelled over its banks" or "The river has swollen over its banks." What does your dictionary say?
6. Suppose you were not sure of the plural form for each of these nouns. What does your dictionary say?
   a. lady-in-waiting
   b. sweepstakes
   c. corona
   d. phenomenon
   e. sheep

47
dict

7. What does your dictionary say is the origin of the word *maverick?*
8. In your dictionary, what is the difference between the labels *slang* and *colloquial?* Browse through the dictionary and try to find an example of a word labeled *slang* and a word labeled *colloquial.*
9. What does your dictionary list as the *-ing* form of the verb *tie?*
10. Suppose you were writing about vitamins and wanted the adjective form of the word. What does your dictionary list for this?

Answer Key for Exercises in Part 4

Exercise 39.1

Turkish people <u>don't</u> think of St. Nicholas as having reindeer or <u>elves</u>, living at the North Pole, or climbing down chimneys with gifts on <u>Christmas</u> Eve. <u>Except</u> for a twist of history, Santa Claus might well speak Turkish, ride a camel, dress for a <u>warmer</u> climate, bring gifts of oranges and tomatoes, and appear on December 5 instead of Christmas Eve. According to the story of the Turkish church about his <u>background</u>, Nicholas was the <u>first</u> bishop of Myra, on the coast of Turkey. Turkish scholars say he was known far and wide for his <u>piety</u> and charity. He was killed around A.D. 245, and after his martyrdom, on December 6, <u>tales</u> of his good deeds lived on. His <u>fame</u> was so great that in the eleventh <u>century</u> when the Italian branch of the Catholic church began a drive to bring to Italy the remains of the most famous

four
ans

saints, <u>thieves</u> stole most of Nicholas's bones from the church tomb in Turkey and took them to a town in <u>southern</u> Italy. Nicholas was abbreviated to Claus, and St. Nick became Santa. Since there are no <u>documents</u> or records of the original Nicholas of Myra, some <u>scholars</u> doubt his <u>existence</u>. But others are convinced there really was a St. Nicholas, even if he didn't have reindeer or live at the North Pole.

Exercise 40.1

1. eight	9. neither
2. received	10. believe
3. niece	11. ceiling
4. thief	12. weigh
5. conceited	13. receipt
6. chief	14. field
7. piece	15. counterfeit
8. freight, neighbors	

Exercise 41.1

Last week Michael <u>planned</u> to have his bicycle repaired, though he admitted that he was <u>hoping</u> he had stopped the leak in the front tire with a patch. Even though he <u>concealed</u> the patch with some heavy tape, he found that he had to keep <u>taping</u> the patch back on the tire. Yesterday, when Michael looked at the bicycle on the way to his first class, he could see that the front tire had become flatter than it should be because it was <u>losing</u> air. With no time to spare, he <u>jogged</u> off to class, resolved that he would take the bicycle to a shop that afternoon.

Exercise 43.1

1. rising, guiding, coming
2. likely, surely, truly
3. careful, useful, stressful

4. continuous, courageous, nervous
5. desirable, noticeable, knowledgeable

Exercise 44.1

1. trays
2. apologies
3. allied
4. steadying
5. accompanying
6. studying
7. loneliness
8. varied
9. ninetieth
10. merciful
11. funnier
12. monkeys
13. burial
14. likelier
15. stories
16. employer
17. studious
18. prettiness

Exercise 45.1

1, 3, 4, 6, 7, 9, 11, 15

Exercise 46.1

1. affects
2. too
3. quiet
4. any one
5. envelope
6. everyday
7. advice
8. any way
9. than
10. by
11. it's
12. stationary
13. all together
14. may be
15. passed
16. assistance
17. all right
18. fourth
19. cite
20. their

Exercise 47.1

1. **a.** begin
   synonyms: commence, start, initiate, inaugurate
   antonyms: end, finish, conclude
   b. big
   synonyms: large, great
   antonyms: small, little
   c. new
   synonyms: fresh, novel, modern and modernistic, original
   antonym: old

2. walk: walk all over [colloquial] 1. to defeat overwhelmingly
   2. to treat in a domineering, unfeeling way
   walk away from: outdistance easily; defeat handily

> walk away with: 1. to steal 2. to win easily
>
> walk off: 1. to go away, esp. without warning 2. to get rid of by walking [*to walk off* pounds]
>
> walk off with: 1. to steal 2. to win (a contest) or gain (a prize), esp. easily
>
> walk out on: [colloquial] to leave; desert; abandon
>
> walk through: to carry out a walk-through, as in a play rehearsal
>
> walk with God: to lead a godly, morally upright life

3. **a.** gog•gle
   b. hon•or•a•ble
   c. met•al•lur•gy
   d. hu•mid•i•ty
   e. pre•sen•ta•tion

4. **a.** break: broke, broken, breaking
   b. lay: laid, laid, laying
   c. swim: swam, swum, swimming
   d. take: took, taken, taking
   e. tread: trod, trodden or trod, treading

5. Either form (*swelled* or *swollen*) is acceptable as the participle.

6. **a.** ladies-in-waiting
   b. sweepstakes
   c. coronas or coronae
   d. phenomena
   e. sheep

7. maverick: After Samuel *Maverick* (1803-70), Texas rancher who did not brand his cattle.

8. Slang: The term or sense is not generally regarded as conventional or standard usage but is used, even by the best speakers, in highly informal contexts. Slang consists of both coined terms and of new or extended meanings attached to established terms. Slang terms either pass into disuse in time or come to have a more formal status.

   Slang: gobbledygook

   Colloquial: The term or sense is generally characteristic of conversational and informal writing. It is not to be regarded

four
ans

as substandard or illiterate.

Colloquial: kid (meaning a small child)

9. tying

10. vitaminic

5

Style and Word Choice

This Part reviews suggestions for choosing the right or most appropriate words and phrases. Included are the following topics:

48. Sexist Language
  a. Alternatives to *Man*
  b. Alternative Job Titles
  c. Alternatives to the Male Pronoun
49. Unnecessary Words
  a. Conciseness
  b. Clichés
  c. Pretentious Language
50. Appropriate Words
  a. Standard English
  b. Colloquialisms, Slang, and Regionalisms
  c. Levels of Formality
  d. Jargon and Technical Terms
  e. Idioms
  f. General and Specific Words
  g. Concrete and Abstract Words
  h. Denotation and Connotation

48 Sexist Language (sexist)

In order to avoid language that either favors the male noun or pronoun or excludes females, consider the following guidelines and suggestions.

48a Alternatives to Man

Man originally referred in a general way to both males and females, but the meaning of the word has become closely associated with adult males only. To avoid this use of *man*, use alternative terms.

Man	*Alternative*
man	person, individual
mankind	people, human beings, humanity
manpower	personnel
the man in the street	the average person
man-made	machine made, synthetic
the common man	the average (or ordinary) person
to man	to operate

48b Alternative Job Titles

Many terms for jobs suggest that only men hold or can hold those jobs. To avoid this, try an alternative term.

Man	*Alternative*
chairman	chairperson, chair, coordinator
foreman	supervisor
mailman	mail carrier, postal worker
fireman	fire fighter
policeman	police officer
congressman	congressional representative
steward, stewardess	flight attendant

**48c
sexist**

48c Alternatives to the Male Pronoun

(See Chapters 3b, 17a.)

Instead of using the pronoun *he* in a general sense to refer back to a noun (the average person . . . he), use an alternative term.

- Use the plural instead.

    Emphasis on the Male: Give the customer his receipt with the change.

    Revised: Give customers their receipts with the change.

- Eliminate the male pronoun or reword to avoid unnecessary problems.

    Emphasis on the Male: The average citizen worries about his retirement benefits.

    Revised: The average citizen worries about retirement benefits.

    Emphasis on the Male: If the taxpayer has questions about the new form, he can call a government representative.

    Revised: The taxpayer who has questions about the new form can call a government representative.

    —or—

    The taxpayer with questions about the new form can call a government representative.

- Replace the male pronoun with *one, you, he* or *she,* or an article (*a, an, the*).

    Emphasis on the Male: The pet owner who can afford it takes his pet to a veterinarian.

    Revised: The pet owner who can afford it takes his or her pet to a veterinarian.

    —or—

    The pet owner who can afford it takes the pet to a veterinarian.

- Repeat a title rather than using a male pronoun.

    Emphasis on the Male: See your doctor first, and he will explain the prescription.

    Revised: See your doctor first, and the doctor will explain the prescription.

- Alternate male and female examples. (But be careful not to confuse your reader.)

    Example of Alternating: A young child is often persuaded by advertisements to buy what he sees on television. When the child goes shopping with a parent, she sees the product on the shelf, remembers it, and asks to have it.

**48c
sexist**

- Address the reader directly in the second person.

    Emphasis on the Male: The applicant must mail his form by Thursday.

    Revised: Mail your form by Thursday.

For the indefinite pronouns *everybody, anybody, everyone,* and *anyone,* some people prefer to continue using the male pronoun (everyone . . . he). But the plural pronoun has also become acceptable (everyone . . . they).

- Use job titles in letters to unknown persons.

    Emphasis on the Male:

    Dear Sir:

    Gentlemen:

    Revised:

    Dear Customer Representative:

    Dear Personnel Director:

    Dear Editor:

Exercise 48.1: Proofreading Practice

In the following paragraph there is some language that could be deemed sexist. Revise the paragraph so that non-sexist language is used consistently.

In the curricula of most business schools, the study of failure has not yet become an accepted subject. Yet the average business student needs to know what he should do when a business strategy fails and how he can learn from his mistakes. Even the chairman of one Fortune 500 company says that the average businessman can learn more from his mistakes than from his successes. Yet the concept of studying failure has been slow in catching on. However, a few business schools and even engineering management majors at one university in California now confront the question of how anyone can recover from his mistakes. Student papers analyze how a typical failed entrepreneur might have better managed his problems. Sometimes, a perceptive student can even relate the lessons to his own personal behavior. One of the typical problems that is studied is that of escalating commitment, the tendency of a manager to throw more and more of his financial resources and manpower into a project that is failing. Another is the tendency of the hapless executive not to

48c
sexist

see that his idea is a bomb. For this reason, computers are being enlisted to help him—and his superiors—make decisions about whether he should bail out or stay in. The study of failure clearly promises to breed success, at least for future businessmen now enrolled in business schools.

Exercise 48.2: Pattern Practice

Using the suggestions for avoiding sexist language offered in Section 48, write a short paragraph about people in a particular profession or group. To gain practice in using various options for using non-sexist language, try to include in your paragraph several of the suggestions in this section.

49 Unnecessary Words

49a Conciseness (con)

> Be as concise as you can in your writing because you will be communicating to your reader more clearly and because you are more likely to keep your reader's interest.

In addition, many readers don't have time for excess words.

To keep your whole paper concise, eliminate what your readers do not need to know, what they already know, and whatever doesn't further the purpose of your paper. That often means resisting the impulse to include everything you know about a subject. Other suggestions for eliminating unnecessary words are offered here.

49a con

- Avoid repetitions. When phrases say the same thing twice, eliminate the repetition. Note the repetition in these phrases:

first beginning	6 P.M. in the evening
final completion	beautiful and lovely
circular in shape	true facts
green in color	prove conclusively
really and truly	each and every
positive benefits	connected together

- Avoid fillers. When phrases say little or nothing, such as "there is" or "there are" or "in view of the fact that," they can be eliminated.

  Wordy: He said that there is a storm approaching.

  Revised: He said that a storm is approaching.

  Wordy: The mayor said that in view of the fact that the budget was overspent, no more projects could be started.

  Revised: The mayor said that because the budget was overspent, no more projects could be started.

  Wordy: It seems to me that it is getting dark out.

  Revised: It is getting dark out.

  Other phrases that can be eliminated include "I will explain," "I am going to discuss," "I will summarize here," and all phrases that tell the reader what you are going to do.

  Wordy: I am going to discuss artificial intelligence, which is an exciting new field of research.

  Revised: Artificial intelligence is an exciting new field of research.

- Combine sentences. When the same nouns or pronouns appear in two sentences, you can combine the two sentences into one so that the repetition is eliminated.

  Wordy: The data will be entered into the reports. It will also be included in the graphs.

  Revised: The data will be entered into the reports and also included in the graphs. (The revised sentence is more concise because it eliminates the pronoun *it* and the repetition of the helping verb *will be.*)

- Eliminate *who, which,* and *that.* Sometimes *who, which,* and *that* can be eliminated without affecting the clarity of your sentence.

  Wordy: The book that was lying on the piano belongs to her.

  Revised: The book lying on the piano belongs to her.

- Turn phrases and clauses into adjectives and adverbs.

the player who was very tired	=	the tired player
all applicants who are interested	=	all interested applicants
touched in a hesitant manner	=	touched hesitantly
the piano that was built out of mahogany	=	the mahogany piano

- Turn prepositional phrases into adjectives.

    an employee with ambition = an ambitious employee
       the entrance of the station = the station entrance
- Use active rather than passive.

    Wordy: An account was opened by Mrs. McDonald.

    Revised: Mrs. McDonald opened an account.

    Wordy: The figures were checked by the research department.

    Revised: The research department checked the figures.

- Remove excess nouns and change whenever possible into verbs.

    Wordy: He made the statement that he agreed with the concept that inflation could be controlled.

    Revised: He agreed that inflation could be controlled.

    Wordy: The function of the box is the storage of excess wire connectors.

    Revised: The box stores excess wire connectors.

- Replace jargon with clearer, shorter words.

Avoid	*Use*
advantageous	beneficial
implement	carry out
procure	acquire
utilize	use
effectuate	carry out
ascertain	find out

Exercise 49.1: Proofreading Practice

The following paragraph is very wordy. Eliminate as many words as you can without losing clarity. You may need to add a few words, too.

It has recently been noted by researchers that there is a growing concern among psychologists that as more parents who are working entrust the responsibility for caring for their infants of a very young age to day care centers, some of these babies may face harm of a psychological nature. The research findings of the researchers in this field focus on children who are less than eighteen months of age who are left in day care centers more than twenty hours a week. For children who are at that most formative age, say the researchers, day care seems to increase the feeling of insecurity. One of the foremost leading researchers in

49a
con

this field says that he isn't sure how the increase in the feeling of insecurity happens, but it is his guess that the stress that a child undergoes each and every day as a result of the separation from the parent can be a contributing causal factor here. Studies of the infants who are in day care for long periods of time each week have shown that more of these infants exhibit feelings of anxiousness and also of hyperactivity. These findings definitely and strongly challenge the older view that day care does not harm or hurt a young child.

Exercise 49.2: Pattern Practice

Listed here are some patterns for eliminating unnecessary words. Following the pattern (and example) given here, make up a wordy sentence and then a more concise revision.

Pattern A: reducing a *who, which,* or *what* clause

> **Wordy:** The cook who was flipping hamburgers . . .
> **Revised:** The cook flipping hamburgers . . .

Pattern B: eliminating fillers

> **Wordy:** It is important that we agree that . . .
> **Revised:** We must agree that . . .

Pattern C: changing a passive verb to active

> **Wordy:** The car was started by the driver.
> **Revised:** The driver started the car.

Pattern D: combine sentences

> **Wordy:** The cereal box was decorated with pictures of famous athletes on one side. On the other side, the box had recipes for candy and snacks.
> **Revised:** The cereal box was decorated with pictures of famous athletes on one side and recipes for candy and snacks on the other side.

Pattern E: turn a phrase or clause into an adjective or adverb

> **Wordy:** The salesperson who sold used cars starred in the TV commercial.
> **Revised:** The used-car salesperson starred in the TV commercial.

49a
con

Pattern F: eliminate repetition

Wordy: When she was first beginning to drive her car, she never drove more than thirty miles per hour.

Revised: When she began to drive her car, she never drove more than thirty miles per hour.

Pattern G: turn a prepositional phrase into an adjective

Wordy: Use the paper with the red lines.

Revised: Use the red-lined paper.

49b Clichés (cl)

Clichés are overused, tired expressions that have lost their ability to communicate effectively.

When you read or hear phrases such as "busy as a beaver" or "a crying shame," you are not likely to think about a beaver busily working or someone actually crying in shame. Avoid such expressions, which are worn out from too much repetition and are no longer vivid.

Some clichés to avoid include the following:

white as snow	rat race
beat around the bush	acid test
dead as a doornail	add insult to injury
in a nutshell	calm before the storm
crack of dawn	better late than never
clear as mud	green with envy
playing with fire	stubborn as a mule
at the drop of a hat	sell like hotcakes

**49b
cl**

Exercise 49.3: Proofreading Practice

Underline the clichés in the following paragraph.

When learning good study habits, some students are sharp as a tack. They know how to make study sessions short and sweet by concentrating only on the most important material. First and foremost, they look at chapter headings and subheadings to get a fix on what the main ideas are. Getting down to business means getting in there and seeing the big picture. Once that is crystal clear, they review arguments or add details. Slowly but surely they go through the material, asking themselves questions that get down to the nitty-gritty. Climbing the ladder of success in college means putting your nose to the grindstone and working hard.

Exercise 49.4: Revision Practice

Revise the paragraph in Exercise 49.3 by using more precise language in place of the clichés.

49c *Pretentious Language* (wc)

> **Pretentious language** is language that is too showy; it calls attention to itself by the use of overly complex sentences and ornate, polysyllabic words used for their own sake.

The following sentence is an example of overblown, pompous language that makes the writer sound pretentious and affected. Plain English that communicates clearly is far better than such attempts at showing off.

Pretenious: The lucidity with which she formulated her questions as she interrogated the indigenous population of the rustic isle drew gasps of admiration from her cohorts.

Revised: Her friends admired her ability to clearly phrase the questions she asked the island's inhabitants.

50 wds

50 Appropriate Words (wds)

Choosing among words is a matter of selecting the correct word, the word that is right in any writing situation. For example, whether an essay is formal or informal, you should always write "between you and *me*" (not "between you and *I*"). But other word choices are not so clear-cut. Instead, it is a question of which word is appropriate for the subject, audience, and purpose of a particular piece of writing.

50a Standard English

Standard English is the generally accepted language of educated people. It is "standard" because it conforms to established rules of grammar, sentence structure, punctuation, spelling, and so on.

Standard English, the language used in magazines, newspapers, and books, is the language you are expected to use in academic writing. If you are not sure if a particular word is standard, check the dictionary. Nonstandard words such as *ain't* are labeled to indicate that they are not acceptable for standard usage.

50b Colloquialisms, Slang, and Regionalisms

Colloquial words are the language of casual conversation and informal writing.

kids (instead of *children*)
sci-fi (instead of *science fiction*)
flunk (instead of *fail*)

Slang words are terms that are made up (such as *barf* or *zonked out*) or are given new definitions (such as *pot* for *marijuana* or *pig* for *police officer*) in order to be novel or unconventional. (Distinguishing between colloquialisms and slang is often difficult, and experts who are consulted when dictionaries are compiled do not always agree.)

hang out
get your act together
bad (in the sense of very good)
cool dude
hit on

Regional words (also called *localisms* or *provincialisms*) are words and phrases more commonly used in one geographic area than in another.

**50b
wds**

pail or *bucket*

bag, sack, poke, or *tote*

porch or *verandah*

seesaw, teeter-totter, or *teeterboard*

Although colloquialisms, slang, and regionalisms are not substandard or illiterate, most readers consider them inappropriate for formal academic writing. Colloquial language is acceptable for informal writing and dialogue, but slang may be unfamiliar to some readers. Slang terms are appropriate for very informal conversations among a group familiar with the current meanings of the terms. After a period of usage, many slang terms become outdated and disappear (for example, *the cat's pajamas, twenty-three skiddoo,* or *a real cool cat*), but some such as *mob, dropout, fan, job,* and *phone,* have become accepted as standard usage.

Some writers are able to make use of an occasional colloquialism or slang term for effect when the writing is not highly formal.

Endowments for the arts and humanities should be underwritten by the private sector, not institutionalized as they are now by government grants. Freedom of artistic expression is at stake when government *has its paws* where they should not be.

The National Park Service is vigorously fighting charges that it *doesn't know beans about* maintaining the ecological health of our national parks. To vindicate its recent actions, park officials have been issuing a series of reports showing the beneficial effects of recent management policies.

**50b
wds**

Exercise 50.1: Dictionary Practice

Look up the following colloquialisms and slang in two or three different dictionaries. What labels and usage suggestions are given for these terms?

1. cop (meaning: a police officer)
2. hot potato (meaning: something likely to cause trouble)
3. schlock (meaning: something of poor quality)
4. cool it (meaning: calm down)
5. buddy (meaning: a friend)
6. split (meaning: leave)
7. flaky (meaning: eccentric, strange)
8. uptight (meaning: very nervous)
9. chicken (meaning: coward)
10. rip off (meaning: cheat)

Exercise 50.2: Writing Practice

List five slang words that you know. Use the words in sentences, and then rewrite the sentence using a standard word with the same definition.

Example: gross out

Slang: He was so **grossed out** by the biology experiment that he was unable to finish.

Revised: He was so **disgusted** by the biology experiment that he was unable to finish.

50c *Levels of Formality*

The **level of formality** is the tone in writing and reflects the attitude of the writer toward the subject and audience. The tone may be highly formal or very informal or somewhere in between.

Informal tone uses words and sentence constructions that are close to ordinary speech and may include slang, colloquialisms, and regionalisms. Like everyday speech, informal writing tends not to have the most precise word choices, uses contractions, uses first and second person pronouns such as "I" and "you" (see Chapter 3a), uses verbs such as "get," "is," and "have," and may include sentence fragments for effect. An informal tone is used by speakers and writers for everyday communication and is appropriate in informal writing.

Informal: He was so <u>sort of</u> irritated because he couldn<u>'t</u> find his car keys and did<u>n't</u> have <u>a whole lot of</u> time to get to his office.

Medium tone is not too casual, not too scholarly. It uses standard vocabulary, conventional sentence structures, and few or no contractions, and it is often the level you'll be expected to use for papers.

Medium: He was <u>somewhat</u> irritated because he could <u>not</u> find his car keys and did <u>not</u> have <u>much</u> time to get to his office.

Formal tone is scholarly and uses sophisticated, multisyllabic words in complex sentence structures not likely to be used when speaking. It often uses the third-person pronoun such as "he or she" or "one" (see Chapter 3a) instead of "I" or "you." Formal

**50c
wds**

writing is preferred by some readers though not by others who find that it is sometimes not as easy to read or understand. Many businesses as well as government and other public offices encourage employees to maintain a medium level of formality.

Formal: Unable to locate his car keys and lacking sufficient time to journey to his office, he was slightly agitated.

In the following example the same information is presented at several levels of formality.

Informal: When someone wants to have a bill passed in this state, he starts off the process by getting it presented in the General Assembly or the Senate. The next thing that happens is that there's a committee that looks at it. The committee meets to decide on changing, accepting, or killing the bill. Usually, there's a lot of discussion when the bill comes back to the General Assembly and Senate. Both places have to okay the bill. If they don't like it, then a committee gets together with people from both the General Assembly and the Senate. They pound out a version that will make both houses happy. When the bill gets passed in both houses, it gets to move on to the governor. If the governor signs the bill or just doesn't do anything, it becomes a law. If the governor says no, it either dies or goes back to the Senate and General Assembly. It's got to get a two-thirds vote in both houses to become a law.

Medium: For a bill to become a law in this state, the first step is to have it introduced in the General Assembly or the Senate. Next, the bill is sent to a committee where hearings are held to change, approve, or kill the bill. When the bill returns to the General Assembly and Senate, there is often a great deal of debate before a vote is taken. If both houses do not pass the bill, a joint committee is appointed, with representatives from both the General Assembly and the Senate. This committee then draws up a bill that is acceptable to both houses. When both houses approve and pass the bill, it moves to the governor's office. For the bill to become a law, the governor can either sign it or take no action. The governor may, however, veto the bill. In this case, it either dies or goes back to both houses where it must pass with a two-thirds majority. If so, it then becomes a law, despite the governor's veto.

Formal: The procedure for passage of legislation in this state originates in either the General Assembly or the Senate. From here the bill is forwarded to a committee where hearings are initiated to determine whether the bill will be endorsed, altered, or terminated. From there, the bill returns to the General Assembly and Senate where extensive debate occurs before voting is completed. In instances in which the bill fails to pass both houses, a joint committee is charged with formulating a compromise bill acceptable to both the Senate and General Assembly. Approval by both houses results in advancing the bill to the governor; the bill will then become law with the governor's signature or

**50c
wds**

with no action being taken in the governor's office. Should the governor reject the bill with a veto, it is either no longer viable or can be resuscitated through a two-thirds favorable vote in both houses, which then constitutes passage into law.

Once you set the level of formality in an essay, keep it consistent. Mixing levels can be distracting and indicates that the writer doesn't have adequate control (see Chapter 17c).

Inconsistent Level of Formality: The economist offered the business executives a lengthy explanation for the recent fluctuation in the stock market. But it was <u>pretty</u> obvious from their questions afterwards that they did<u>n't get it</u>.

Revised: The economist offered the business executives a lengthy explanation for the recent fluctuation in the stock market. But it was <u>quite</u> obvious from their questions afterwards that they did <u>not understand his explanation</u>.

For an example of a paragraph with an inconsistent level of formality, see the paragraph in Exercise 50.3. A revised version appears in the Answer Key for Exercise 50.3.

Exercise 50.3: Proofreading Practice

The following paragraph is intended to be written in a medium to formal tone, but the writer lost control and slipped into some inappropriate choices of informal words and phrases. Rewrite the paragraph so that the wording is consistently at a medium to formal level.

To eliminate sexual harassment in the workplace, companies should come up with clearly defined guidelines that help you figure out which actions to avoid. Merely telling people not to engage in sexual harassment doesn't do much to illustrate things to cut out. Therefore, to sensitize their personnel, some companies hold seminars in which employees who have complaints act out unpleasant or demeaning stuff directed at them by their bosses or fellow workers. Seeing such actions portrayed often helps the offender recognize how insulting some act was, even if the offending person didn't mean it like that. Discussions that get going later also help people realize how their actions affect those they work with, and further definitions or memos often aren't needed.

**50c
wds**

Exercise 50.4: Pattern Practice

The tone of the following sentences can be changed by changing some of the key terms. If the sentence is informal, change it to a more formal tone. Similarly, if the sentence is formal, change it to a more informal tone. A sample sentence has been changed from a formal sentence to an informal one.

Original: Scientists are issuing warnings that one procedure for alleviating the menace of global warming is to reduce carbon dioxide emissions.

Revised to a More Informal Tone: Scientists warn that one way to reduce the threat of global warming is to cut down on carbon dioxide exhaust.

1. A step in the right direction would be to lean on automobile makers and make them raise the fuel efficiency of the gas-guzzling cars they are turning out.
2. But an even quicker way to drop fuel use would be to hike the gas tax.
3. Environmentalists are also requesting stricter limitations on smokestack emissions of sulfur dioxide, a major contributor to acid rain.
4. But states now producing high-sulfur coal aren't happy about the damage this will do to their economy.

50d *Jargon and Technical Terms*

**50d
wds**

Jargon (also called **technical terms**) is the specialized language of various trades, professions, and groups, such as lawyers, plumbers, electricians, biologists, horse racers, and pharmacists. These terms are used by specialists within a group to communicate with each other in a concise way when referring to various complex concepts, objects, techniques, and so on. However, jargon is also a negative term that refers to the use of unnecessarily technical or inflated expressions.

Specialized Language: Psychologists talk about *syndromes* and *cognitive styles;* doctors talk about a *subcutaneous hemorrhage* and *metabolic disorders;* and auto mechanics discuss *carburetors, fuel injectors,* and *exhaust manifolds.*

Inflated Expressions: *learning facilitator* (teacher)
monetary remuneration (pay)

When you are writing about a specialized subject for a general audience, you can use technical terms if needed and then define the terms so that they are easily understood by your readers.

One of the great challenges for the future is the development of superconductors, metallic ceramics that when cooled below a certain critical temperature offer no resistance to the flow of an electric current. (Having defined superconductors, this author can now use the word and not lose the reader.)

Unnecessary jargon indicates the writer's inability to write clearly. Some writers mistakenly think that business documents, government reports, and other public and impersonal writing should have this inflated tone. Note the wordiness and pompous tone of this example:

Original: Utilize this receptacle, which functions as a repository for matter to be disposed of.

Revised: Deposit litter here.

50e Idioms

An **idiom** is an expression that means something beyond the simple definition or literal translation into another language. An idiom such as "kick the bucket" (meaning "die") is not understandable from the meanings of the individual words.

par for the course
live high on the hog
the old college try
by and large
with the naked eye
fresh as a daisy
put someone in the driver's seat

**50e
wds**

For a list of idiomatic prepositions that follow certain words, see Chapter 5a. Because the meaning of phrasal verbs (see Chapter 1g) is not the same as the literal meaning of each of the words, phrasal verbs are also idioms.

50f General and Specific Words

General words refer to whole categories or large groups and classes of items. Other words are more **specific** in that they identify items in a group.

Tree is more general than *maple*, and *maple* is more general than *sugar maple*, a particular kind of maple tree.

General	Specific	More specific
animal	dog	cocker spaniel
plant	flower	rose
clothing	shoes	loafers

Sometimes, a general word is adequate or appropriate for the occasion. For example, *car* is a more general word than *Ford*, and it is more appropriate in the following brief account of a trip:

This year we visited several parts of the country that we had not seen before. Last fall, we flew to New Mexico for a week, and during spring vacation we traveled by car from New York to Chicago.

The focus in these sentences is on the places that were visited, not the particular kind of car in which the writer rode.

While general terms are useful in some contexts, specific words are often better choices because they are more precise and vivid and can help the reader's imagination in seeing, hearing, feeling, and smelling what is described (if that is the writer's purpose). Compare these examples.

General: He walked across the street to see the merchandise in the store window.

More Specific: He ambled across Lexington Avenue to see the velvet ties in Bloomingdale's window.

General: To help our economy, America needs to sell more products on the world market.

More Specific: To decrease our trade deficit, American industries should develop their best high-tech products such as high-resolution television and communications satellites to sell to growing markets in China and Europe.

Some general words are too vague to convey a writer's meaning:

bad child

(Is the child rude? evil? ungrateful?)

**50f
wds**

bad food

(Is the food overcooked? contaminated? tasteless? unhealthy?)

Exercise 50.5: Pattern Practice

Listed next are some general terms. What are more specific words that could be used instead?

General	Specific	More specific
food	vegetable	carrot

1. music
2. book
3. animal
4. clothes
5. field of study
6. machine
7. car
8. food
9. place of business
10. athlete

50g Concrete and Abstract Words

Concrete words refer to people and things that can be perceived by the senses. We are able to form images in our minds of concrete terms: the *thick white foam* in the *glass, dog, garden gate, smoke.*

Abstract words refer to qualities, concepts, conditions, and ideas: *truth, economics, slow, happy, ethical.*

We need both abstract terms to communicate complex ideas and also concrete words to convey what we see, hear, taste, touch, and feel. However, dull writing tends to be unnecessarily abstract and overuses words such as *aspects, factors,* and *means.*

Abstract: Rain forest trees constitute more than 20 percent of the industrial world's consumption of wood. The harvest from rainforest trees is a valuable crop because of the ability of such trees to resist disease and infestations common in other woods. In addition, because these trees have greater strength and durability than softwood trees, they are useful for wooden structures that require the ability to withstand heavy weights and external pressures. Their characteristic colors and growth patterns make rainforest trees well suited for use in furniture and other wooden products where color is a prized commodity. Thus, in recent years, global demand for tropical hardwoods has increased dramatically.

Concrete: More than 20 percent of the wood used throughout the world is cut from rainforests. The trees from these forests are valued for their ability to resist termites, fungi, and other common diseases of wood. In addition, because rainforest hardwood such as teak and mahogany resists breaking, cracking, and buckling more than softer wood, it is used for flooring, boat frames, wood siding for houses, and other wooden structures that must withstand pressure from heavy weights. The dark reddish color and interesting graining patterns of rosewood are particularly attractive when made into chairs, tables, and beds; dark brown or black ebony wood is used in billiard cues, and the black keys of pianos. Thus, in the last five years, countries throughout the world have ordered and imported more tropical wood than they used in the last fifty years.

Exercise 50.6: Revision Practice

The following description in a travel magazine has some abstract and general terms that could be revised to be more specific and concrete. Rewrite the paragraph so that it is more specific and concrete.

Traveling to the Bahamas, a group of islands fifty miles across the water from the United States, is an easy trip for private boats. Since gambling is a popular sport, people go on weekends to gamble and to enjoy other sports. Tourism is the nation's leading industry, and Bahamanian planners predict a sharp rise in the future. Because of this expectation, developers are building more housing of different types. Nassau, which has suffered from increased crime, is no longer the primary location for tourist development, but boats continue to stop there to let people look around.

50h
wds

50h Denotation and Connotation

The **denotation** of a word is the explicit dictionary meaning, the definition.

The **connotation** is the group of ideas implied but not directly indicated by the word. The connotation conveys attitudes and emotional overtones beyond the direct definition. These associations can be positive or negative and may be different for different individuals. But there is also a large group of shared connotations.

A pig is an animal (the denotation), but there are also negative connotations of *sloppiness, dirt,* and *fat* associated with pigs.

Famous and *notorious* have similar denotative meanings, but *notorious* has a negative connotation, whereas *famous* connotes a positive quality.

Groups of words with similar meaning can often be distinguished by their different negative, neutral, and positive connotations. For example, *fat, plump,* and *obese* describe the same condition, but *fat* has a more negative connotation than *plump,* and *obese,* a medical term, is generally considered to be a more neutral term.

Exercise 50.7: Pattern Practice

The following groups of words have similar denotative meanings, but their connotations differ. Arrange each group so that they go from most positive to most negative.

Most positive	Neutral	Most negative
slender	lean	scrawny

1. canine, mutt, puppy
2. law-enforcement officer, police officer, cop
3. cheap, inexpensive, economical
4. ornate, embellished, garish
5. counterfeit, replica, copy
6. scholar, egghead, intellectual
7. determined, stubborn, uncompromising
8. scared, apprehensive, paranoid
9. explanation, excuse, reason
10. gabby, talkative, chatty

50h
wds

Answer Key for Exercises in Part 5

Exercise 48.1

One possible revision is as follows:

In the curricula of most business schools, the study of failure has not yet become an accepted subject. Yet average business students need to know what they should do when a business strategy fails and how they can learn from their mistakes. Even the chairperson of one Fortune 500 company says that the average business executive can learn more from mistakes than from successes. Yet the concept of studying failure has been slow in catching on. However, a few business schools and even engineering management majors at one university in California now confront the question of how anyone can recover from his or her mistakes. Student papers analyze how a typical failed entrepreneur might have better managed his or her problems. Sometimes, perceptive students can even relate the lessons to their own personal behavior. One of the typical problems that is studied is that of escalating commitment, the tendency of a manager to throw more and more financial resources and personnel into a project that is failing. Another is the tendency of a hapless executive not to see that an idea is a bomb. For this reason, computers are being enlisted to help executives—and their superiors—make decisions about whether to bail out or stay in. The study of failure clearly promises to breed success, at least for future business executives now enrolled in business schools.

five
ans

Exercise 49.1

One possible revision is as follows:

Researchers note a growing concern among psychologists that as more working parents entrust infants to day care centers, some of these babies may face psychological harm. The research findings focus on children less than eighteen months of age left in day care centers more than twenty hours a week. For children at that formative age, say the researchers, day care seems to increase the feeling of insecurity. One of the foremost researchers in this field says he isn't sure how the increase in insecurity happens, but he guesses that the stress a child undergoes each day as a result of the separation from the parent can be a contributing factor. Studies of infants in day care for long periods of time each week have shown that more of these infants exhibit feelings of anxiousness and also of hyperactivity. These findings challenge the older view that day care does not harm a young child.

Exercise 49.3

When learning good study habits, some students are <u>sharp as a tack</u>. They know how to make study sessions <u>short and sweet</u> by concentrating only on the most important material. <u>First and foremost</u>, they look at chapter headings and subheadings <u>to get a fix on</u> what the main ideas are. <u>Getting down to business</u> means <u>getting in there</u> and <u>seeing the big picture</u>. Once that is <u>crystal clear</u>, they review arguments or add details. <u>Slowly but surely</u> they go through the material, asking themselves questions that <u>get down to the nitty-gritty</u>. <u>Climbing the ladder of success</u> in college means <u>putting your nose to the grindstone</u> and working hard.

Exercise 49.4

One possible revision is as follows:

When learning good study habits, some students are very knowledgeable. They know how to make study sessions concise by concentrating only on the most important material. First, they look at chapter headings and subheadings to get a clear idea of what the main ideas are. They get to work by looking for the major ideas. Once that is clear, they review arguments or add details. They methodically go through the material asking themselves questions that focus on basic points. Being successful in college means expending effort and working hard.

Exercise 50.3

One possible revision is as follows:

To eliminate sexual harassment in the workplace, companies should construct clearly defined guidelines that help employees recognize actions to avoid. Merely telling people not to engage in sexual harassment does not adequately illustrate specific acts from which they should refrain. Therefore, to sensitize their personnel, some companies hold seminars in which employees who have complaints act out unpleasant or demeaning actions

five
ans

directed at them by their supervisors or fellow workers. Seeing such actions portrayed often helps the offender recognize how insulting some act was, even if the offending person did not intend any disrespect. Discussions that follow also help people realize how their actions affect those they work with, and further definitions or memos often are not needed.

Exercise 50.4
Possible revisions:

1. Revised to a more formal tone:

An appropriate measure would be to exert pressure on automobile manufacturers and force them to increase the fuel efficiency of the current models which consume excessive amounts of gasoline.

2. Revised to a more formal tone:

However, a more rapid method of reducing fuel consumption would be to increase taxation on gasoline.

3. Revised to a less formal tone:

People interested in protecting the environment are also asking for tighter limits on smokestacks pouring out sulfur dioxide, a major cause of acid rain.

4. Revised to a more formal tone:

However, states currently producing high-sulphur coal are expressing concern about the resulting destruction of their economic base.

Exercise 50.5
Some possible answers are as follows:

General	*Specific*	*More specific*
1. music	song	*Star-Spangled Banner*
2. book	novel	*David Copperfield*
3. animal	cat	Siamese kitten
4. clothes	pants	white linen shorts
5. field of study	economics	agricultural economics
6. machine	saw	chain saw
7. car	sports car	Honda CRX
8. food	bread	dark rye bread
9. place of business	grocery store	fruit and vegetable market
10. athlete	football player	linebacker

Exercise 50.7
Possible answers are as follows:

	Most positive	*Neutral*	*Most negative*
1.	puppy	canine	mutt
2.	law-enforcement officer	police officer	cop
3.	economical	inexpensive	cheap
4.	ornate	embellished	garish
5.	replica	copy	counterfeit
6.	scholar	intellectual	egghead
7.	uncompromising	determined	stubborn
8.	apprehensive	scared	paranoid
9.	explanation	reason	excuse
10.	chatty	talkative	gabby

five
ans

6

Special Writing Concerns

Previous parts have covered general concepts and matters of grammar, punctuation, spelling, and mechanics. These are concerns for all writing. This part, however, deals with special writing concerns when you are using sources including how to summarize, paraphrase, avoid plagiarism, use quotations, and document your sources. Another special writing concern is the preparation of your résumé, and you will find several formats and strategies for preparing this important document. The topics covered in this part include the following:

51. Working with Sources
  a. Summaries and Paraphrases
  b. Plagiarism
  c. Quotations
  d. MLA Documentation Format
  e. APA Documentation Format

52. Résumés
  a. Sections of the Résumé
  b. Résumé Styles

51 Working with Sources

51a Summaries and Paraphrases

A **summary** is a brief restatement of a writer's main ideas.

As you write, you'll find it useful to include summaries of other people's writing when you refer to the main idea of another writer but do not wish to quote that person. Good reasons for using summaries are that the source has unnecessary detail, the writer's phrasing is not particularly memorable or worth quoting, or you want to keep your writing concise. When you include a summary of a source, you need to refer to that source to give credit to the writer. (See Chapters 51d and 51e for information on how to cite your sources.) If you do not include a reference to your source, you may be guilty of plagiarism (see Chapter 51b).

Characteristics of your summaries include the following:

- Are written in your own words, not those of the source you are summarizing
- Give the main points only, omitting details, facts, examples, illustrations, direct quotations, and other specifics
- Use fewer words than the source being summarized (see Chapter 49a for suggestions on how to make your writing more concise)
- Do not follow the organization of the source
- Are objective and do not include your own interpretation or slant on the material

Original Source "As human beings have populated the lands of the earth, we have pushed out other forms of life. It seemed to some that our impact must stop at the ocean's edge, but that has not proved to be so. By overharvesting the living bounty of the sea and by flushing the wastes and by-products of our societies from the land into the ocean, we have managed to impoverish, if not destroy, living ecosystems there as well."

(Source: Thorne-Miller, Boyce, and John G. Catena. *The Living Ocean: Understanding and Protecting Marine Biodiversity*. Washington, D.C.: Island Press, 1991. 3–4.)

Summary: Humans have destroyed numerous forms of life on land and are now doing the same with the oceans. Overfishing as well as flushing waste products into the waters have brought about the destruction of various forms of ocean life.

51a

....

HINT: Some useful strategies for writing a summary follow:
When you are writing a summary, begin by reading the original source carefully and thoughtfully. After the first

reading, ask yourself what major point the author is making. When you have that answer in mind, go back and re-read the source, making a few notes in the margin if that helps you. Then, look away from your source and like a newscaster, panelist, or speaker reporting to a group, say the following and finish the sentence: "This person is saying that...." Write down what you've said, and then go back and re-read both the source and your notes in the margins to check that you've correctly remembered and included the main point or points. You may find that you then need to revise your summary.

If you plan to use your summary in a report or research paper, make notes of the page references that you will need. In your paper, signal your readers that you are using information from your summary and include a page reference in parentheses.

A **paraphrase** restates information from a source but in your own words.

A paraphrase has the following characteristics:

- Has approximately the same number of words as the source (a summary, conversely, is much shorter)
- Uses your own words, not those of the source
- Keeps the same organization as the source
- Is more detailed than a summary
- Is objective and does not include your own interpretation or slant on the material

Original Source: "The automobile once promised a dazzling world of speed, freedom, and convenience, magically conveying people wherever the road would take them. Given these alluring qualities, it is not surprising that people around the world enthusiastically embraced the dream of car ownership. But societies that have built their transport systems around the automobile are now waking up to a much harsher reality. The problems created by overreliance on the car are outweighing its benefits."

(Lowe, Marcia D. "Rethinking Urban Transport." *State of the World 1991.* New York: Norton, 1991. 56.)

51a

Unacceptable Paraphrase: (This paraphrase borrows words, phrases, and sentence structures from the original. Exact or overly close borrowing of words and phrases are underlined. Note also the similar sentence structures.)

Automobiles used to <u>promise us a dazzling world of speed, freedom, and con-venience,</u> taking <u>people wherever roads led them</u>. With these kinds of attractive qualities, we should <u>not be surprised that people</u> everywhere happily took to the idea of owning their own cars. <u>But</u> nations that have structured their systems of transportation on using cars are beginning <u>to wake up</u> to the idea of a harder <u>reality</u>. <u>Relying too much on cars causes problems that outweigh its benefits</u> (Lowe 56).

Acceptable Paraphrase: Automobiles, which offered swift, easy, and independent transportation, allowed people to travel wherever there were roads. Owning a car became everyone's dream, a result that is not surprising, given the benefits of car travel. Nations built their transportation systems on the car, but despite its advantages, societies that rely heavily on cars are beginning to recognize that they cause severe problems as well. Heavy dependence on automobiles creates problems which offset their advantages (Lowe 56).

....

HINT: Some useful advice when paraphrasing follows:
    It is easy to fall into the trap of borrowing the language of the source, but if you do, you are in danger of plagiarizing (see Chapter 51b). When you prepare to write a paraphrase, begin by reading the original passage as many times as is needed to understand its full meaning. Take notes, using your own words, if that helps. Then, put the original source aside and write a draft of the paraphrase, using your notes if needed. Check your version against the original source by re-reading the original to be sure that you have included all the ideas and followed the same organization as the source. If you find some phrase worth quoting later, when you include information from the paraphrase in your own writing, use quotation marks in the paraphrase to identify what you have borrowed from the source and make a note of the page reference that you will need. In your paper, you need to signal your readers when you are using information from your paraphrase and include a page reference in parentheses.

51a
....

Exercise 51.1: Writing Practice

a. *To practice summarizing and paraphrasing, rewrite both of the following quotations, first as a summary of the contents and then as a para-phrase. These quotations are not from any real source, but when you cite them in the second part of this exercise, create a fictitious source to cite.*

1. The National Rifle Association (NRA), which was founded in 1871 to teach safety and marksmanship to gun owners, has become the nation's most powerful lobbying group in the bitter fight against gun-control laws. Arguing that the Second Amendment to the Constitution guarantees the rights of citizens to own guns, the NRA promotes people's right to protect themselves and their property. Most gun owners, claims the NRA, are law-abiding people who use guns for sport or for self-defense. While the NRA acknowledges the widespread use of guns by criminals and the ever-increasing numbers of innocent children killed by guns, NRA officials also point out that criminals are the ones who kill, not guns. Stricter laws and law enforcement, argues the NRA, can reduce crime, not gun-control laws. No matter how strict the laws become for the purchase of guns, those bent on illegally owning a gun can find ways to get one if they have the money.

2. Gun-control supporters, who lobby for stricter ownership laws and against the National Rifle Association (NRA), argue that guns are not useful for self-defense and do not inhibit crime. Various groups calling for stronger legislation against gun ownership point out that guns promote killing. When a gun is present, they note, the level of violence can increase rapidly. Research shows that a gun kept for protection is far more likely to be used to kill someone the gun owner knows than to be used to kill a thief. Moreover, guns in the home result in accidents in which children are killed. Opponents of the NRA answer the charge that they are ignoring the Second Amendment by citing the First Amendment which guarantees the right to hold public meetings and parades. Although Americans have the right to hold parades, they point out, people have to get a permit to do so, and gun permits are no more of an infringement on the rights of Americans than are parade permits.

b. *To practice incorporating summaries and paraphrases into your own writing, write a paragraph either for or against stronger gun-control laws, and make use of the sources you have just summarized and paraphrased previously. Remember to cite the made-up source you create. For help with citing sources, see Chapters 51d or 51e.*

51a

51b Plagiarism

Plagiarism means failing to cite a source so that the words and ideas of someone else are presented as the writer's own work.

Writers who quote the wording (see Chapter 51c) or who summarize or paraphrase (see Chapter 51a) the words, ideas, data, conclusions, arguments, results, and other material from sources must acknowledge this by using documentation (see Chapters 51d and 51e). If you consciously or unconsciously pass off as your own the work of someone else, you commit the very serious offense of stealing known as plagiarism. The result can be failing courses or even being expelled from a school. Summarizing or paraphrasing which follows the wording of a source too closely is one form of unconscious plagiarism; depending too heavily on quotations from a source is another form of plagiarism.

> **HINT:** To avoid plagiarism, read over your paper and ask yourself whether your readers can properly identify which ideas and words are yours and which are from the sources you cite. If that is clear, if you have not let your paper become merely a string of quotations from sources, and if the paper is predominantly your words, phrases, and integration of ideas, then you are not plagiarizing.

While you document the use of other people's ideas, words, and results, you do not have to cite material that is common knowledge. At first, it may be difficult to decide what is common knowledge and what needs to be cited, but as you become better acquainted with a field, this becomes clear. Common knowledge is that body of general ideas your readers share. For example, if your audience is American educators, it is common knowledge among this group that American school children are not well acquainted with geography. More specific information, however, needs to be cited. If you cite test results that prove the extent of the problem or use the words and ideas of some knowledgeable person about the causes of the problem, that is not common knowledge and needs documentation. Similarly, it is common knowledge among most Americans who are aware of current

51b

energy problems that the use of solar power is one answer to future energy needs. But any forecasts about how widely solar power may be used twenty years from now would be the work of some person or group studying the subject, and documentation would be needed. Common knowledge also consists of facts widely available in a variety of standard reference books.

Source: (The following excerpt is from pages 105–106 of Laura Tangley's *The Rainforest: Earth at Risk*. New York: Chelsea House, 1992.)

"One of the most obvious—and most important—approaches to saving rainforests is to protect them in national parks, the same way that industrialized nations such as the United States and Canada safeguard their tropical wonders. Yet so far fewer than 5% of the world's tropical forests are included in parks or other kinds of protected areas. Most of the developing countries that house these forests simply do not have enough money to buy land and set up park systems. And many of the nations that do establish parks are then unable to pay park rangers to protect the land. These unprotected parks routinely are invaded by poor, local people who desperately need the forest's wood, food, land, or products to sell. The areas are often called "paper parks" because they exist on paper but not in reality."

Accidental Plagiarism: *In this paragraph the words, phrases, and ideas from the original source are underlined. Note how much comes from the original source and how the author has neglected to signal to the reader that this material comes from another source.*

The problem of saving the world's rainforests has become a matter of great public concern. There are a number of solutions being offered, <u>but the most obvious and most important approach is to protect them in national parks</u>. This is <u>the same way that industrialized nations such as the United States and Canada safeguard their natural wonders</u>. In poorer nations this does not work because <u>they do not have enough money to buy land and set up park systems</u>. What happens is that when they don't have money, <u>they are unable to pay park rangers to protect the land</u>. Without any protection from rangers, poor people come in and invade because they <u>desperately need the forest's wood, food, land, or products to sell</u>. These parks then don't really exist as parks.

51b

Revised Version: The problem of saving the world's rainforests has become a matter of great public concern. Of the approaches being considered, Laura Tangley, in *The Rainforest*, considers one of the most important solutions to be turning rainforests into national parks. Tangley points out, however, that this is only a solution for industrialized nations such as the United States and Canada because they have the funding to keep national parks protected from poachers. In developing nations which cannot afford park rangers, the local populations are not prevented from taking wood, food, land, or forest products that they can sell. Tangley states that such forests, because they are not protected from human destruction, "exist on paper but not in reality" (106).

Exercise 51.2: Writing Practice

To practice citing sources and avoiding plagiarism, add citations in MLA format to the paragraph which incorporates the sources listed here. For information on parenthetical references in MLA format, see Chapter 51d.

Sources:

A. The quotations included here are from the following source:
   Lowe, Marcia D. "Rethinking Urban Transport." *State of the World 1991*. New York: Norton, 1991.

- "Cities with streets designed for cars instead of people are increasingly unlivable" (56).
- "Traffic congestion, now a fact of life in major cities, has stretched daily rush hours to 12 hours or longer in Seoul and 14 in Rio de Janeiro. In 1989, London traffic broke a record with a 53-kilometer backup of cars at a near standstill" (57).
- "Roaring engines and blaring horns cause distress and hypertension, as in downtown Cairo, where noise levels are 10 times the limit set by health and safety standards" (57).

B. The quotations included here are from the following source:
   Lipperman, Irwin. *Planning for a Livable Tomorrow*. New York: Nathanson, 1992.

- "City space is rapidly being eaten up by automobiles. Parking in a city center can use up to 20 or 30% of the available space, and suburban malls often have parking lots bigger than the malls themselves" (99).
- "Automobile pollutants in the air inhaled by urbanites increases the likelihood of lung disorders and makes bronchial problems more severe, especially among the elderly" (108).

The following paragraph is part of a research paper on the topic of city planning:

51b

Another important concern in city planning is to formulate proposals to eliminate or reduce problems caused by automobiles. Cities with streets designed for cars instead of people are increasingly unlivable, for cars cause congestion, pollution, and noise. While more public transportation can reduce these problems, it is not likely that city dwellers will give up owning cars. Therefore, solutions are needed for parking, which already uses up as much as 20 or 30% of the space available in downtown areas, and for rush hour traffic, which now causes rush hours to be extended to as much as twelve hours or longer in Seoul and to fourteen hours in Rio de Janeiro. Pollution, another urban problem caused partly by cars, needs to be controlled by reducing automobile emissions, which increases lung disorders and aggravates bronchial problems. In addition, noise from automobiles must be curbed as it has already become a health problem in cities such as Cairo where noise levels are already ten times the acceptable standard for human health.

51c Quotations (quotes)

Quotations are records of the exact words of a written or spoken source and are set off by quotation marks. All quotations should make reference to the source of the quotation.

Follow these guidelines to use quotations effectively:

- *Use quotations as evidence, as support, or as further explanation of what you have written.* Quotations are not substitutes for stating your point in your own words.
- *Use quotations sparingly.* Too many quotations strung together with very little of your own writing makes a paper look like a scrapbook of pasted-together sources, not a thoughtful integration of what is known about a subject.
- *Use quotations that illustrate the author's own viewpoint or style or excerpts that would not be as effective if rewritten in different words.* This includes quotations that are succinct or particularly well phrased.

51c
quotes

Original #1: When asked to comment on the recent investigations of government fraud, Senator Smith said, "Their ability to undermine our economy is exceeded only by their stupidity in thinking that they wouldn't get caught." (This statement is worth quoting because restating it in different words would probably take more words and have less punch.)

Original #2: When asked to comment on the recent investigations of government fraud, Senator Smith said, "These huge payments for materials that should have cost less will now cost the government money because they will increase our budget deficit more than we anticipated." (This statement is a good candidate for rewriting in your own words, with a reference to Senator Smith, because the statement is not particularly concise, well-phrased, or characteristic of a particular person's way of saying something.)

Revision of #2: When asked to comment on the recent investigations of government fraud, Senator Smith noted that overpayments on materials will cause an unexpected increase in the budget deficit.

• *Integrate the quotation smoothly into your own writing by showing how it fits into the ideas being expressed. Because you do not want to drop an undigested quotation into your writing, you can explain the connection, draw out the point being made, show a logical link, or add a follow up comment.*

Original: Modern farming techniques are different from those used twenty years ago. John Adams, an Iowa soybean grower, says, "Without a computer program to plan my crop allotments or to record my expenses, I'd be back in the dark ages of guessing what to do." (The quotation here is presented somewhat abruptly, without an introduction and without a clear indication from the writer as to how Mr. Adams' statement fits into the ideas being discussed.)

Revised: Modern farming techniques differ from those of twenty years ago, particularly in the use of computer programs for planning and budgeting. John Adams, an Iowa soybean grower who relies heavily on computers, explains, "Without a computer program to plan my crop allotments or to record my expenses, I'd be back in the dark ages of guessing what to do." (This revision explains how Mr. Adams' statement confirms the point being made.)

**51c
quotes**

HINT: Some words and phrases you can use when integrating quotations:

according to [name]	[name] has found that
as [name] puts it	[name] notes
as [name] explains	[name] says
[name] concludes	[name] suggests
[name] observes	[name] writes

In her 1992 study of new medications that fight depression, Smith writes, "The result of . . . ."

Arguments for more funding of public transportation emphasize the efficiency of buses and trains when compared to private transportation, for, as John H. Windover notes, "An underground metro can carry 40,000 passengers past a certain point in a single lane in one hour while a lane of private cars—even with four passengers in every car—can move only about 6,000 people an hour."

(1) Types of Quotations

Quoting Prose

If your quotation is no more than four lines (either handwritten or typed), include the quotation in your paragraph and use quotation marks (see Chapter 28a).

During the summer of 1974, at a crucial stage of
development in the Apollo program, national interest
in NASA was sharply diverted by the Watergate
affair. As Joseph Trento, an investigative reporter,
explains in his book on the Apollo program: "The
nation was sitting on the edge of its collective
seat wondering if Richard Nixon would leave us in
peace or pull the whole system down with him" (142).

Source: Trento, Joseph. <u>Prescription for Disaster</u>.
New York: Crown, 1987.

If the quotation is more than four handwritten or typed lines, set it off by indenting ten spaces from the left margin. Double-space the quotation, and do not use quotation marks. If the first line of the quotation is the beginning of the paragraph in the source, indent that line an additional five spaces.

> While the Apollo program accomplished many of its goals, it was not without difficulties even at the very end of the program. In his book on the Apollo and space shuttle programs, Joseph Trento reports on the final mission in the Apollo program:

> > The last mission involving the Apollo hardware nearly ended in tragedy for the American crew. After reentry the crew opened a pressure release valve to equalize the command module atmosphere with the earth's atmosphere. But the reaction control rockets failed to shut down and deadly nitrogen tetroxide oxydizer gas entered the cabin's breathing air. The crew survived the incident, but some at Houston and in Washington wondered if the layoff from manned flight hadn't put the crew at risk (144).

> > Source: Trento, Joseph. <u>Prescription for Disaster.</u> New York: Crown, 1987.

Quoting Poetry

If you are quoting a line of poetry, include it in your paragraph and use quotation marks. For two lines of poetry, which can also be included in your paragraph, use a slash mark (/) to mark the end of the first line, and follow the capitalizing of the original (see Chapter 28a).

```
Twice in the poem "The Love Song of J. Alfred
Prufrock" T.S. Eliot repeats, like a chorus, the
lines "In the room the women come and go / Talking
of Michelangelo."
```

When you are quoting more than two lines of poetry, set them off by indenting ten spaces. Double-space, and do not use quotation marks. (The number in parentheses in the example indicates the line numbers in the original poem.)

```
In "The Waste Land" T.S. Eliot provides us with
fleeting glimpses of London seen through the
speaker's eyes and mind:

          Unreal city,
          Under the brown fog of a winter dawn,
          A crowd flowed over London Bridge, so many,
          I had not thought death had undone so many
          (60-63).
```

Quoting Dialogue

When you are quoting the speech of two or more people who are talking, write each person's speech as a separate paragraph. Verbs, identification of the speaker, and closely related short comments and narrative can be included in the paragraph (see Chapter 28a).

51c
quotes

For generations, fathers have been telling sons who are nearing the end of their college days, "Son, your mother and I don't care what career you finally decide to pursue because the important thing is that you will be going forth." The key word here is <u>forth</u>. Every time you attend a graduation, you hear a dean or president say, "And so, young men and women, as you go forth..." For years, I had thought that forth meant going out into the world on their own; I had thought that forth meant leaving home. But then I discovered that I was wrong. Every time that they go forth, they come back, so forth must mean home. My father, however, gave to forth its old traditional meaning. On the day I was graduated from college, he presented to me a Benrus watch and then he said with a smile, "All right, now give me the keys to the house."

"Why, Dad?" I replied.

"Because you're going forth, which is any direction but to this house."

But I got my mother to let me back in (142-43).

Source: Cosby, Bill. <u>Fatherhood</u>. New York: Doubleday, 1986.

(2) Capitalization of Quotations

Capitalize the first word of directly quoted speech. If the quotation is interrupted and then continues on in the same sentence, don't capitalize the second part of the quotation. However, the first word of a fragment in dialogue is capitalized.

She said, "He likes to talk about football, especially when the Super Bowl is coming up."

"He likes to talk about football," she said, "especially when the Super Bowl is coming up."

"He likes to talk about football," she said. "Especially when the Super Bowl is coming up."

(3) Punctuation of Quotations

Commas

When you introduce quotations, use the comma to set off less formal expressions such as *he said, she asked,* or *Brady stated.*

As R. F. Notel explains, "The gestures people use to greet each other differ greatly from one culture to another."

But when the quotation is integrated into the sentence, especially when it follows *that,* do not use capitalization or punctuation.

The public relations director noted that "newsletters to alumni are the best source of good publicity—and donations."

Colon

Use the colon to introduce formal quotations and quotations that have two or more sentences.

The selection of juries has become a very complex and closely researched process: "In addition to employing social scientists, some lawyers now practice beforehand with 'shadow juries,' groups of twelve people demographically similar to an actual jury."

End Punctuation

Put periods before the second quotation mark. If the quotation has an exclamation mark or question mark, include that before

51c
quotes

the second quotation mark. But if the exclamation mark or question mark is part of the sentence but not the quotation, put the mark after the second quotation mark.

The stage director issued his usual command to the actor: "Work with me!" Did she really say, "I quit"?

Brackets

Occasionally, you may need to add some information within a quotation, insert words to make the quotation fit your sentence, or indicate with *sic* that you are quoting your source exactly even though you recognize an error there. When you insert any words within the quotation, set off your words with brackets. (See Chapter 34 for more on brackets.)

"During President Carter's administration, Press [Frank Press, Carter's Science Adviser] indicated his strong bias against funding applied research."

Original Source: *"Contributing editors* are people whose names are listed on the masthead of a magazine, but who are usually not on the staff. Basically, they're freelance writers with a good track record of producing ideas and articles prolifically."

Use of Quotation: Not all the names listed on the masthead of a magazine are regular staff members. Some are "freelance writers [who have] . . . a good track record of producing ideas and articles prolifically."

Ellipsis (for omitted words)

When you omit words from a quotation, use an ellipsis (three dots) to indicate that material has been left out. (See Chapter 35 for more information on ellipsis.)

Single Quotation Marks

When you are enclosing a quotation within a quotation, use a single quotation mark (the apostrophe mark on a typewriter).

In his book on the history of the atomic bomb, Richard Rhodes describes Enrico Fermi, one of the creators of the first atomic bomb, as he stood at his window in the physics tower at Columbia University and gazed out over New York City: "He cupped his hands as if he were holding a ball. 'A little bomb like that,' he said simply, for once not lightly, 'and it would all disappear'" (275).

SOURCE: Rhodes, Richard. *The Making of the Atomic Bomb.* New York, Simon & Schuster, 1986.

For more information on the use of punctuation with quotation marks, see Chapter 28d.

(4) Alternatives to Quotations

Other ways to make reference to sources of information include summaries and paraphrases. For information on summaries and paraphrases, see Chapter 51a. For information on how to document your sources for quotations, see Chapters 51d and 51e.

Exercise 51.2: Writing Practice

Assume that you are writing a paper on the topics listed here and want to quote from the source given for each topic. Using the information in Chapter 51c write a paragraph that quotes the source directly. Include some paraphrasing and summarizing also (see Chapter 51a).

1. Possible topics: the history of racing cars, aerodynamics in car design, famous old racing cars

SOURCE: Hill, Phil. "Salon: Bugatti 57G." *Road and Track* July 1987: 126–32.

In the Fifties, Grand Prix teams like Vanwall, Mercedes and Maserati experimented with wind-cheating bodywork, but abandoned the endeavor. Racing teams then didn't have the resources to study the entire aero package—lift, drag, driver cooling, etc.—and there were tragic reminders, such as Bernd Rosemeyer's death in an Auto Union record car, that the black art could also be deadly.

Ettore Bugatti had made an early unsuccessful attempt at racing car aerodynamics with "Tank" bodies on Type 32s in 1923. But there was another Bugatti Tank, built in the next decade, that became an example of how effective an aero body could be. In 1937 a supercharged Bugatti Type 57 with an all-enveloping body was driven by those two wonderful French drivers Robert Benoist and Jean-Pierre Wimille in the 24 hours of Le Mans. The car won the race at an average 85.13 mph, nearly 4 mph better than the old record. It was the first to travel more than 2000 miles during the 24-hour event (126).

2. Possible topics: George Gershwin, American musicals, history of musical theater, popular music

SOURCE: Livingston, "Gershwin." *Stereo Review* Aug. 1987: 63–66.

Among the songwriters Americans love best Gershwin ranks very high. His success went beyond the realm of popular music, however, to the concert hall

51c
quotes

and opera house, and he may well be the greatest composer the United States has ever produced.

The best of his so-called serious works—*Rhapsody in Blue, An American in Paris,* and *Porgy and Bess*—have grown in stature since his death, as have such songs as *Embraceable You, The Man I Love,* and *Fascinating Rhythm.* Writing of his songs in the book *The Gershwin Years,* Edward Jablonski and Robert D. Lawrence said: "Each year since 1937 we hear them more delightedly and gratefully than ever before—ever discovering in them a resilient charm, a durable brilliance, a permanent beauty" (63).

3. Possible topics: coping at college, verbal self-defense

SOURCE: Elgin, Suzette Haden. *The Gentle Art of Verbal Self-Defense.* n.p.: Dorset, n.d.

Sometimes, in spite of all your best intentions, you find yourself in a situation where you have *really* fouled it up. You are 100 percent in the wrong, you have no excuse for what you've done, and disaster approaches. Let us say, for example, that you enrolled in a class, went to it three or four times, did none of the work, forgot to drop it before the deadline, and are going to flunk. Or let's say that you challenged an instructor on some information and got nowhere trying to convince him or her that you were right; then you talked to a counselor, who got nowhere trying to convince you that you were wrong; next you spent quite a lot of time doing your duty to the other students in the class by telling them individually that the instructor is completely confused; and how, much too late, you have discovered that it is *you* who are in error. Either of these will do as a standard example of impending academic doom.

In such a case, there's only one thing you can do, and you're not going to like it. Go to the instructor's office hour, sit down, and level. Say that you are there because you've done whatever ridiculous thing you have done, that you already know you have no excuse for it, and that you have come in to clear it up as best you can. Do not rationalize; do not talk about how this would never have happened if it hadn't been for some other instructor's behavior; do not mention something the instructor you are talking to should have done to ward this off; do not, in other words, try to spread your guilt around. Level and be done with it (260–61).

51c
quotes

When you are using material from other sources, you must acknowledge these sources by citing them. If you do not, you are committing a form of stealing known as plagiarism (see Chapter 51b). Formats for documenting sources vary among fields. For English and other humanities, use the format of the Modern Language Association (MLA). For the social sciences, use the format of the American Psychological Association (APA). These two are explained here, but for formats in the natural sciences and technology, consult a style manual or journal in the field. Newspapers and other publishing companies, businesses, and large organizations often have their own formats, which are explained in their own style manuals.

51∂ MLA Documentation Format (MLA)

Modern Language Association (MLA) format is used to document papers in the humanities.

At the end of papers where you have used material from other sources, include a list of the sources from which you have quoted, summarized, or paraphrased. In the MLA format, used for papers in English and other humanities, this list is titled "Works Cited." In your paper you will need parenthetical references to these sources. You may also need endnotes to add material that would disrupt your paper if it were included in the text. Parenthetical references, endnotes, and works cited are formatted as follows:

(1) Parenthetical References

Parenthetical references to material you have quoted, paraphrased, or summarized provide brief information to help the reader locate the full reference in the works cited at the end of the paper. You may have previously used footnotes to indicate each source as you used it, but for the MLA form now in use, select among the following forms of parenthetical reference, depending on how much information you include in your sentence or in your introduction to a quotation:

Author's Name Not Given in the Text

If you do not mention the author's name in your sentence, put the author's last name in parentheses, leave a space with no punctuation, and then put the page number.

Recent research on sleep and dreaming indicates that dreams move backward in time as the night progresses (Dement 72).

51d
MLA

Author's Name Given in the Text

If you state the author's name in the sentence, include only the page number in parentheses.

Freud states that "a dream is the fulfillment of a wish" (154).

Two or More Works by the Same Author

If you used two or more different sources by the same author, put a comma after the author's last name and include a shortened version of the title and the page reference. If the author's name is in the text, include only the title and page reference.

One current theory emphasizes the principle that dreams express "profound aspects of personality" (Foulkes, *Sleep* 144).

But investigation shows that young children's dreams are "rather simple and unemotional" (Foulkes, "Children's Dreams" 90).

(2) Notes

When you have additional comments or information that would disrupt the paper, cite the information in notes numbered consecutively through the paper. Put the number at the end of the phrase, clause, or sentence containing the material you are referring to or quoting and after the punctuation. Raise the number above the line, with no punctuation. Leave no extra space before the number and one extra space after if the reference is in the middle of the sentence and two extra spaces when the reference number is at the end of the sentence.

The treasure hunt for sixteenth-century pirate loot buried in Nova Scotia began in 1927,[3] but hunting was discontinued when the treasure seekers found the site flooded at high tide.[4]

At the end of your paper, begin a new sheet with the heading "Notes," but do not underline this heading or put it in quotation marks. Leave a one-inch margin at the top, center the heading, double-space, and begin listing your notes. For each note, indent five spaces, raise the number above the line, and begin the note. Double-space, and if the note continues on the next line, begin that line at the left margin. The format is slightly different from that used in the Works Cited section in that the author's name appears in normal order, followed by a comma, the title, publisher, date in parentheses, and a page reference.

---

[3] Some historians argue that this widely accepted date is inaccurate. See Jerome Flynn, *Buried Treasures* (New York: New port, 1978): 29–43.

[4] Avery Jones and Jessica Lund, "The Nova Scotia Mystery Treasure," *Contemporary History 9* (1985): 81–83.

(3) Works Cited

The Works Cited section at the end of your paper (after the Notes, if you have any) is a list of all the sources you referred to in your paper and does not include other materials you may have read but not referred to. This list is arranged alphabetically by the last name of the author (to help the reader find the reference more easily). If the source has no author, use the first word of the title (but not the articles *a*, *and*, or *the*). There are three parts to each reference: author, title, and publishing information. Each part is followed by a period and two spaces.

For the Works Cited section, begin a new sheet of paper, leave a one-inch margin at the top, center the heading "Works Cited" (with no underline or quotation marks), and then double-space before the first entry. For each entry, begin at the left margin for the first line and indent five spaces for additional lines in the entry. Double space throughout.

Books (and Pamphlets)

One Author

    Joos, Martin. The Five Clocks. New York:
          Harcourt, Brace, and World, 1962.

Two or Three Authors

    Duggan, Stephen, and Betty Drury. The Rescue of
          Science and Learning. New York: Macmillan,
          1948.

```
Mellerman, Sidney, John Scarcini, and Leslie
      Karlin. Human Development: An Introduction
      to Cognitive Growth. New York: Harper,
      1981.
```

More than Three Authors

```
Spiller, Robert, et al. Literary History of the
      United States. New York: Macmillan, 1960.
```

More than One Work by the Same Author

```
Newman, Edwin. A Civil Tongue. Indianapolis:
      Bobbs-Merrill, 1966.
---. Strictly Speaking. New York: Warner Books,
      1974.
```

(Put the author's name in the first entry only. From then on, instead of the name, type three hyphens and a period, skip two spaces, and begin the next title. Alphabetize by title.)

Editor or Translator

```
Lash, Joseph, ed. From the Diaries of Felix
      Frankfurter. Boston: Norton, 1975.
```

Corporate Author

```
United States Capitol Society. We, the People:
      The Story of the United States Capitol.
      Washington, National Geographic Soc., 1964.
```

Anonymous

> Report of the Commission on Tests. New York:
>
>   College Entrance Examination Board, 1970.

More than One Volume

> Rutherford, Ernest. The Collected Papers. 3
>
>   vols. Philadelphia: Allen and Unwin,
>
>   1962-65.

(Specific references to the volume numbers belong in the parenthetical reference. If you are using only one of the volumes, put that number at the end of the reference, two spaces after the final period.)

Work with an Editor

> Dreiser, Theodore. Sister Carrie. Ed. Kenneth S.
>
>   Lynn. New York: Rinehart, 1959.

Work in an Anthology

> Dimock, George E., Jr. "The Name of Odysseus."
>
>   Essays on the Odyssey. Ed. Charles Taylor.
>
>   4th ed. 2 vols. Bloomington: Indiana UP,
>
>   1963. 2:54-72.

Introduction, Foreword, Preface, or Afterword

> Bruner, Jerome. Introduction. Thought and
>
>   Language. By Lev Vygotsky. Cambridge:
>
>   M.I.T., 1962. v-xiii.

Second or Later Edition

Ornstein, Robert E. <u>The Psychology of
Consciousness.</u> 2nd ed. New York: Harcourt,
1977.

Modern Reprint

Weston, Jessie L. <u>From Ritual to Romance.</u> 1920.
Garden City: Anchor-Doubleday, 1957.

Articles in Periodicals

Journal with Continuous Paging

Delbruch, Max. "Mind from Matter." <u>American
Scholar </u>47 (1978): 339-53.

Journal without Continuous Paging

Barthla, Frederick, and Joseph Murphy.
"Alcoholism in Fiction." <u>Kansas Quarterly</u>
17.2 (1981): 77-80.

Monthly or Bimonthly Magazine

Diamond, Jared. "The Worst Mistake in Human
History." <u>Discover</u> May 1987: 64-67.

Weekly or Biweekly Magazine

Isaacson, Walter. "Will the Cold War Fade Away?"
<u>Time</u> 27 July 1987: 40-45.

Newspaper Article

Strout, Richard L. "Another Bicentennial." <u>New York Times</u> 10 Nov. 1978, late ed.: A9.

Other Sources

Computer Service

Sampter, Jessica. "American Indian Mining Rights." <u>Business Monthly</u> June 1984: 14-22. DIALOGUE file 180, item 991432478723.

Computer Software

Tepper, Kenneth. <u>Time is Money</u>. Computer software. Turning Point, 1983. Apple, 64K, disk.

Government Publication

United States. Office of Education. <u>Tutor-Trainer's Resource Handbook.</u> Washington: GPO, 1973.

Information Service

Farmer, W. L. <u>Individualized Evaluation as a Method of Instruction to Improve Writing Ability in Freshman College Composition</u>. Urbana: ERIC Clearinghouse on Reading and Communication Skills, 1976. ED 133 759.

51d
MLA

Interview

```
Kochem, Prof. Alexander, Personal interview. 18
     April 1985.
Faulkner, William. Interview. With J. S. van den
     Heuvel. Writers at Work: The Paris Review
     Interviews. Ed. Malcolm Cowley. New York:
     Penguin, 1957. 119-41.
```

Radio and TV

```
American Folklore. Narr. Hugh McKenna. Writ. and
     Prod. Carl Tannenberg. PBS. WFYI,
     Indianapolis. 14 Mar. 1987.
```

Reference Book

```
"Mandarin." Encyclopedia Americana, 1980 ed.
```

For additional information on MLA format, see Joseph Gibaldi and Walter J. Acktert, *MLA Handbook for Writers of Research Papers,* 3rd ed., New York: MLA, 1988 (or more recent edition, if available).

51e APA Documentation Format (APA)

American Psychological Association (APA) format is used to document papers in the behavioral and social sciences.

If you are asked to use APA format, consult *The Publication Manual of the American Psychological Association,* 3d ed. Washington, D.C.: American Psychological Association, 1983.

APA style is like MLA style in that you have parenthetical references in your paper to refer readers to the list at the end of the paper, numbered notes that are to be used only to include information that would disrupt the writing if included there, and at the end of the paper, a reference list of works cited. References in this list include only the sources used in the research and preparation of your paper.

(1) Parenthetical References

When you use APA format, follow the author-date method of citation. Include the author's last name and year of publication in your text.

Millard (1970) compared reaction times . . .

In a recent study of reaction times (Millard, 1970) . . .

In 1970 Millard compared reaction times . . .

When a work has two authors, always cite both names every time the reference occurs in the text. When a work has more than two authors and fewer than six, cite all the authors the first time the reference occurs. In later references, include only the first name followed by et al.

Ellison, Mayer, Brunerd, and Keif (1987) studied . . .

When Ellison et al. (1987) continued . . .

When a work has no author, cite the first few words of the reference list entry.

One newspaper article ("When South Americans") indicates . . .

(2) Reference List

Arrange all entries in alphabetical order by the author's last name, and for several works by one author, arrange by year of publication with the earliest one first. Start each entry at the left margin and indent the rest of the entry lines three spaces. Double-space throughout. For authors' names, give all surnames first and then the initials. Use commas to separate a list of two or more names, and use an & (ampersand) before the last name in the list. Capitalize only the first word of the title and the subtitle (and any proper names) of a book or article, but capitalize the name of the journal. Underline (or italicize) book titles, names of journals, and the volume number of the journal.

51e
APA

Books

One Author

Rico, G. L. (1983). <u>Writing the natural way</u>. Los Angeles: J. P. Tarcher.

Two or More Authors

Strunk, W., Jr., & White, E. B. (1979). <u>The elements of style </u>(3rd ed.). New York: Macmillan.

Edited Volume

Maher, B. A. (Ed.). (1964-72). <u>Progress in experimental personality research</u> (6 vols.). New York: Academic Press.

Article in Edited Book

Riesen, A. H. (1966). Sensory deprivation. In E. Stellar & J. M. Sprague (eds.), <u>Progress in physiological psychology</u> (pp. 224-54). New York: Academic Press.

Government Publication

Clements, S. D. (1966). <u>Minimal brain dysfunction in children</u> (NINDS Monograph No. 3, U.S. Public Health Service Publication No. 1415). Washington, D.C.: U.S. Government Printing Office.

Technical and Research Report

Birney, A. F., & Hall, M. M. (1981). <u>Early iden-
    tification of children with written language
    disabilities</u> (Report No. 81-502).
    Washington, D.C.: National Education
    Association.

Article in Reference Book

Neptune, (1986). <u>Encyclopedia Brittanica.</u>

Published Interview

Newman, P. (1990, January). [Interview with
    William Epstein, editor of <u>JEP: Human
    Perception and Performance</u>]. <u>APA Monitor</u>,
    pp. 7, 39.

(Use brackets to indicate that the material is a description of
form and content, not a title. Use the format appropriate for
the published source of the interview, which in this example is
a newspaper.)

Review of a Book

Carmody, T. P. (1982). A new look at medicine
    from the social perspective [Review of <u>Social
    contexts of health, illness, and patient
    care</u>]. <u>Contemporary Psychology, 27</u>, 208-209.

51e
APA

If the review is untitled, use the material in brackets as the title;
keep the brackets to indicate that the material is a description of
form and content, not a title.)

Periodicals

One Author

Boice, R. (1985). Cognitive components of block-
ing. <u>Written Composition</u>, 2, 91-104.

Two or More Authors

Flower, L., & Hayes, J. R. (1981). A cognitive
process theory of writing. <u>College
Composition and Communication</u>, 32, 365-387.

No Author

The blood business. (1972, September 11). <u>Time,</u>
pp. 47-48.

Magazine Article

Timmons, H. (1985, November). Changing our buying habits. <u>American Consumer,</u> pp. 29-36.

Newspaper Article

Leftlow, B. S. (1986, December 18). Corporate
take-overs confuse stockmarket predictions.
<u>Wall Street Journal</u>, pp. 1, 14.

Monograph

Rotter, P. B. (1966). Generalized expectancies of
early childhood speech patterns. <u>Monographs of
the Childhood Education Society</u>, 36(2, Serial
No. 181).

Nonprint Media

Computer Program

Hazen, L. C. (1992). <u>Journalism ethics for
reporting on public figures</u> [computer pro-
gram]. Orange City, CA: Greenway Software.

(To reference the manual for a computer program, give the same information provided for the computer program. However, identify the source as a computer program manual in the brackets after the title.)

Film, Videotape, Audiotape, or Slides

Chaim, L. A. (Producer), & Klug, A. F.
(Director). (1990). <u>Veterinary diagnostics
for small animal clinics</u> [Film]. Hillside,
NJ: Multimedia Arts.

(Give the names and, in parentheses, the function of the originator or primary contributors; specify the medium in brackets after the title; and give the location and name of the distributor, which in this example is Multimedia Arts.)

52 *Résumés* (res)

> Your résumé is a tool to help you sell yourself to a prospective employer.

Like the effective business letter that emphasizes the reader's perspective, the effective résumé focuses on the particular organization to which you are sending it. Choose the details that relate your particular skills and achievements to the job for which you are applying. If you intend to apply for several different jobs, you will need to revise your résumé so that it is tailored for each job.

52a Sections of the Résumé

Listed here are the major sections of a résumé arranged in the order that you might use for your own résumé. You can use any of these headings or make up new sections more appropriate for your special abilities.

```
                         NAME
COLLEGE ADDRESS                      PERMANENT ADDRESS
PROFESSIONAL/CAREER OBJECTIVE/GOAL
EDUCATION/EDUCATIONAL RECORD
SIGNIFICANT COURSES/PERTINENT COURSEWORK
WORK EXPERIENCE
SKILLS/QUALIFICATIONS
COLLEGE ACTIVITIES and HONORS/ACTIVITIES/MEMBERSHIPS
REFERENCES
```

(1) Name
Generally, you should use your full name rather than initials or a nickname.

(2) Address
Include both your college and permanent addresses if they are different so that your prospective employer can contact you at either place. Include phone numbers and the dates that you will be at both addresses.

```
MARK DANIEL KANE
COLLEGE ADDRESS                 PERMANENT ADDRESS
421 Cary Quadrangle             1523 Elmwood Drive
West Lafayette, IN 47906        Nobleton, IN 46623
     317-555-0224               317-200-8749
(Until May 15, 19XX)            (After May 15, 19XX)
```

(3) Career Objective

Relate this section directly to the job you want and make sure you tie in the skills you have acquired from previous work experience, your education, and outside activities. Include the job title you seek and the type of work or skills you want to use. Write a concise phrase or clause, not a full sentence.

```
A summer internship with a construction company
that requires skills in field engineering, cost
controlling, planning, scheduling, and estimat-
ing.

A systems analyst position, stressing technical,
communication, and supervisory skills.
```

(4) Education

This is a major section for most students. Include the following:

- Name of college(s) attended
- Degree(s) and graduation dates(s) (month and year)
- Major, minor, or specialization
- Grade point average (optional) (Include your own GPA first, then a slash mark, and then the highest possible GPA at the school.)

Put these in the order of whichever aspect you want to emphasize, the degree or the college.

```
Purdue University
   Bachelor of Science, May 1999
   Major: Electrical Engineering; GPA: 5.7/6.0

      -or-

Bachelor of Science in Electrical Engineering,
   May 1999 Purdue University, GPA: 5.7/6.0
```

**52a
res**

You may also include important coursework and related experience such as workshops, special courses, conferences, projects, and/or reports.

Significant Courses

List the courses that are different from the ones everyone in your major must take or the few upper-level courses that are particularly significant. Use a more specific heading, if possible, such as "Public Relations Courses" rather than "Significant Courses."

Special Projects

Here you can point out some features of your particular education that make you unique and help you to stand out. Describe the projects, reports, or conferences briefly and give the most important details.

(5) Work Experience

This section can be arranged in several ways. Before deciding, list for yourself the following items:

- Job titles, places worked, locations, and dates. Include part time, temporary and volunteer work as well as cooperative programs and internships.
- Duties you performed and skills you acquired, using action verbs.

You can organize this information as a functional, skills, chronological, or imaginative résumé. See Section B on styles of a résumé.

```
Research Analyst
Kellogg Co.; Montack, Michigan; Summer 1987
– Supervised 9 assistants gathering information
  on cows' eating habits
– Researched most recent information on cows'
  nutritional needs
– Analyzed data to determine how to reduce num-
  ber of feeding hours while maintaining nutri-
  tional quality
```

**52a
res**

If the company you worked for is particularly impressive, you may want to begin with the company's name to highlight it.

(6) Skills

Not all résumés include a skills section, but this is a useful way to emphasize the skills you have acquired from various jobs or activities. To prepare this section, list the following for yourself:

- Jobs, club activities, projects, special offices or responsibilities
- Skills you have developed from these experiences. For example, as president of a club you had to lead meetings, delegate responsibilities, coordinate activities, etc.

Group the skills under three to five skills categories that relate to the job you are seeking and use these as your skills headings.

```
Management
    — Led a committee to prepare and institute new
      election procedures for Student Union Board
    — Evaluated employees' work progress for
      monthly reports
Communication
    — Wrote weekly advertisements for student gov-
      ernment entertainment activities
    — Represented sorority in negotiations with
      university administrators
    — Spoke to potential funding groups for stu-
      dent-organized charity events
Programming
    — Analyzed and designed a program to record
      and average student grades for faculty mem-
      ber
    — Designed a program to record and update
      items of sorority's $90,000 annual budget
```

HINT: To make your skills section effective and to help the prospective employer see you as an active worker, use action verbs such as the following:

Action Verbs

act	generate	persuade
adapt	get	plan
administer	govern	prepare
advise	guide	present
analyze	handle	process

assess	head	produce
build	hire	program
calculate	implement	promote
catalogue	improve	provide
compile	increase	raise
complete	initiate	recommend
conduct	install	recruit
coordinate	integrate	represent
create	maintain	revise
decide	manage	schedule
define	market	select
demonstrate	modify	sell
design	monitor	send
develop	motivate	speak
direct	negotiate	supervise
distribute	obtain	survey
edit	operate	train
establish	order	transmit
evaluate	organize	update
examine	oversee	write
forecast	perform	

(7) College Activities

This section demonstrates your leadership and involvement and can include college activities, honors, and official positions or responsibilities you have had. You may need to explain in a phrase or two what various organizations are because prospective employers will probably not be familiar with the fact that the Tomahawk Club is an honorary service organization on your campus or that Alpha Gamma Alpha is a freshman honors council at your school.

52a
res

(8) References

You can include three or four references on your résumé, but many people prefer to be selective about who gets a copy of their list. If you also wish to be selective, list the names on a separate sheet of paper that matches your résumé, and include the name, address, and phone number of each reference. Add a sentence or two that explain your connection with that person. On the résumé, include the following statement:

```
References: available on request.
```

52b *Résumé Styles*

In choosing between the functional, skills, chronological, or imaginative style for your résumé, consider what you want to highlight. Examples of functional, skills, and chronological résumés are included at the end of this section.

(1) Functional Résumés

This style categorizes each job by function (for example, program designer, case worker, field consultant) with the most significant listed first. Then, each function is described by detailing responsibilities held, actions taken, and results achieved. Subordinate employers' names and dates. This approach is useful if you have impressive job titles and duties to feature.

(2) Skills Résumés

This emphasizes skills and abilities gained through jobs, other experiences, and school activities. Arrange the skills from the most relevant to the least. You can include the name and location of companies and dates of employment. This approach is particularly appropriate when the skills you've acquired are more impressive than the jobs you've had or when you want to highlight a significant skill acquired from different experiences and jobs. It also allows you to relate your skills to the job you want.

(3) Chronological Résumés

This style, which highlights your current job and employer's name, was once the standard approach, but it has been replaced in many fields. However, some conservative employers may still prefer it. It is also appropriate if you want to emphasize your cur-

52b
res

rent job as the most important, if your work experience is closely related to the job you are seeking, or if you are older and have extensive work experience to offer. When you are stressing extensive work experience as your strongest qualification, place the Work Experience before the Education section. You may prefer to include only your most recent jobs or those that best relate to the job you seek.

For this approach, begin each entry with the employer's name and your dates of employment. Then include a brief description of your job, including titles and responsibilities. Arrange this list chronologically, beginning with the most recent.

(4) Imaginative Résumés

This résumé style highlights your artistic ability and creativity. It is particularly appropriate when you are seeking an artistic or creative position. It contains the same information as the others but can be structured in your own style and arranged in some unique and interesting way on the page. You can use borders or special pictures and/or graphics that you create.

When you are ready to assemble your résumé, decide how you want to organize the sections. For example, is your work experience more important than your education? Are your college activities more important than your past jobs?

> **HINT:** Consider developing a skills résumé if your activities are more important than the jobs you've had.

Use white space and lists to make your résumé visually appealing, easy to read, and uncluttered. Highlight your headings with different kinds of type, underlining, boldface, capital letters, and indenting to show your organizing ability. And be sure that your headings are all parallel. Many companies prefer one-page résumés, but this may vary according to your field and career objective. Above all, make the résumé highlight your unique capabilities.

Leslie James Edelon

CURRENT ADDRESS   PERMANENT ADDRESS
(until June 1, 1991)   (after June 1, 1991)

230 Grant Street   Route #2, Box 30-A
West Grandville, KS 67608   Rinard, KS 62339
(214) 743-9881   (214) 681-0099

CAREER OBJECTIVE

    An entry-level position in installment loans working towards a career
    as a farm loan officer

EDUCATION

    North Kansas State College, Bachelor of Science in Agriculture
    Finance, May 1991
    GPA: 4.02/5.00

    Areas of Study
    Finance/Management: Agriculture Finance, Financial Accounting,
    Financial Management, Farm Management, Farm Organization

    Sales/Marketing: Marketing Management, Agri-Sales and Marketing, Grain
    Marketing, Managerial Accounting, Quantitative Techniques

EXPERIENCE

    Bookkeeper, Farmers & Merchants State Bank; Summer 1990
              - Answered customer inquiries and complaints
              - Balanced customer checkbooks
              - Verified $3,000-$5,000 currency daily

    Assistant Manager, Family Farm; 1984-present
              - Contributed management input
              - Assisted in financial planning
              - Operated heavy equipment

    Special Sales Chairman, State College Tractor Pull Foundation; August
    1989
              - Coordinated National College Tractor Pullers
                Association souvenir sales
              - Sold advertising space on tickets

ACTIVITIES

    Tractor Pull Foundation
    Agriculture Economics Club
    Alpha Zeta Professional Fraternity
    Ceres Honorary Fraternity

REFERENCES: Available on request

52b
res

Example of a functional résumé

ALETHA WATMAN

UNTIL May 15, 1991   **AFTER** May 15, 1991
210 Waldron Drive   12955 Bleekman Street
University City, LA 71213   Pontosa, OK 75337

PROFESSIONAL OBJECTIVE
      A career in personnel management which would involve coordinating,
      communicating, and training

EDUCATION
      Carlman College; expected graduation, May 1991
      Bachelor of Arts degree in Organization Psychology
            Minor: General Management

      GPA (6.0 scale): Major and Minor 5.9; Overall 5.6

      Major Related Courses:
            Personnel Management, Interviewing, Labor Relations, Industrial
            Psychology, Organizational Communications, Persuasion, Public
            Relations, Psychological Testing, Business Writing, Marketing

SKILLS

      Coordinating
            - Planned and organized campaign for Homecoming Queen candidate
            - Supervised dining room preparation at the Sheraton Plaza

      Communicating
            - Underwent 150 hours of training to learn peer counseling
              techniques
            - Developed and delivered a seminar on peer counseling for the
              American Personal Guidance Convention, Washington, D.C., 1989
            - Handled customer complaints

      Training
            - Supervised peer counseling program in college dormitory
            - Instructed other employees in proper food and beverage service

WORK EXPERIENCE (paid for 100% of college expenses)
      Waitress, Carlman Memorial Union; Fall 1987 to present
      Salesperson, University Book Store, Carlman College; Fall 1987, Spring
            1988, Spring 1989
      Waitress, Sheraton Plaza, University City, Louisiana; Summer 1987

ACTIVITIES AND HONORS
      Peer Counselor (Student Dormitory)
      Campaign Manager for Homecoming Queen candidate
      Member of Psi Chi (Psychology Honor Society)
      Dean's List (8 semesters)

REFERENCES
      Available upon request

52b
res

Example of a skills résumé

NOAH ALLAN MARMOR

Campus Address
Box 218, Daniels Hall
Oshkego, NY 14945
217/ 332-1617

Permanent Address
6545 Country Inn Lane
Roxton Falls, NY 17190
314/ 991-2387

PROFESSIONAL OBJECTIVE
An engineering career in aircraft structural analysis or structural
dynamics

EDUCATION
Milman Polytechnic Institute; Oshkego, New York
Bachelor of Science in Aeronautical Engineering, December 1985
Structures and Materials Major/Dynamics and Control Minor

Significant Courses
Advanced Matrix Methods, Mechanics of Composite Materials, Elasticity
in Aerospace Engineering, Flight Mechanics, Aircraft Design I and II,
Jet Propulsion Power Plants

Special Projects
 - Proposed and performed wind tunnel test of composite laminates
    to study aeroelastic divergence
 - Worked on a team designing a supersonic fighter aircraft with
    short take-off and landing capabilities
 - Learned the use of a computer program to analyze aeroelastic
    stability of a wing

WORK EXPERIENCE
Bell Helicopter Textron, Fort Worth, Texas: September 1987 to present
 - Use flight dynamics simulation computer programs such as DNAW06
    and C81
 - Evaluate rotors and rotor-fuselage combinations

Prisler and Associates, Dallas, Texas: December 1985 to September 1987
 - Draft rotor parts for research and flight test programs

Hughes Aircraft, Los Angeles, California (Engineering Co-op): January
    1984 to June 1984
 - Tested composite specimens to verify material specifications
 - Fabricated composite structures for research programs

ACTIVITIES
Hillel Foundation Coordinator
Alpha Omicron (Engineering Honorary Society)
AIPAC Public Relations Chairman

REFERENCES: Available on request

**52b
res**

Example of a chronological résumé

JILLIAN CHAPLER
125 East Maynard Place
Gary, IN 46801
(312) 555-1818

CAREER OBJECTIVE
A career in the sales, marketing, or public relations department
of a large and growing hotel chain

WORK EXPERIENCE
Howard Johnson's O'Hare International (Chicago) - Sales

Sales Manager	June 1988—present
Sales Representative	March 1982—January 1986
Trade Shows Organizer	June 1981—February 1982

Howard Johnson's, (Kokomo, IN) - Management

Management Office Staff	October 1980—April 1981
Employee Training Supervisor	May 1979—September 1980

Nippersink Manor Resort (O'Dare Lake, MI) - Management

Scheduling Supervisor	May 1977—May 1979
Promotional Staff	January 1974—May 1977
Accounting Department	October 1973—December 1973

Lakeview Manor (Benton City, MI) - Public Relations

Public Relations Assistant	June 1972—October 1973

EDUCATION
Northern Indiana State University (Kendleberg, IN): Restaurant and
Hotel Management Major, 1986-1988

Linton Community College (Linton, IN): Liberal Arts Major, 1970-
1972
Degrees: Bachelor of Science in Restaurant and Hotel
Management, N.I.S.U., 1991
Associate of Arts and Sciences, L.C.C., 1972

AFFILIATIONS
American Management Association
American Society of Hotel Managers
National Hotel Association

ACTIVITIES, AWARDS, INTERESTS
Chairman of Awards: Outstanding Service Awards (Howard Johnson's)
Macintosh Users Club (Chicago)
President, Kokomo Chapter of National Hotel Association

REFERENCES
Available upon request

Example of a chronological résumé that emphasizes extensive work
experience rather than the education section

Answer Key for Exercises in Part 6

Exercise 51.2

One possible revision is as follows:

Another important concern in city planning is to formulate proposals to eliminate or reduce problems caused by automobiles. As Marcia D. Lowe notes, "Cities with streets designed for cars instead of people are increasingly unlivable" (56), for cars cause congestion, pollution, and noise. While more public transportation can reduce these problems, it is not likely that city dwellers will give up owning cars. Therefore, solutions are needed for parking, which already uses up as much as 20 or 30% of the space available in downtown areas (Lipperman 99), and for rush hour traffic, which now causes rush hours to be extended to as much as twelve hours or longer in Seoul and to fourteen hours in Rio de Janeiro (Lowe 57). Pollution, another urban problem caused partly by cars, needs to be controlled by reducing automobile emissions, which as Irwin Lipperman points out, increases lung disorders and aggravates bronchial problems (108). In addition, noise from automobiles must be curbed as it has already become a health problem in cities such as Cairo where noise levels are already ten times the acceptable standard for human health (Lowe 57).

six
ans

Paper Format (format)

Included here is information to help you prepare your papers to be read by others. The following topics are covered:

1. Titles
2. Headings and Subheadings
3. Page Preparation
4. Spacing for Punctuation

1   Titles

Choosing a Title

The title serves several purposes. It helps readers by indicating what they can expect as to the topic and the author's perspective in the essay. Some titles state in a straightforward manner what the essay will be about; for example, the title "Nutritional Benefits of High-Fiber Foods" is a clear indication of the content and the author's intention to address it directly, in a formal manner. Other titles, particularly of personal essays, may offer the reader only a hint about the topic, a hint that becomes clearer after reading the essay. "At Sea over the Ocean" might be the title for an essay describing a ride in a hot-air balloon lost over the Atlantic. The tone of this title also suggests a possibly light, informal approach.

A title also helps the writer organize a topic and select the emphasis for a particular essay. Writers who select the title before or during the early stages of writing may need to check at a later stage to see that the title still relates to the essay as it evolves and develops. Good titles have the following characteristics:

- *They are clear and specific.* An example of an overly general title for a short essay would be "Divorce" because it does not indicate what aspect of divorce will be discussed. Even a title such as "Recent Trends in Automotive Design" is too general for a short essay because so much material could be discussed under this heading.
- *They are brief.* Most titles are no more than six or seven words.

format

Titles should stand alone and not be part of the first sentence or be referred to by a pronoun in the first sentence. For example, in a research paper entitled "The Influence of Television Advertisements in Presidential Elections," the first sentence should not be as follows:

Incorrect Opening Sentence: *This* is a topic of great concern both to politicians and to those who think that *these* elections have become popularity contests.

Revised: The degree to which television advertisements influence voters' choices in presidential elections worries politicians and others who think that national elections have become popularity contests.

Capitalizing a Title

The first and last words of a title, plus all other words except articles (*a, an, the*), short prepositions (*by, for, in, to, on,* etc.) and short joining words (*but, and, or,* etc.) should be capitalized. Capitalize both words of a hyphenated word. Capitalize the first word of a subtitle that appears after a colon.

Choosing a Career in Retailing

A History of Anti-Imperialism

Myths Through the Ages

Short but Sweet

My Childhood: The Plight of Growing Up Black

(For more information about capitalization, see Chapter 36.)

Punctuating a Title

For your own essays, do not put the title in quotation marks, and do not use a period after the title. (For information on using quotations marks and underlining when you cite other titles either in your own title or in your paper, see Chapters 28 and 29.)

format

Spacing a Title on the Page

For Typed Cover Pages   If a cover page is requested for research papers and reports, space the title one-third down from the top of the page. Double-space the title, and then move down to list the rest of the information, as illustrated in the section on spacing in this Chapter.

For the First Typed Page   If you have a cover page, include only the title on the first page and begin the first line four spaces down the page. See the illustration in the section on spacing in this Chapter.

If you do not have a cover page, leave a one-inch margin at the top and include at the left-hand margin your name, your instructor's name, the course number and section, and date submitted. Double-space this information. Then double-space and type the title, centered on the page. If more than one line is needed, double space. Then leave two double-spaces (four lines) and begin the paper. See the illustration in the section on spacing in this Chapter.

For Handwritten Papers   Follow the format for typed papers by leaving a one-inch margin at the top and then writing your name, your instructor's name, the course and section number, and date submitted at the left-hand margin. Put the title on the first ruled line of the page, skip a line, and then begin writing your paper.

2   *Headings and Subheadings*

Headings are the short titles that define sections and subsections in long reports and outlines. In a report, headings provide visual emphasis by breaking the report into manageable portions that are easily seen and identified. Headings with numbers—in reports, outlines, and tables of contents—also indicate relationships because the numbers tell the reader which parts are segments of a larger part, which are equal, and which are of less importance. Subheadings are the headings of less importance within a series of headings.

format

Headings for outlines and in most reports are numbered, either in the decimal system or with Roman numerals. While the decimal system is used more often in technical and professional fields than Roman numerals, some of these fields still follow traditional use of Roman numerals. Decimals can also be combined with letters.

Decimal numbers	*Roman numerals*
1.0	I.
1.1 —or— 1.a. —or— 1a	A.
1.2 —or— 1.b. —or— 1b	1.
1.2.1 —or— 1.a.1.	2.
1.2.2 —or— 1.a.2.	B.
1.2.2.1	1.
2.0	a.
2.1 —or— 2.a	1)
	a)
	2.
	I.

....

HINT: For all headings and subheadings, be sure to use the same grammatical form (parallelism) to start each phrase.

Not Parallel: I.   For Preliminary Planning
                II.   The Rough Draft
              III.   Polishing the Draft

Revised: I. Planning the Paper
II. Writing the Rough Draft
III. Polishing the Draft

—or—

I. The Preliminary Draft
II. The Rough Draft
III. The Polished Draft

3 *Page Preparation*

Paper: Use only 8 1/2-by-11-inch white, unlined paper for typing. Do not use onionskin or other very thin paper or erasable paper. For handwritten papers, use lined paper. For both handwritten and typed papers, use only one side of each sheet.

Line Spacing: Double-space typewritten papers, and write on every other line for handwritten papers. Writing on every other line allows you room for making corrections and gives your teacher space in which to write comments.

Ink: Use black ribbon for typewritten papers and black ink for handwritten papers. Do not use pencil.

Margins: Leave an inch at the top, on the right-hand side, and at the bottom of the page. Leave a 1 1/2-inch margin on the left-hand side of the page.

Indentations: At the beginning of each paragraph, indent five spaces when typing and one inch for handwritten pages. For long quotations within paragraphs, indent ten spaces for typing and two inches for handwritten pages.

Page Numbers: Use Arabic numerals (1, 2, 3, and so on), and place them in the upper right-hand corner, 1/2 inch from the top of the page. Do not place a number on the first page; begin numbering with 2 on the second page.

Word-Processed Papers: Papers written on computers with easily read printing are generally acceptable, but you should check with your teacher. Tear off the edging of the paper, and separate the sheets.

Page Spacing:

1. Cover Page

If a cover page is requested, include the title, double-spaced, about one-third of the way down the page. Slightly below the middle of the page type *by* in the center. Then, double-space and type your name. Leave space and then include the following information in a double-spaced, centered list: the course number and section, the instructor, and the date submitted. See the illustration.

format

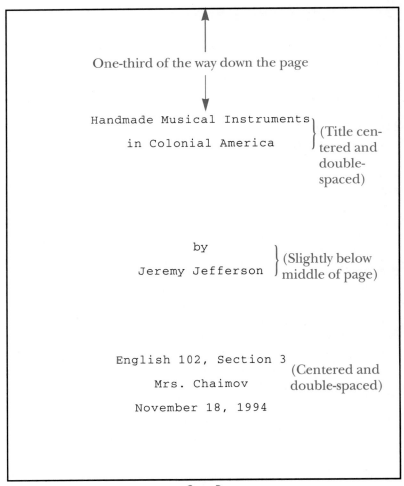

Cover Page

2. First Page:

If you have a typed cover page: Leave a one-inch margin at the top, and then repeat only the paper title. Leave two double-spaces (four spaces) before the first line of text.

If you do not have a typed cover page: Leave a one-inch margin at the top and include the following information in a double-spaced list at the left-hand margin: your name, your instructor's name, the course number and section, and date submitted. Then double-space and type the title, centered on the page. If more than one line is needed, double space. Then leave two double spaces (four lines) and begin the paper. See the illustration.

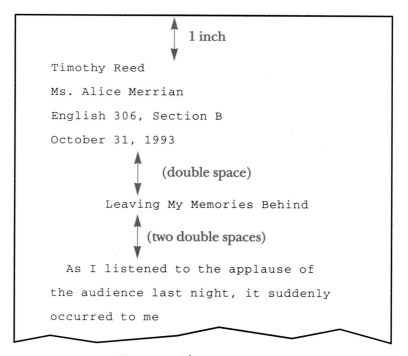

First page with no cover page

If your paper is handwritten: Follow the format for first pages of typed papers without cover pages by leaving a one-inch margin at the top and then writing your name, your instructor's name, the course and section number, and date submitted at the left-hand margin. Put the title on the first ruled line of the page, skip a line, and then begin writing your paper.

3. Later Pages

Leave a one-inch margin at the top. In the upper right-hand corner, 1/2 inch from the top, put your last name and the page number with no punctuation. If you have lengthy quotes, indent ten spaces. See the illustration.

format

1/2 inch

Smith 3

1 inch

When the first discoveries of the ozone hole in the Antarctica atmosphere were reported, scientists from the British Antarctic Survey described its pattern:

> The ozone hole would open in the stratospheric ozone layer over the pole in September, with the first light of the Antarctic sunrise. It would close in mid-October, by which time the sun would be up round the clock and ozone-rich air of the lower latitudes would flood over the pole in an event known as the final warming.

As the Survey team noted, each year there was less ozone in the hole. By 1985, when the British finally published the results

4. Works Cited Page

On the right-hand side of the page, 1/2 inch from the top, type your last name and page number. One inch from the top, centered on the page, type *Works Cited*. Type the first line of each entry with the last name first. Indent five spaces for all further lines in that entry. Continue with your entries double-spaced down the page. See the illustration.

format

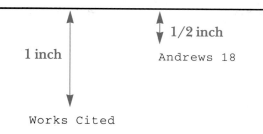

```
                                      1/2 inch

              1 inch              Andrews 18


                       Works Cited


Nemelman, Barry. Life of Darwin. New York:

     Doubleday, 1981.

Nystand, Alice. The Battle for Evolution

     in the Schools. Philadelphia: Dighton,

     1978.

---. "Biology Teaching in Secondary

     Schools."Science Teaching 45 (1982):

     422-504.

Orfine, Michael. Understanding Evolution.

     San Francisco: Josten and Parks, 1989.
```

4 *Spacing for Punctuation*

End punctuation (. ? !)
Leave no space before the end punctuation and two spaces
  before the next sentence.

> next year. After the term of . . .

Periods after abbreviations (.)
Leave no space before the period and one space after. When a
  sentence ends with an abbreviation, use only one period to
  indicate both the abbreviation and the period that ends the
  sentence.

> Dr. Smith was noted for . . .
> . . . at 8 A.M. The next day there was . . .

Commas, semicolons, colons (, ; :)
Leave no space before the mark and one space after.

> happy, healthy child
> John, a musician; Josh, a doctor; and . . .

Apostrophes (')
Leave no space within a word. At the end of a word, leave no
  space before the apostrophe, with one space after.

> don't
> boy's hat
> boxes' lids

Quotation marks (" " ' ')
Leave no space between the quotation marks and what they
  enclose, no space between double and single quotation marks,
  and one space afterward in the middle of a sentence.

> "No way" was his favorite expression.
> " 'Battle Hymn of the Republic' should be the last song on the program,"
> she explained.

Hyphen (-)

Leave no space before or after. If the hyphen shows the connection of two prefixes to one root word, put one space after the first hyphen.

a six-page report
the pre- and post-test scores

Dash (-- —)

In a typewritten paper, type two hyphens, with no space before or after. For handwritten papers, write a longer line than the hyphen, leaving no space before or after. For papers written on a computer, there may be a dash mark to use.

```
Not one of us--Tobias, Matthew, or Nick--thought it
mattered.
Not one of us—Tobias, Matthew, or Nick—thought it
mattered.
```

Slash (/)

Leave no space before or after except for marking lines of poetry, when one space is left before and after.

and/or
He read his favorite two lines from the poem, "slipping, sliding on his tongue / the sound of music in his soul."

Brackets, parentheses [] ()

Leave no space before or after the material being enclosed.

"When [the fund-raising group] presented its report (not previously published), the press covered the event."

Ellipsis (. . .)

Leave one space before each period, one space between, and one space after. If you are using four dots to indicate that you are omitting one or more sentences, treat the first dot like a period, with no space after the last word, and then space evenly.

No one . . . noticed the error.

Every worker signed the contract. . . . No one opposed the new guidelines for health care.

Underlining (<u>abcdef</u>) *or italics (abcdef)*

When using a typewriter or writing by hand, use underlines with or without breaks between words, but be consistent once you choose to use or not use breaks. If your computer has italic type, ask your instructor whether italics or underlining is preferred.

format

<u>Wind in the Willows</u>

<u>Wind</u> <u>in</u> <u>the</u> <u>Willows</u>

<u>Wind in the Willows</u>

Wind in the Willows

Glossary of Usage

This list includes words and phrases you may be uncertain about when writing. If you have questions about words not included here, try the index to this book to see whether the word is discussed elsewhere. You can also check a recently published dictionary. (The dictionary used here as a source of information is the *Oxford American Dictionary*, Oxford University Press, 1980.)

usage

A, An: Use *a* before words that begin with a consonant (for example, *a* cat, *a* house) and before words beginning with a vowel that sounds like a consonant (for example, *a* one-way street, *a* union. Use *an* before words that begin with a vowel (for example, *an* egg, *an* ice cube) and before words with a silent *h* (for example, *an* hour). See Chapter 4b.

Accept, Except: *Accept*, a verb, means *to agree to, to believe,* or *to receive.*

The detective **accepted** his account of the event and did not hold him as a suspect in the case.

Except, a verb, means *to exclude* or *leave out,* and *except,* a preposition, means *leaving out.*

Because he did not know any of the answers, he was **excepted** from the list of contestants and asked to leave.

Except for brussel sprouts, which I hate, I eat most vegetables.

Advice, Advise: *Advice* is a noun, and *advise* is a verb.

She always offers too much **advice**.

Would you **advise** me about choosing the right course?

Affect, Effect: Most frequently, *affect*, which means *to influence*, is used as a verb, and *effect*, which means a *result* is used as a noun.

> The weather **affects** my ability to study.

> What **effect** does too much coffee have on your concentration?

However, *effect*, meaning *to cause* or *bring about*, is also used as a verb.

> The new traffic enforcement laws **effected** a great change in people's driving habits.

Common phrases with *effect* include the following:

> in effect
> to that effect

usage

Ain't: This is a nonstandard way of saying *am not, is not, has not, have not*, etc.

All ready, Already: *All ready* means *prepared*; *already* means *before* or *by this time*.

> The courses for the meal are **all ready** to be served.

> When I got home, she was **already** there.

All Right, Alright: *All right* is two words, not one. *Alright* is an incorrect form.

All Together, Altogether: *All together* means *in a group*, and *altogether* means *entirely, totally*.

> We were **all together** again after having separate vacations.

> He was not **altogether** happy about the outcome of the test.

Alot, A Lot: *Alot* is an incorrect form of *a lot*.

a.m., p.m. (or) A.M., P.M.: Use these with numbers, not as substitutes for the words *morning* or *evening*.

> **Wrong:** We meet every a.m. for an exercise class.

> **Revised:** We meet every morning at 9 A.M. for an exercise class.

Among, Between: Use *among* when referring to three or more things and *between* when referring to two things.

> The decision was discussed **among** all the members of the committee.

> It was difficult to decide **between** the chocolate mousse pie and the almond ice cream for dessert.

Amount, Number: Use *amount* for things or ideas that are general or abstract and cannot be counted. For example, furniture is a general term and cannot be counted. That is, we cannot say "one furniture" or "two furnitures." Use *number* for things that can be counted, as, for example, four chairs, or three tables.

> He had a huge **amount** of work to finish before the deadline.
>
> There were a **number** of people who saw the accident.

An: See the entry for *a, an.*

And: While some people discourage the use of *and* as the first word in a sentence, it is an acceptable word with which to begin a sentence.

And Etc.: Adding *and* is redundant because *et* means "and" in Latin. See the entry for *etc.*

usage

Anybody, Any Body: See the entry for *anyone, any one.*

Anyone, Any One: *Anyone* means *any person at all. Any one* refers to a specific person or thing in a group. There are similar distinctions for other words ending in *-body* and *-one* (for example, *everybody, every body; anybody, any body;* and *someone, some one*).

> The teacher asked if **anyone** knew the answer.
>
> **Any one** of those children could have taken the ball.

Anyways, Anywheres: These are nonstandard forms for *anyway* and *anywhere.*

As, As If, As Though, Like: Use *as* in a comparison (not *like*) when there is an equality intended or when the meaning is *in the function of.*

> Celia acted **as** [not *like*] the leader when the group was getting organized. (Celia = leader)

Use *as if* or *as though* for the subjunctive.

> He spent his money **as if** [or **as though**] he were rich.

Use *like* in a comparison (not *as*) when the meaning is *in the manner of* or *to the same degree as.*

> The boy swam **like** a fish.

Don't use *like* as the opening word in a clause in formal writing:

Informal: Like I thought, he was unable to predict the weather.

Formal: As I thought, he was unable to predict the weather.

Assure, Ensure, Insure: *Assure* means *to declare* or *promise, ensure* means *to make safe* or *certain,* and *insure* means *to protect with a contract of insurance.*

I **assure** you that I am trying to find your lost package.

Some people claim that eating properly **ensures** good health.

This insurance policy also **insures** my car against theft.

Awful, Awfully: *Awful* is an adjective meaning *inspiring awe* or *extremely unpleasant.*

He was involved in an **awful** accident.

Awfully is an adverb used in very informal writing to mean *very.* It should be avoided in formal writing.

Informal: The dog was **awfully** dirty.

Awhile, A While: *Awhile* is an adverb meaning a *short time* and modifies a verb:

He talked **awhile** and then left.

A *while* is an article with the noun *while* and means a *period of time.*

I'll be there in **a while**.

Bad, Badly: *Bad* is an adjective and is used after linking verbs. *Badly* is an adverb.

The wheat crop looked **bad** [not *badly*] because of lack of rain.

There was a **bad** flood last summer.

The building was **badly** constructed and unable to withstand the strong winds.

Beside, Besides: *Beside* is a preposition meaning *at the side of, compared with,* or *having nothing to do with. Besides* is a preposition meaning *in addition to* or *other than. Besides* as an adverb means *also* or *moreover.* Don't confuse *beside* with *besides.*

That is **beside** the point.

Besides the radio, they had no other means of contact with the outside world.

Besides, I enjoyed the concert.

Between, Among: See the entry for *among, between.*

Breath, Breathe: *Breath* is a noun, and *breathe* is a verb.

> She held her **breath** when she dived into the water.
>
> Learn to **breathe** deeply when you swim.

But: While some people discourage the use of *but* as the first word in a sentence, it is an acceptable word with which to begin a sentence.

Can, May: *Can* is a verb that expresses ability, knowledge, or capacity:

> He **can** play both the violin and the cello.

May is a verb that expresses possibility or permission. Careful writers avoid using *can* to mean permission:

> **May** [not *can*] I sit here?

Can't Hardly: This is incorrect because it is a double negative.

> **Wrong:** She **can't hardly** hear normal voice levels.
>
> **Revised:** She **can hardly** hear normal voice levels.

Choose, Chose: *Choose* is the present tense of the verb, and *chose* is the past tense:

> Jennie always **chooses** strawberry ice cream.
>
> Yesterday, she even **chose** strawberry-flavored popcorn.

Cloth, Clothe: *Cloth* is a noun, and *clothe* is a verb.

> Here is some **cloth** for a new scarf.
>
> His paycheck helps to feed and **clothe** many people in his family.

Compared To, Compared With: Use *compared to* when showing that two things are alike. Use *compared with* when showing similarities and differences.

> The speaker **compared** the economy **to** a roller coaster because both have sudden ups and downs.
>
> The detective **compared** the fingerprints **with** others from a previous crime.

Could Of: This is incorrect. Instead use *could have.*

Data: This is the plural form of *datum*. In informal usage, *data* is used as a singular noun, with a singular verb. However, since dictionaries do not accept this, use *data* as a plural form for academic writing.

> **Informal Usage:** The **data** is inconclusive.
> **Formal Usage:** The **data** are inconclusive.

Different From, Different Than: *Different from* is always correct, but some writers use *different than* if there is a clause following this phrase.

> This program is **different from** the others.
> That is a **different** result **than** they predicted.

usage

Done: The past tense forms of the verb *do* are *did* and *done*. *Did* is the simple form that needs no additional verb as a helper. *Done* is the past form that requires the helper *have*. Some writers make the mistake of interchanging *did* and *done*.

> **Wrong:** They **done** it again.
> **Correct:** They **did** it again.
> —or—
> They **have done** it again.

Effect, Affect: See the entry for *affect, effect*.

Ensure: See the entry for *assure, ensure, insure*.

Etc.: This is an abbreviation of the Latin *et cetera*, meaning *and the rest*. Because it should be used sparingly if at all in formal academic writing, substitute other phrases such as *and so forth* or *and so on*.

Everybody, Every Body: See the entry for *anyone, any one*.

Everyone, Every One: See the entry for *anyone, any one*.

Except, Accept: See the entry for *accept, except*.

Farther, Further: While some writers use these words interchangeably, dictionary definitions differentiate them. *Farther* is used when actual distance is involved, and *further* is used to mean *to a greater extent, more*.

> The house is **farther** from the road than I realized.
> That was **furthest** from my thoughts at the time.

Fewer, Less: *Fewer* is used for things that can be counted (fewer trees, fewer people), and *less* is used for ideas, abstractions, things that are thought of collectively, not separately (less trouble, less furniture), and things that are measured by amount, not number (less milk, less fuel).

Fun: This noun is used informally as an adjective.

> **Informal:** They had a **fun** time.

Goes, Says: *Goes* is a nonstandard form of *says*.

> **Wrong:** Whenever I give him a book to read, he **goes**, "What's it about?"
> **Correct:** Whenever I give him a book to read, he **says**, "What's it about?"

Gone, Went: The past tense forms of the verb *go* and *went* and *gone*. *Went* is the simple form that needs no additional verb as a helper. *Gone* is the past form that requires the helper *have*. Some writers make the mistake of interchanging *went* and *gone*.

> **Wrong:** They already **gone** away.
> **Correct:** They already **went** away.
> —or—
> They **had gone** before I woke up.

usage

Good, Well: *Good* is an adjective and therefore describes only nouns. *Well* is an adverb and therefore describes adjectives, other adverbs, and verbs. The word *well* is used as an adjective only in the sense of "in good health."

> **Wrong:** The stereo works **good**.
> **Wrong:** I feel **good**.
> **Correct:** The stereo works **well**.
> **Correct:** I feel **well**.
> **Correct:** She is a **good** driver.

Got, Have: *Got* is the past tense of *get* and should not be used in place of *have*. Similarly, *got to* should not be used as a substitute for *must*. *Have got to* is an informal substitute for *must*.

> **Wrong:** Do you **got** any pennies for the meter?
> **Correct:** Do you **have** any pennies for the meter?
> **Wrong:** I **got** to go now.
> **Correct:** I **must go** now.

Informal: You **have got to** see that movie.

Great: This adjective is overworked in its formal meaning of *very enjoyable, good,* or *wonderful* and should be reserved for its more exact meanings such as *of remarkable ability, intense, high degree of,* and so on.

> **Informal:** That was a **great** movie.
> **More Exact Uses of *Great*:** The vaccine was a **great** discovery.
> The map went into **great** detail.

Have, Got: See the entry for *got, have.*

Have, Of: *Have,* not *of,* should follow verbs such as *could, might, must,* and *should.*

> **Wrong:** They **should of** called by now.
> **Correct:** They **should have** called by now.

Hisself: This is a nonstandard substitute for *himself.*

Hopefully: This adverb means *in a hopeful way.* Many people consider the meaning *it is to be hoped* as unacceptable.

> **Acceptable:** He listened **hopefully** for the knock at the door.
> **Often Considered Unacceptable: Hopefully**, it will not rain tonight.

I: While some people discourage the use of *I* in formal essays, it is acceptable. If you wish to eliminate the use of *I,* see Chapters 1d, 17d, and 20f on passive verbs.

Imply, Infer: Some writers use these interchangeably, but careful writers maintain the distinction between the two words. *Imply* means *to suggest without stating directly, to hint. Infer* means *to reach an opinion from facts or reasoning.*

> The tone of her voice **implied** that he was stupid.
> The anthropologist **inferred** that this was a burial site for prehistoric Indians.

Insure: See the entry for *assure, ensure, insure.*

Irregardless: This is an incorrect form of the word *regardless.*

Is When, Is Why, Is Where, Is Because: These are incorrect forms for definitions. See Chapter 18 on faulty predication.

Faulty Predication: Nervousness **is when** my palms sweat.
Revised: When I am nervous, my palms sweat.

—or—

Nervousness is a state of being very uneasy or agitated.

Its, It's: *Its* is a personal pronoun in the possessive case. *It's* is a contraction for *it is*.

The kitten licked **its** paw.
It's a good time for a vacation.

Kind, Sort: These two forms are singular and should be used with *this* or *that*. Use *kinds, sorts* with *these* or *those*.

This kind of cloud often indicates that there will be heavy rain.
These sorts of plants are regarded as weeds.

Lay, Lie: *Lay* is a verb that needs an object and should not be used in place of *lie*, a verb that takes no direct object.

Wrong: He should **lay** down and rest awhile.
Correct: He should **lie** down and rest awhile.
Correct: You can **lay** that package on the front table.

Leave, Let: *Leave* means *to go away*, and *let* means to permit. It is incorrect to use *leave* when you mean *let*:

Wrong: Leave me get that for you.
Correct: Let me get that for you.

Less, Fewer: See the entry for *fewer, less*.

Let, Leave: See the entry for *leave, let*.

Like, As: See the entry for *as, as if, like*.

Like For: The phrase "I'd like for you to do that" is incorrect. Omit *for*.

May, Can: See the entry for *can, may*.

Most: It is incorrect to use *most* as a substitute for *almost*.

Nowheres: This is an incorrect form of *nowhere*.

Number, Amount: See the entry for *amount, number*.

Of, Have: See the entry for *have, of*.

usage

Off Of: It is incorrect to write *off of* for *off* in such phrases as *off the bus* or *off the table*.

O.K., Ok, Okay: These can be used informally but should not be used in formal or academic writing.

Reason ... Because: This is redundant. Instead of *because*, use *that*:

> **Wordy:** The **reason** she dropped the course is **because** she couldn't keep up with the homework.
>
> **Revised:** The **reason** she dropped the course is **that** she couldn't keep up with the homework.
>
> —or—
>
> She dropped the course **because** she couldn't keep up with the homework.

Reason Why: Using *why* is redundant. Drop the word *why*.

> **Wordy:** The **reason why** I called is to remind you of your promise.
>
> **Revised:** The **reason** I called is to remind you of your promise.

Saw, Seen: The past tense forms of the verb *see* and *saw* and *seen*. *Saw* is the simple form that needs no additional verb as a helper. *Seen* is the past form that requires the helper *have*. Some writers make the mistake of interchanging *saw* and *seen*.

> **Wrong:** They **seen** it happen.
>
> **Correct:** They **saw** it happen.
>
> —or—
>
> They **have seen** it happen.

Set, Sit: *Set* means *to place* and is followed by a direct object. *Sit* means *to be seated*. It is incorrect to substitute *set* for *sit*.

> **Wrong:** Come in and **set** down.
>
> **Correct:** Come in and **sit** down.
>
> **Correct:** **Set** the flowers on the table.

Should of: This is incorrect. Instead use *should have*.

Sit, Set: See the entry for *set, sit,*

Somebody, Some Body: See the entry for *anyone, any one*.

Someone, Some One: See the entry for *anyone, any one*.

Sort, Kind: See the entry for *kind, sort*.

Such: This is an overworked word when used in place of *very* or *extremely*.

Sure: The use of *sure* as an adverb is informal. Careful writers use *surely* instead.

> **Informal:** I **sure** hope you can join us.
> **Revised:** I **surely** hope you can join us.

That There, This Here, These Here, Those There: These are incorrect forms for *that, this, these, those*.

That, Which: Use *that* for essential clauses and *which* for non-essential clauses. Some writers, however, also use *which* for essential clauses.

Their, There, They're: *Their* is a possessive pronoun; *there* means *in, at,* or *to that place*; and *they're* is a contraction for *they are*.

> **Their** house has been sold.
> **There** is the parking lot.
> **They're** both good swimmers.

Theirself, Theirselves, Themself: These are all incorrect forms for *themselves*.

Them: It is incorrect to use this in place of either the pronoun *these* or *those*.

> **Wrong:** Look at **them** apples.
> **Correct:** Look at **those** apples.

Thusly: This is an incorrect substitute for *thus*.

To, Too, Two: *To* is a preposition; *too* is an adverb meaning *very* or *also*; and *two* is a number.

> He brought his bass guitar **to** the party.
> He brought his drums **too**.
> He had **two** music stands.

Toward, Towards: Both are accepted forms with the same meaning.

Use to: This is incorrect for the modal meaning "formerly."

usage

Instead, use *used to.*

Want for: Omit the incorrect *for* in phrases such as "I want for you to come here."

Well, Good: See the entry for *good, well.*

Went, Gone: See the entry for *gone, went.*

Where: It is incorrect to use *where* to mean *when* or *that.*

> **Wrong:** The Fourth of July is a holiday **where** the town council shoots off fireworks.
>
> **Correct:** The Fourth of July is a holiday **when** the town council shoots off fireworks.
>
> **Wrong:** I see **where** there is now a ban on shooting panthers.
>
> **Correct:** I see **that** there is now a ban on shooting panthers.

Where . . . at: This is a redundant form. Omit the *at.*

> **Wordy:** This is **where** the picnic is at.
>
> **Revised:** This is **where** the picnic is.

Which, That: See the entry for *that, which.*

While, Awhile: See the entry for *awhile, a while.*

Who, Whom: Use *who* for the subject case; use *whom* for the object case.

> He is the person **who** signs that form.
>
> He is the person **whom** I asked for help.

Who's, Whose: *Who's* is a contraction for *who is; whose* is a possessive pronoun.

> **Who's** included on that list?
>
> **Whose** wristwatch is this?

Your, You're: *Your* is a possessive pronoun; *you're* is a contraction for *you are.*

> **Your** hands are cold.
>
> **You're** a great success.

Glossary of Grammatical Terms

Absolutes: Words or phrases that modify whole sentences rather than parts of sentences or individual words. An absolute phrase, which consists of a noun and participle, can be placed anywhere in the sentence but needs to be set off from the sentence by commas.

> <u>The snow having finally stopped,</u> the football game began.
>
> (absolute phrase)

Abstract Nouns: Nouns that refer to ideas, qualities, generalized concepts, and conditions and that do not have plural forms. (See Chapters 2a and 50g.)

> happiness, pride, furniture, trouble, sincerity

Active Voice: See **voice.**

Adjectives: Words that modify nouns and pronouns. (See Chapter 4.) Descriptive adjectives (*red, clean, beautiful, offensive,* for example) have three forms:

> **Positive:** red, clean, beautiful, offensive
>
> **Comparative:** (for comparing two things): redder, cleaner, more beautiful, less offensive
>
> **Superlative:** (for comparing more than two things): reddest, cleanest, most beautiful, least offensive

Adjective Clauses: See **dependent clauses.**

Adverbs: Modify verbs, verb forms, adjectives, and other adverbs. (See Chapter 4.) Descriptive adverbs (for example, *fast, graceful, awkward*) have three forms:

Positive: fast, graceful, awkward

Comparative: (for comparing two things): faster, more graceful, less awkward

Superlative: (for comparing more than two things): fastest, most graceful, least awkward

Adverb Clauses: See **dependent clauses**.

Agreement: The use of the corresponding form for related words in order to have them agree in number, person, or gender. (See Chapters 3b, 12, and 17a.)

John runs. (Both subject and verb are singular.)

It is necessary to flush the **pipes** regularly so that **they** don't freeze. (Both subjects, *it* and *they*, are in third person; *they* agrees in number with the antecedent, *pipes*.)

Antecedents: Words or groups of words to which pronouns refer.

When the **bell** was rung, **it** sounded very loudly. (*Bell* is the antecedent of *it*.)

Antonyms: Words with opposite meanings.

Word	*Antonym*
hot	cold
fast	slow
noisy	quiet

Appositives: Non-essential phrases and clauses that follow nouns and identify or explain them. (See Chapter 9.)

My uncle, <u>who lives in Wyoming</u>, is taking windsurfing lessons in Florida.
          (appositive)

Articles: See **noun determiners**.

Auxiliary Verbs: Verbs used with main verbs in verb phrases.

<u>should be</u> going   <u>has</u> taken
(auxiliary verb)   (auxiliary verb)

Cardinal Numbers: See **noun determiners**.

Case: The form or position of a noun or pronoun that shows its use or relationship to other words in a sentence. The three cases in English are (1) *subject* (or *subjective* or *nominative*), (2) *object* (or *objective*), and (3) *possessive* (or *genitive*). (See Chapter 3a).

Clauses: Groups of related words that contain both subjects and predicates and that function either as sentences or as parts of sentences. Clauses are either *independent* (or *main*) or *dependent* (or *subordinate*). (See Chapter 8.)

Collective Nouns: Nouns that refer to groups of people or things, such as a *committee, team*, or *jury*. When the group includes a number of members acting as a unit and is the subject of the sentence, the verb is also singular. (See Chapters 2a and 12.)

The jury **has** made a decision.

Comma Splices: Punctuation errors in which two or more independent clauses in compound sentences are separated only by commas and no coordinating conjunctions. (See Chapter 11.)

Comma Splice: Jessie said that he could not help, that was typical of his responses to requests.

Revised: Jessie said that he could not help, but that was typical of his responses to requests.

—or—

Jessie said that he could not help; that was typical of his responses to requests.

Common Nouns: Nouns that refer to general rather than specific categories of people, places, and things and are not capitalized. (See Chapter 2a.)

basket, person, history, tractor

Comparative: The form of adjectives and adverbs used when two things are being compared. (See Chapter 4d.)

higher, more intelligent, less friendly

terms

Complement: When linking verbs link subjects to adjectives or nouns, the adjectives or nouns are complements.

> Phyllis was <u>tired.</u>
>   (complement)
>
> She became a <u>musician.</u>
>   (complement)

Complex Sentences: Sentences with at least one independent clause and at least one dependent clause arranged in any order. (See Chapter 10c.)

Compound Nouns: Words such as *swimming pool, dropout, roommate,* and *stepmother,* in which more than one word is needed.

Compound Sentences: Sentences with two or more independent clauses and no dependent clauses. (See Chapter 10b.)

Compound-Complex Sentences: Sentences with at least two independent clauses and at least one dependent clause arranged in any order. (See Chapter 10d.)

Conjunctions: Words that connect other words, phrases, and clauses in sentences. Coordinating conjunctions connect independent clauses; subordinating conjunctions connect dependent or subordinating clauses with independent or main clauses.

> **Coordinating Conjunctions:** *and, but, for, or, nor, so, yet*
>
> **Some Subordinating Conjunctions:** *after, although, because, if, since, until, while,* and so on.

Conjunctive Adverbs: Words that begin or join independent clauses. (See Chapters 8a and 21.)

> consequently, however, therefore, thus, moreover

Connotation: The attitudes and emotional overtones beyond the direct definition of a word. (See Chapter 50h.)

> The words *plump* and *fat* both mean fleshy, but *plump* has a more positive connotation than *fat.*

Consistency: Maintaining the same voice with pronouns, the same tense with verbs, and the same tone, voice, or mode of discourse. (See Chapter 17.)

Coordinating Conjunctions: See **conjunctions**.

terms

Coordination: Of equal importance. Two independent clauses in the same sentence are coordinate because they have equal importance and the same emphasis. (See Chapters 8a and 19a-c.)

Correlative Conjunctions: Words that work in pairs and give emphasis.

both . . .and	neither . . . nor
either . . . or	not . . . but also

Dangling Modifiers: Phrases or clauses in which the doer of the action is not clearly indicated. (See Chapter 14.)

Wrong: <u>Missing an opportunity to study</u>, the exam seemed especially difficult.   (clause with no doer of the action)

Revised: Missing an opportunity to study, Tim thought the exam seemed especially difficult.

Declarative Mood: See **mood**.

Demonstrative Pronouns: Pronouns that refer to things. (See **noun determiners** and Chapter 2b.)

this, that, these, those

Denotation: The explicit dictionary definition of a word. (See Chapter 50h.)

terms

Dependent Clauses (Subordinate Clauses): Clauses that cannot stand alone as complete sentences. (See Chapter 8b.) There are two kinds of dependent clauses: adverb clauses and adjective clauses.

Adverb clauses begin with subordinating conjunctions such as *after, if, because, while, when*, and so on.

Adjective clauses tell more about nouns or pronouns in sentences and begin with words such as *who, which, that, whose, whom*.

Determiner: See **noun determiner**.

Diagrams: See **sentence diagrams**.

Direct Discourse: See **mode of discourse**.

Direct/Indirect Quotations: Direct quotations are the exact words said by someone or the exact words in print that are being copied. Indirect quotations are not the exact words but the rephrasing or summarizing of someone else's words. (See Chapter 28a.)

Direct Objects: Nouns or pronouns that follow a transitive verb and complete the meaning or receive the action of the verb. The direct object answers the question *what?* or *whom?*

Ellipsis: A series of three dots to indicate that words or parts of sentences are being omitted from material being quoted (See Chapter 35.)

Essential and Nonessential Clauses and Phrases: *Essential* (also called *restrictive*) clauses and phrases appear after nouns and are necessary or essential to complete the meaning of the sentence. *Nonessential* (also called *nonrestrictive*) clauses and phrases appear after nouns and add extra information, but that information can be removed from the sentence without altering the meaning. (See Chapter 9.)

> Apples <u>that are green</u> are not sweet.
> (essential clause)
>
> Golden Delicious apples, <u>which are yellow</u>, are sweet.
> (nonessential clause)

Excessive Coordination: Occurs when too many equal clauses are strung together with coordinators into one sentence. (See Chapter 19c.)

Excessive Subordination: Occurs when too many subordinate clauses are strung together in a complex sentence. (See Chapter 19f.)

Faulty Coordination: Occurs when two clauses that are either unequal in importance or that have little or no connection to each other are combined in one sentence and written as independent clauses. (See Chapter 19b.)

Faulty Parallelism: See **parallel construction**.

Faulty Predication: Occurs when a predicate does not appropriately fit the subject. This happens most often after forms of the *to be* verb. (See Chapter 18.)

> **Faulty:** The reason he was late was because he had to study.
> **Revised:** He was late because he had to study.

Fragments: Groups of words punctuated as sentences that either do not have both a subject and a complete verb or that are dependent clauses. (See Chapter 13.)

> **Fragment:** Whenever we wanted to pick fresh fruit while we were staying on my grandmother's farm.
>
> **Revised:** Whenever we wanted to pick fresh fruit while we were staying on my grandmother's farm, we would head for the apple orchard with buckets.

Fused Sentences: Punctuation errors (also called *run-ons*) in which there is no punctuation between independent clauses in the sentence. (See Chapter 11.)

> **Fused:** Jennifer never learned how to ask politely she just took what she wanted.
>
> **Revised:** Jennifer never learned how to ask politely; she just took what she wanted.

Gerunds: Verbal forms ending in *-ing* that function as nouns. (See **phrases**, **verbals**, and Chapter 1b.)

> Arnon admitted that he enjoys <u>cooking</u>.
> (gerund)
>
> <u>Jogging</u> is a form of exercise that does not require much equipment.
> (gerund)

Homonyms: Words that sound alike but are spelled differently and have different meanings. (See Chapter 46.)

> hear/here
> passed/past
> buy/by

Idioms: Expressions meaning something beyond the simple definition or literal translation into another language. For example, idioms such as *short and sweet* or *to the point* are expressions in English that cannot be translated literally into another language. (See Chapter 50e.)

Imperative Mood: See **mood**.

Indefinite Pronouns: Pronouns that make indefinite reference to nouns. (See Chapters 2b, 3b, and 17a.)

> anyone, everyone, nobody, something

terms

Independent Clauses: Clauses that can stand alone as complete sentences because they do not depend on other clauses to complete their meanings. (See Chapter 8a.)

Indirect Discourse: See **mode of discourse**.

Indirect Objects: Words that follow transitive verbs and come before direct objects. They indicate the one to whom or for whom something is given, said, or done and answer the questions *to what?* or *to whom?* Indirect objects can always be paraphrased by a prepositional phrase beginning with *to* or *for*.

> Alice gave <u>me</u> some money.
>   (indirect object)
> **Paraphrase:** Alice gave some money to me.
>
> Terry made <u>everyone</u> fresh lemonade.
>   (indirect object)
> **Paraphrase:** Terry made fresh lemonade for everyone.

Infinitives: Phrases made up of the present form of the verb preceded by *to*. Infinitives can have subjects, objects, complements, or modifiers. (See **phrases** and Chapter 1b.)

> Everyone wanted <u>to swim</u> in the new pool.
>   (infinitive)
> There were no houses <u>to rent</u> on that street.
>   (infinitive)

Intensifiers: Modifying words used for emphasis.

> She **most certainly** did fix that car!

Interjections: Words used as exclamations.

> **Oh**, I don't think I want to know about that.

Interrogative Pronouns: Pronouns used in questions. (See Chapter 2b.)

> who, whose, whom, which, that

Irregular Verbs: Verbs in which the past tense forms and/or the past participles are not formed by adding *-ed* or *-d*. (See Chapter 1c4.)

> do, did, done

Jargon: Words and phrases that are either the specialized language of various fields or, in a negative sense, unnecessarily technical or inflated terms. (See Chapter 50d.)

Intransitive Verbs: See **verbs**.

Linking Verbs: Verbs linking the subject to the subject complement. The most common linking verbs are *appear, seem, become, feel, look, taste, sound* and *be.*

> I <u>feel</u> sleepy.
> (linking verb)
>
> He <u>became</u> the president.
> (linking verb)

Misplaced Modifiers: Modifiers not placed next to or close to the word(s) being modified. (See Chapter 15.)

> **Wrong:** We saw an advertisement for an excellent new stereo system with dual headphones <u>on television</u>.
> (misplaced modifier)
>
> **Revised:** We saw an advertisement on television for an excellent new stereo system with dual headphones.

Modal Verbs: Helping verbs such as *shall, should, will, would, can, could, may, might, must, ought to,* and *used to* that express an attitude such as interest, possibility, or obligation. (See Chapter 1f.)

Mode of Discourse: Direct discourse repeats the exact words that someone says, and indirect discourse reports the words but changes some of the words. (See Chapter 17e.)

> Everett said, <u>"I want to become a physicist."</u>
> (direct discourse)
>
> Everett said <u>that he wants to become a physicist.</u>
> (indirect discourse)

Modifiers: Words or groups of words that describe or limit other words, phrases, and clauses. The most common modifiers are adjectives and adverbs. (See Chapter 4.)

Mood: Verbs indicate whether a sentence expresses a fact (the declarative or indicative mood), express some doubt or something contrary to fact or state a recommendation (the subjunctive mood), or issue a command (the imperative mood). (See Chapter 1e.)

terms

Nonessential Clauses and Phrases: See **essential and nonessential clauses and phrases**.

Nonrestrictive Clauses and Phrases: See **essential and nonessential clauses and phrases**.

Nouns: Words that name people, places, things, and ideas and have plural or possessive endings. Nouns function as subjects, direct objects, predicate nominatives, objects of prepositions, and indirect objects. (See Chapter 2a.)

Noun Clauses: Subordinate clauses used as nouns.

> <u>What I see here</u> is adequate.
> (noun clause)

Noun Determiners: Words that signal that a noun is about to follow. They stand next to their nouns or can be separated by adjectives. Some noun determiners can also function as nouns. There are five types of noun determiners:

1. Articles
   definite: *the*
   indefinite: *a, an*
2. Demonstratives: *this, that, these, those*
3. Possessives: *my, our, your, his, her, its, their*
4. Cardinal numbers: *one, two, three,* and so on
5. Miscellaneous: *all, another, each, every, much,* and others

Noun Phrases: See **phrases**.

Number: The quantity expressed by a noun or pronoun, either singular (one) or plural (more than one).

Objects: See **direct objects** and **object complements**.

Object Complements: The adjectives in predicates modifying the object of the verb (not the subject).

> The enlargement makes the picture <u>clear</u>.
>   (object complement)
> I consider Jolene <u>successful</u>.
>   (object complement)

terms

Object of the Preposition: Noun following the preposition. The preposition, its object, and any modifiers make up the *prepositional phrase.*

For <u>Daniel</u>
(object of the preposition *for*)

She knocked twice *on the big wooden door.*
(prepositional phrase)

Objective Case of Pronouns: The case needed when the pronoun is the direct or indirect object of the verb or the object of a preposition. (See Chapters 3a and 17a.)

Singular
First person: *me*
Second person: *you*
Third person: *him, her, it*

Plural
First person: *us*
Second person: *you*
Third person: *them*

Parallel Construction: When two or more items are listed or compared, they must be in the same grammatical form as equal elements. When items are not in the same grammatical form, they lack parallel structure (often called *faulty parallelism*). (See Chapter 16b.)

She was sure that **being an apprentice in a photographer's studio** would be more useful than **being a student in photography classes.** (The phrases in bold type are parallel because they have the same grammatical form.)

Parenthetical Elements: Nonessential words, phrases, and clauses set off by commas, dashes, or parentheses.

Participles: Verb forms that may be part of the complete verb or function as adjectives or adverbs. The present participle ends in *-ing,* and the past participle usually ends in *-ed, -d, -n* or *-t.* (See **phrases** and Chapter 1a.)

Present participles: *running, sleeping, digging*
Past participles: *walked, deleted, chosen*

She is **running** for mayor in this campaign. (present participle)
The **elected** candidate will take office in January. (participle)

Parts of Speech: The eight classes into which words are grouped according to their function, place, meaning, and use in a sentence: nouns, pronouns, verbs, adjectives, adverbs, prepositions, conjunctions, and interjections.

Passive Voice: See **voice**.

Past Participle: See **participles**.

Perfect Progressive Tense: See **verb tenses**.

Perfect Tenses: See **verb tenses**.

Person: There are three "persons" in English:

First person: the person or persons speaking (*I* or *we*)
Second person: the person or persons spoken to (*you*)
Third person: the person or persons spoken about (*he, she, it, they* or *anyone, everybody,* etc.)

(See Chapter 3a.)

Personal Pronouns: Refer to people or things. (See Chapter 3a.)

	Subject	*Object*	*Possessive*
Singular			
First person	I	me	my, mine
Second person	you	you	your, yours
Third person	he, she, it	him, her, it	his, her, hers, its

	Subject	*Object*	*Possessive*
Plural			
First person	we	us	our, ours
Second person	you	you	your, yours
Third person	they	them	their, theirs

Phrases: Groups of related words without subjects and predicates. (See Chapter 7.) Verb phrases function as verbs.

She <u>has been eating</u> too much sugar.
(verb phrase)

Noun phrases function as nouns.

A <u>major winter storm</u> hit <u>the eastern coast of Maine</u>.
(noun phrase)   (noun phrase)

Prepositional phrases usually function as modifiers.

> That book <u>of hers</u> is overdue at the library.
> (prepositional phrase)

Participial phrases, gerund phrases, infinitive phrases, appositive phrases, and absolute phrases function as adjectives, adverbs, or nouns.

> **Participial Phrase:** I saw people **staring at my peculiar looking haircut.**
> **Gerund Phrase: Making copies of videotapes** can be illegal.
> **Infinitive Phrase:** He likes **to give expensive presents.**
> **Appostive Phrase:** You ought to see Dr. Elman, **a dermatologist.**
> **Absolute Phrase: The test done,** he sighed with relief.

Possessive Pronouns: See **personal pronouns, noun determiners**, and Chapters 3a and 24d.

Predicate Adjectives: See **subject complements.**

Predicate Nominatives: See **subject complements.**

Predication: Words or groups of words that express action or state of beginning in a sentence and consist of one or more verbs, plus any complements or modifiers.

terms

Prefixes: Word parts added to the beginning of words. (See Chapter 42.)

Prefix	*Word*
bio- (life)	biography
mis- (wrong, bad)	misspell

Prepositions: Link and relate their objects (usually nouns or pronouns) to some other word or words in a sentence. Prepositions usually precede their objects but may follow the objects and appear at the end of the sentence. (See Chapter 5.)

> The waiter gave the check <u>to my date</u> by mistake.
>   (prepositional phrase)
> I wonder <u>what</u> she is asking <u>for</u>.
>   (object of the   (preposition)
>   preposition)

Prepositional Phrases: See **phrases.**

Progressive Tenses: See **verb tenses.**

Pronouns: Words that substitute for nouns. (See Chapter 2b.) Pronouns should refer to previously stated nouns, called antecedents.

> When <u>Josh</u> came in, <u>he</u> brought some firewood.
> (antecedent) (pronoun)

Forms of pronouns: personal, possessive, reflexive, interrogative, demonstrative, indefinite, and relative

Pronoun Case: Refers to the form of the pronoun that is needed in a sentence. See **subject**, **object**, and **possessive cases** and Chapter 3a.

Proper Nouns: Refer to specific people, places, and things. Proper nouns are always capitalized. (See Chapters 2a and 36.)

> Copenhagen, Honda, House of Representatives, Spanish

Reflexive Pronouns: Pronouns that show someone or something in the sentence is acting for itself or on itself. Because a reflexive pronoun must refer to a word in a sentence, it is not the subject or direct object. If used to show emphasis, reflexive pronouns are called *intensive pronouns.*

Singular	Plural
First person: *myself*	First person: *ourselves*
Second person: *yourself*	Second person: *yourselves*
Third person: *himself, herself, itself*	Third person: *themselves*

Relative Pronouns: Pronouns that show the relationship of a dependent clause to a noun in the sentence. Relative pronouns substitute for nouns already mentioned in sentences and introduce adjective or noun clauses. (See Chapter 3b.)

Relative pronouns: *that, which, who, whom, whose*

> This was the movie **that** won the Academy Award.

Restrictive Clauses and Phrases: See **essential and nonessential clauses and phrases**

Run-on Sentences: See **fused sentences** and Chapter 11.

Sentences: Groups of words that have at least one independent clause (a complete unit of thought with a subject and predicate).

(See Chapter 10.) Sentences can be classified by their structure as *simple, compound, complex,* and *compound-complex.*

Simple: one independent clause
Compound: two or more independent clauses
Complex: one or more independent clauses and one or more dependent clauses
Compound-complex: Two or more independent clauses and one or more dependent clauses

Sentences can also be classified by their function as *declarative, interrogative, imperative,* and *exclamatory.*

Declarative: makes a statement
Interrogative: asks a question
Imperative: issues a command
Exclamatory: makes an exclamation

Sentence Diagrams: A method of showing relationships within a sentence.

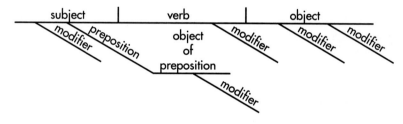

Marnie's cousin, who has no taste in food, ordered a hamburger with coleslaw at the Chinese restaurant.

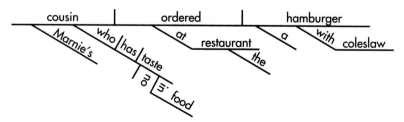

Sentence Fragment: See **fragment.**

Simple Sentence: See **sentence** and Chapter 10a.

Simple Tenses: See **verb tenses**.

Split Infinitives: Phrases in which modifiers are inserted between *to* and the verb. Some people object to split infinitives, but others consider them grammatically acceptable.

> to quickly turn
> to easily reach
> to forcefully enter

Subject: The word or words in a sentence that act or are acted upon by the verb or are linked by the verb to another word or words in the sentence. The *simple subject* includes only the noun or other main word or words, and the *complete subject* includes all the modifiers with the subject. (See Chapter 6.)

> **Harvey** objected to his roommate's alarm going off at 9 a.m. (*Harvey* is the subject.)
> **Every single one of the people in the room** heard her giggle. (The simple subject is *one*; the complete subject is the whole phrase.)

Subject Complement: The noun or adjective in the predicate (*predicate noun* or *adjective*) that refers to the same entity as the subject in sentences with linking verbs, such as *is/are, feel, look, smell, sound, taste,* and *seem*.

> She feels <u>happy</u>.
>   (subject complement)
> He is a <u>pharmacist</u>.
>   (subject complement)

Subject Case of Pronouns: See **personal pronouns** and Chapter 3a.

Subjunctive Mood: See **mood**.

Subordinating Conjunctions: Words such as *although, if, until,* and *when*, which join two clauses and subordinate one to the other.

> She is late. She overslept.
> She is late **because** she overslept.

Subordination: The act of placing one clause in a subordinate or dependent relationship to another in a sentence because it is less important and is dependent for its meaning on the other clause. (See Chapters 19d, 19e, and 19f.)

terms

Suffix: Word part added to the end of a word. (See Chapter 43.)

Suffix	*Word*
-ful	careful
-ness	nameless

Superlative Forms of Adjectives and Adverbs: See **adjectives** and **adverbs** and Chapter 4d.

Synonyms: Words with similar meanings.

Word	*Synonym*
damp	moist
pretty	attractive

Tense: See **verb tense**.

Tone: The attitude or level of formality reflected in the word choices of a piece of writing. (See Chapters 17c and 50c.)

Transitions: Words in sentences that show relationships between sentences and paragraphs. (See Chapter 21.)

Transitive Verbs: See **verbs**.

terms

Verbals: Words that are derived from verbs but do not act as verbs in sentences. Three types of verbals are *infinitives, participles,* and *gerunds.* (See Chapter 1b.) Infinitives: *to* + verb

> to wind
>
> to say

Participles: words used as modifiers or with helping verbs. The present participle ends in *-ing,* and many past participles end in *-ed.*

> The dog is <u>panting</u>.
>   (present participle)
> They blew on the <u>glowing</u> coals.
>   (present participle)
> They have <u>used</u> all the dishes.
>   (past participle)
> He bought only <u>used</u> clothing.
>   (past participle)

Gerunds: present participles used as nouns.

<u>Smiling</u> was not a natural act for her.
(gerund)

Her favorite sport is <u>sailing</u>.
                                    (gerund)

Verbs: Words or groups of words (verb phrases) in predicates that express action, show a state of being, or act as a link between the subject and the rest of the predicate. Verbs change form to show time (tense), mood, and voice and are classified as *transitive, intransitive,* and *linking verbs.* (See Chapter 1.)

- Transitive verbs require objects to complete the predicate.

He <u>cut</u> the cardboard <u>box</u> with his knife.
(transitive verb)   (object)

- Intransitive verbs do not require objects.

My ancient cat often <u>lies</u> on the porch.
                                (intransitive verb)

- Linking verbs link the subject to the following noun or adjective.

The trees <u>are</u> bare.
            (linking verb)

Verb Conjugations: The forms of verbs in various tenses. (See Chapter 1c.)

Regular:
Present
    Simple present: I walk   we walk
        you walk   you walk
        he, she, it walks   they walk
    Present progressive:
        I am walking   we are walking
        you are walking   you are walking
        he, she, it is walking   they are walking
    Present perfect:
        I have walked   we have walked
        you have walked   you have walked
        he, she, it has walked   they have walked

Present perfect progressive:

I have been walking	we have been walking
you have been walking	you have been walking
he, she, it has been walking	they have been walking

Past

Simple past: I walked   we walked

you walked	you walked
he, she, it walked	they walked

Past progressive:

I was walking	we were walking
you were walking	you were walking
he, she, it was walking	they were walking

Past perfect:

I had walked	we had walked
you had walked	you had walked
he, she, it had walked	they had walked

Past perfect progressive:

I had been walking	we had been walking
you had been walking	you had been walking
he, she, it had been walking	they had been walking

Future

Simple future:

I shall walk	we shall walk
you will walk	you will walk
he, she, it will walk	they will walk

Future progressive:

I shall be walking	we shall be walking
you will be walking	you will be walking
he, she, it will be walking	they will be walking

Future perfect:

I shall have walked	we shall have walked
you will have walked	you will have walked
he, she, it will have walked	they will have walked

Future perfect progressive:

I shall have been walking	we shall have been walking
you will have been walking	you will have been walking
he, she, it will have been walking	they will have been walking

terms

Irregular:

Present

   Simple present:

I go	we go
you go	you go
he, she, it goes	they go

   Present progressive:

I am going	we are going
you are going	you are going
he, she, it is going	they are going

   Present perfect:

I have gone	we have gone
you have gone	you have gone
he, she, it has gone	they have gone

   Present perfect progressive:

I have been going	we have been going
you have been going	you have been going
he, she, it has been going	they have been going

Past

   Simple past:

I went	we went
you went	you went
he, she, it went	they went

   Past progressive:

I was going	we were going
you were going	you were going
he, she, it was going	they were going

   Past perfect:

I had gone	we had gone
you had gone	you had gone
he, she, it had gone	they had gone

   Past perfect progressive:

I had been going	we had been going
you had been going	you had been going
he, she, it had been going	they had been going

Future

   Simple:

I shall go	we shall go
you will go	you will go
he, she, it will go	they will go

terms

Future progressive:

I shall be going	we shall be going
you will be going	you will be going
he, she, it will be going	they will be going

Future perfect:

I shall have gone	we shall have gone
you will have gone	you will have gone
he, she, it will have gone	they will have gone

Future perfect progressive:

I shall have been going	we shall have been going
you will have been going	you will have been going
he, she, it will have been going	they will have been going

Verb Phrases: See **verbs**.

Verb Tenses: The times indicated by the verb forms in the past, present, or future. (For the verb forms, see **verb conjugations** and Chapter 1c.)

Present

Simple present: describes actions or situations that exist now and are habitually or generally true

I **walk** to class every afternoon.

Present progressive: indicates activity in progress, something not finished, or something continuing

He **is studying** Swedish.

Present perfect: describes single or repeated actions that began in the past and lead up to and include the present

She **has lived** in Alaska for two years.

Present perfect progressive: indicates action that began in the past, continues to the present, and may continue into the future

They **have been building** that parking garage for six months.

Past

Simple past: describes completed actions or conditions in the past

They **ate** breakfast in the cafeteria.

terms

Past progressive: indicates past action that took place over a period of time

He **was swimming** when the storm began.

Past perfect: indicates an action or event was completed before another event in the past

No one **had heard** about the crisis when the newscast began.

Past perfect progressive: indicates an ongoing condition in the past that has ended

I **had been planning** my trip to Mexico when I heard about the earthquake.

Future

Simple future: indicates actions or events in the future

The store **will open** at 9 A.M.

Future progressive: indicates future action that will continue for some time

I **will be working** on that project next week.

Future perfect: indicates action that will be completed by or before a specified time in the future

Next summer, they **will have been** here for twenty years.

Future perfect progressive: indicates ongoing actions or conditions until a specific time in the future.

By tomorrow, I **will have been waiting** for the delivery for one month.

Voice: Verbs are either in the *active* or *passive* voice. In the active voice, the subject performs the action of the verb. In the passive, the subject receives the action. (See Chapters 1d and 17d.)

The dog <u>bit</u> the boy.
(active verb)

The boy <u>was bitten</u> by the dog.
(passive verb)

Using Compare and Correct and Question and Correct

When you know the terms you want to look up, you can use the table of contents or the index to this book. But when you do not know the term, there are two ways you can find the section you need.

1. **Compare and Correct**

   On the following pages you will find examples of problems or errors that may be like one you want to correct. When you recognize a sentence with a problem similar to one in your sentence, you will be referred to the chapter in this book that will help you make the needed revision.

2. **Question and Correct**

   Inside the back cover of the book is a series of questions writers often ask. When you read a question similar to the one you have in mind, you will find a reference to the chapter of the book that will give you the answer. Though the topic headings for the questions will help you locate your question, you can also check the back cover flap where you will find an alphabetical list of key words used in those commonly asked questions.

Both the questions and examples are grouped in sets as follows:

- About sentences
- About punctuation and mechanics
- About spelling
- About style and word choices
- About special writing concerns
- About paper format

Compare and Correct

Examples of Sentence Errors	Error and Corresponding Chapter Number
1. He has *broke* his bike light and needs a new one. **Revised:** He has broken his bike light and needs a new one.	1. Irregular verb. See Chapter **1c**.
2. Mr. Villus is one of those people who *is* never on time. **Revised:** Mr. Villus is one of those people who are never on time.	2. Incorrect subject-verb agreement. See Chapter **12**.
3. The library has a dozen *computer* and some *printer* for students to use. **Revised:** The library has a dozen computers and some printers for students to use.	3. Incorrect use of plurals. See Chapter **2a**.
4. The committee had to make a choice between *him and I*. **Revised:** The committee had to make a choice between him and me.	4. Incorrect pronoun case. See Chapter **3a**.
5. In Hollywood *they* think that moviegoers are too conservative to appreciate really interesting background music.	5. Vague pronoun reference. See Chapter **3b**.

Revised: In Hollywood composers who write music for movies think that moviegoers are too conservative to appreciate really interesting background music.

6. Whenever the class does experiments with the help of the lab assistants, *they* wind up leaving *their* equipment all over the lab tables.
   Revised: Whenever the class does experiments with the help of the lab assistants, the students wind up leaving the lab assistants' equipment all over the lab tables.

6. Incorrect pronoun reference. See Chapter **3b**.

7. He learned how to play the bass guitar *real* well.
   Revised: He learned how to play the bass guitar very well.

7. Incorrect use of adjective. See Chapter **4a**.

8. It will take *a* hour to finish this project.
   Revised: It will take an hour to finish this project.

8. Incorrect use of *a*. See Chapter **4b**.

9. Taking the main street through town is more quicker than the bypass road.
   Revised: Taking the main street through town is quicker than taking the bypass road.

9. Incorrect comparison. See Chapter **4d**.

10. He had *much* problems with his computer.
    Revised: He had many problems with his computer.

10. Incorrect choice of *much/many*. See Chapter **4c**.

11. She was bored *on* the subject of safe driving.
    Revised: She was bored with the subject of safe driving.

11. Incorrect preposition. See Chapter **5a**.

12. The meeting will be *at* Monday.
Revised: The meeting will be on Monday.

12. Incorrect preposition. See Chapter **5b**.

13. We decided to shift to a zone defense, this gave us better coverage on Maravich.
Revised: We decided to shift to a zone defense, and this gave us better coverage on Maravich.

13. Comma splice. See Chapter **11a**.

14. Senator Levadi led the fight against salary hikes in Congress he hoped in that way to attract public favor.
Revised: Senator Levadi led the fight against salary hikes in Congress; he hoped in that way to attract public favor.

14. Fused or run-on sentence. See Chapter **11b**.

15. Usually Tim *ride* to his class on his bike.
Revised: Usually Tim rides to his class on his bike.

15. Incorrect subject-verb agreement. See Chapter **12**.

16. Either the book or the magazines *is* a good source of information on that topic.
Revised: Either the book or the magazines are a good source of information on that topic.

16. Incorrect subject-verb agreement. See Chapter **12**.

17. One hundred miles *are* a long distance between gas stations.
Revised: One hundred miles is a long distance between gas stations.

17. Incorrect subject-verb agreement. See Chapter **12**.

18. *Living Legends* sound like a collection of sport stories.
Revised: *Living Legends* sounds like a collection of sport stories.

18. Incorrect subject-verb agreement. See Chapter **12**.

19. There is so many problems with that television set that it should be returned to the store.

19. Incorrect subject-verb agreement. See Chapter **12**.

Revised: There are so many problems with that television set that it should be returned to the store.

20. Owning a pet has many advantages. *Such as learning to care for an animal and learning responsibility.*
    Revised: Owning a pet has many advantages such as learning to care for an animal and learning responsibility.

20. Sentence fragment. See Chapter **13**.

21. *Being in Chem 114,* it was useful to have a hand calculator at all times.
    Revised: Being in Chem 114, I found it useful to have a hand calculator at all times.

21. Dangling modifier. See Chapter **14**.

22. The weather reporter announced that a tornado had been sighted *on the evening news.*
    Revised: The weather reporter announced on the evening news that a tornado had been sighted.

22. Misplaced modifier. See Chapter **15**.

23. In the training camp our mornings started with *6:30 A.M. wake-up calls* and *eating breakfast at 8:30 A.M.*
    Revised: In the training camp our mornings started with 6:30 A.M. wake-up calls and breakfasts at 8:30 A.M.

23. Faulty parallelism. See Chapter **16b**.

24. The best way to spend *one's* free time is to work on an activity *you* haven't done for a long time.
    Revised: The best way to spend one's free time is to work on an activity one hasn't done for a long time.

24. Shift in person. See Chapter **17a**.

25. The hardest part for beginning skiers is to keep *their* skis pointed straight forward. To succeed *you* have to concentrate on the skis.

25. Shift in person. See Chapter **17a**.

Revised: The hardest part for beginning skiers is to keep their skis pointed straight forward. To succeed they have to concentrate on the skis.

26. Suddenly, as we *were driving* along, smoke or steam *starts* coming out from under the hood of the car.
Revised: Suddenly, as we were driving along, smoke or steam started coming out from under the hood of the car.

26. Shift in verb tense. See Chapter **17b**.

27. We *were riding* along, enjoying the scenery and not thinking about how long it *had been* since we stopped for gas. Suddenly, the motor *dies*.
Revised: We were riding along, enjoying the scenery and not thinking about how long it had been since we stopped for gas. Suddenly, the motor died.

27. Shift in verb tense. See Chapter **17b**.

28. It was desirable for all the candidates to have fluent speaking abilities, good social skills, and a *with-it* appearance.
Revised: It was desirable for all the candidates to have fluent speaking abilities, good social skills, and fashionably current clothing.

28. Shift in tone. See Chapter **17c**.

29. The boy had to stay home and do his homework, but this was not wanted by him.
Revised: The boy had to stay home and do his homework, but he did not want this.

29. Shift in voice. See Chapter **17d**.

30. The secretary said *that her boss was busy* and *could you wait in the reception area.*

30. Shift in discourse. See Chapter **17e**.

Revised: The secretary said that her boss was busy and that they could wait in the reception area.

31. Loneliness *is when* you have no real friend to turn to.
    Revised: Loneliness is a condition in which you find that you have no real friend to turn to.

31. Faulty predication. See Chapter **18**.

32. He drank too much on his job, and he was fired.
    Revised: Because he drank too much on the job, he was fired.

32. Inappropriate coordination. See Chapter **19b**.

33. The crowd objected to the referee's decision, and they began yelling insults, so the referee blew her whistle to call for quiet, but people didn't stop their hooting and stomping.
    Revised: When the crowd objected to the referee's decision, they began yelling insults. As a result, the referee blew her whistle to call for quiet. But people didn't stop their hooting and stomping.

33. Excessive coordination. See Chapter **19c**.

34. When I finally decided to major in public relations and advertising, it was a difficult decision.
    Revised: I finally decided to major in public relations and advertising, which was a difficult decision.

34. Inappropriate subordination. See Chapter **19e**.

35. The future is bright for the high school vocational agriculture student who has had training in microcomputers because they are so necessary on the modern farm, which requires planning and record keeping.

35. Excessive subordination. See Chapter **19f**.

Revised: The high school vocational agriculture student who has trained in microcomputers has a bright future. Computers are necessary on the modern farm because farming requires planning and record keeping.

36. *Instead of a motorcycle helmet, which I would have preferred, a gift of a dictionary* was what my aunt chose for a graduation present for me.
    Revised: As a graduation present for me, my aunt chose a gift of a dictionary, though I would have preferred a motorcycle helmet.

36. Sentence moves from unknown to known material. See Chapter **20a**.

37. Courses with large enrollments lack appeal because there is less attention paid to each student.
    Revised: Courses with small enrollments are more appealing because there is more attention paid to each student.

37. Negative language. See Chapter **20b**.

38. She *couldn't hardly* refuse the gift.
    Revised: She could hardly refuse the gift.

38. Double negative. See Chapter **20c**.

39. Preparation of the chemical was the hardest part of the lab.
    Revised: The students found that the hardest part of the lab was preparing the chemical.

39. Uses a noun instead of a verb. See Chapter **20d**.

40. It was the wish of my parents for me to go to college.
    Revised: My parents wished that I would go to college.

40. Sentence subject is not the intended subject. See Chapter **20e**.

41. A mistake *was made* in my order for a sandwich by the waiter.
    Revised: The waiter made a mistake in my order for a sandwich.

41. Uses passive instead of active. See Chapter **20f**.

42. The tension in the arena was obvious. The crowd was not cheering noisily or tossing popcorn boxes around. We knew that without Terry our team wouldn't be able to win and go on the semifinals. We tried to psyche ourselves up anyway.
Revised: The tension in the arena was obvious. For example, the crowd was not cheering noisily or tossing popcorn boxes around. We knew that without Terry our team wouldn't be able to win and go on the semifinals. But we tried to psyche ourselves up anyway.

42. Needs transitions. See Chapter **21**.

43. The homecoming queen waved enthusiastically to the crowd. She was teary-eyed but happy. She kept smiling at the TV camera as she rode by. It was easy to see how happy she was.
Revised: Teary-eyed but happy, the homecoming queen waved enthusiastically to the crowd. As she rode by, she kept smiling at the TV camera. It was easy to see how happy she was.

43. Monotonous sentence rhythm. See Chapter **22**.

Examples of Punctuation Errors

Error and Corresponding Chapter Number

44. Kari studied the catalog of summer courses and she decided that she should sign up for an introduction to anthropology.
Revised: Kari studied the catalog of summer courses, and she decided that she should sign up for an introduction to anthropology.

44. No comma in a compound sentence. See Chapter **23a**.

45. When the sun had set the owls started to hoot.
Revised: When the sun had set, the owls started to hoot.

45. No comma after introductory clause. See Chapter **23b**.

46. Laura *who is my cousin's daughter* is coming for a visit.
Revised: Laura, who is my cousin's daughter, is coming for a visit.

46. No commas setting off nonessential clause. See Chapter **23c**.

47. Jerrys old VW is faster than my car but not hers'.
Revised: Jerry's old VW is faster than my car but not hers.

47. No apostrophe with the possessive. See Chapter **24a**.

48. The jury announced it's decision.
Revised: The jury announced its decision.

48. Apostrophe incorrectly used with possessive pronoun "its." See Chapter **24a**.

49. Wade showed up on time for the meeting, however, he came on the wrong day.
Revised: Wade showed up on time for the meeting; however, he came on the wrong day.

49. No semicolon between independent clauses. See Chapter **25a**.

50. He preferred health foods, such as: whole wheat bread, organically grown vegetables, and caffeine-free drinks.
Revised: He preferred health foods, such as whole wheat bread, organically grown vegetables, and caffeine-free drinks.

50. Unnecessary colon. See Chapter **26f**.

51. Was Karl the one who said, "I'll bring the beer?"
Revised: Was Karl the one who said, "I'll bring the beer"?

51. Incorrect use of question mark with quotation. See Chapter **27b**.

52. The 6 P.M. news announced that "the White House said it would not confirm the truth… of this story."

52. Incorrect use of quotation marks with quotation. See Chapter **28a**.

53. "I would like to learn more about how tornadoes form," I said. "Here's a useful book," responded the librarian.
Revised: "I would like to learn more about how tornadoes form," I said.
   "Here's a useful book," responded the librarian.

53. Incorrect presentation of dialogue. See Chapter **28a**.

54. One of his favorite old movies, "Casablanca," was on the late show last night.
Revised: One of his favorite old movies, *Casablanca*, was on the late show last night.

54. Titles of long works should be italicized. See Chapter **29a**.

55. She was a well known medieval historian. She was not, however, as well-known as her husband, a musician.
Revised: She was a well-known medieval historian. She was not, however, as well known as her husband, a musician.

55. Incorrect hyphenation of two word units. See Chapter **30c**.

56. They were hardly ever a-part after they met.
Revised: They were hardly ever apart after they met.

56. Incorrect word division. See Chapter **30a**.

57. The puppy returned with some black and white shreds in its mouth—my morning newspaper. I gulped—again.
Revised: The puppy returned with some black and white shreds in its mouth—my morning news-paper. I gulped, again.

57. Overuse of dashes. See Chapter **31**.

58. I took two Economics courses this semester and one History course.
Revised: I took two economics courses this semester and one history course.

58. Incorrect capitalization. See Chapter **36.**

59. When European tourists travel in the U. S., they are surprised that so few Americans speak other languages.
Revised: When European tourists travel in the United States, they are surprised that so few Americans speak other languages.

59. Incorrect abbreviation. See Chapter **37.**

60. 43 more names were added to the list.
Revised: Forty-three more names were added to the list.

60. Incorrect use of numbers. See Chapter **38.**

Examples of Problems with Spelling

Error and Corresponding Chapter Number

61. When winter comes, I always enjoy planing trip to warm beaches, even if don't always go.
Revised: When winter comes, I always enjoy planning a trip to warm beaches, even if I don't always go.

61. Needs proofreading. See Chapter **39.**

62. She *recieved* a B.A. in the *feild* of art history.
Revised: She received a B.A. in the field of art history.

62. Spelling error (*ie/ ei*). See Chapter **40.**

63. After I took a course in *writting,* I was *begining* to improve my spelling.
Revised: After I took a course in writing, I was beginning to improve my spelling.

63. Incorrect doubling of consonants. See Chapter **41.**

64. She *discribed* the hill she would climb *tommorrow*.
Revised: She described the hill she would climb tomorrow.

65. Echo Bay is a *desireable* place to go *picnicing*.
Revised: Echo Bay is a desirable place to go picnicking.

66. The comedian was *funnyer* than the last time I heard her, when she told *storys* of her childhood.
Revised: The comedian was funnier than the last time I heard her, when she told stories of her childhood.

67. Of all the various electronic *mediums*, broadcasting via *radioes* is the most popular.
Revised: Of all the various electronic media, broadcasting via radios is the most popular.

68. *There* train *past* through *to* quickly to see much of the town *accept* the station.
Revised: Their train passed through too quickly to see much of the town except the station.

69. At the *beginning* of the basketball game, the referee *began* to blow his whistle whenever the coach *began* to yell at the opposing players.
Revised: At the start of the basketball game, the referee began to blow his whistle whenever the coach launched into yelling at the opposing players.

---

64. Incorrect prefixes. See Chapter **42**.

65. Incorrect suffixes. See Chapter **43**.

66. Spelling error (*y* to *i*). See Chapter **44**.

67. Spelling error (plurals). See Chapter **45**.

68. Incorrect sound-alike words. See Chapter **46**.

69. Unnecessary word repetition— need to consult dictionary. See Chapter **47**.

Examples of Problems with Words	*Error and Corresponding Chapter Number*
70. In the last ten years, the *mailman* has had an increased workload because of the tide of bulk *he* must deliver. **Revised:** In the last ten years, mail carriers have had an increased workload because of the tide of bulk mail they must deliver.	**70.** Sexist language. See Chapter **48**.
71. At 8 a.m. *in the morning I first* began to feel ill. **Revised:** At 8 A.M. I began to feel ill.	**71.** Unnecessary words. See Chapter **49a**.
72. Tina is usually *a quick study* and can learn new skills *with lightening speed*. But the computer programming course *was over her head*. **Revised:** Tina is usually a quick learner who masters new skills in jet-speed time. But in the computer programming course, she groped helplessly, unable to cope with the material that was too advanced for her.	**72.** Clichés. See Chapter **49b**.
73. The legal system is intended to protect the average *guy's* rights. **Revised:** The legal system is intended to protect the average person's rights.	**73.** Mixture of formal and informal language. See Chapter **50c**.

ESL Index

Index

terms

index

index

index

Symbol	Explanation	Chapter
ab	abbreviation error	37
ad	adjective/adverb error	4
agr	agreement error	12
awk	awkward construction	
ca	case error	3
cap	capitalization error	36
coord	coordination error	19a–c
cs	comma splice	11
dm	dangling modifier	14
emph	needs emphasis	
frag	sentence fragment	13
fs	fused sentence	11
hyph	hyphenation error	30
ital	italic/underlining error	29
lc	use lower case	36
mm	misplaced modifier	15
num	number use error	38
¶	new paragraph	
//	parallelism error	16
pl	plural needed	2
pred	predication error	18
p	punctuation error	23–34
.	period error	27
?	question mark error	27
!	exclamation point error	27
,	comma error	23
;	semicolon error	25
:	colon error	26
'	apostrophe error	24
" "	quotation marks error	28
—	dash error	31
( )	parentheses error	33
[ ]	brackets error	34
. . .	ellipses error	35
/	slash error	32
ref	reference error	3b, 19a
shft	shift error	17
sp	spelling error	39–47
subord	subordination error	19d–f
t	tense error	17b
trans	transition needed	21
v	verb error	1
var	variety needed	22
w	wordy	49
wc	word choice error	50
ww	wrong word	50
x	obvious error	
^	insert	
∩	transpose	
ℑ	delete	

Key Topics in the 62 Most Commonly Asked Questions About Grammar, Punctuation, Mechanics, and Style

Question and Correct: 62 Most Commonly Asked Questions About Grammar, Punctuation, Mechanics, and Style

Questions about Sentences

1. Should sentences have a certain number of words?   Chapter 10
2. Are there words that should not be used to start sentences?   Chapter 10
3. When are the different verb tenses used?   Chapter 1c
4. Does this verb have the right ending?   Chapter 12
5. When are singular and plural verbs used for
   confusing subjects?   Chapter 12
6. Is this a complete sentence?   Chapter 13
7. Does this sentence have a problem with a phrase   Chapters 14,
   or group of words?   15, 16
8. Is this phrase in the right place in the sentence?   Chapter 15
9. Which is correct, *between you and I* or *between you and me*?   Chapter 3a
10. Why are phrases such as *sure good* and *real well* incorrect?   Chapter 4
11. When are *a* and *an* used correctly?   Chapter 4b
12. When two or more things are compared, when is *-er* and
    -est correct and when should *more* and *most* be used?   Chapter 4d
13. When should a sentence or group of sentences keep
    the same verb tenses or persons?   Chapter 17b
14. What is wrong with sentences with *is when, is where,* or *is because*?   Chapter 18
15. These sentences are grammatically correct,   Chapters 19,
    but they could be better. What's needed?   20, 21, 22
16. When is it appropriate to use the passive voice?   Chapter 20f
17. These sentences sound choppy. What can be done?   Chapters 21, 22
18. What can be done when sentences don't seem to flow?   Chapter 21

Questions about Punctuation and Mechanics

19. When should a comma be used before *and* and *but*?   Chapters 11, 23a
20. How do you avoid putting in commas
    where they are not necessary?   Chapter 23h
21. Do pronouns like *it* and plural nouns have apostrophes?   Chapter 24
22. When do you use a semicolon instead of a comma?   Chapter 25a
23. Does a semicolon go before or after quotation marks?   Chapter 25c, 28d
24. What punctuation is used with a list?   Chapter 26a
25. Which abbreviations have periods?   Chapter 37
26. Do periods and question marks go inside
    or outside quotation marks?   Chapter 28d
27. How is dialogue punctuated and written on the page?   Chapters 28a, 51c
28. How do you know where to put punctuation marks
    when you also use quotation marks?   Chapters 28d, 51c
29. What punctuation is used for titles, names of movies,
    plays, and so on?   Chapter 28b, 29a
30. Which words in directly quoted speech are capitalized?   Chapters 28, 36
31. Which words are hyphenated?   Chapter 30
32. What do you do when the whole word
    won't fit at the end of the line?   Chapter 30a

"I chose your text because I found
the size, format, and 'feel' of the book so appealing.
I congratulate you on coming up with a text
that has so many attractive features that distinguish
it from the dozens of other handbooks on the
market. . . . I'm very happy to have discovered your
reference book and look forward to using it."

Elsie Ervin Bock
Lynchburg College

"We have been especially impressed with
the non-authoritarian, 'tutorial' tone of the book,
which is rare in sentence-level handbooks. . . .
Please keep the exercise combination of
'Proofreading Practice' and 'Pattern Practice.'
Students need both to master the skills."

Rebecca Innocent
Southern Methodist University

"The author has done a tremendous job
of designing a very inclusive handbook that keeps
terminology to a minimum. . . . Her illustrations
are often stronger than those in most handbooks,
and her outlining of concepts clearer. Her exercises
are more contextual than in standard handbooks."

Larry Hert
Delta Community College

ISBN 0-13-22   X

9 780132 256247